JOEY 22

Matt Gryta (signature)

JOEY 22

By Matt Gryta

Getzville Grove Press, Ltd.
TOLEDO, OHIO

First Publication 2014

Getzville Grove Press, Ltd. P.O. Box 9479 Toledo, Ohio 43697
www.getzvillegrove.com

Book layout ©2013 BookDesignTemplates.com
Cover design by Studiosansnom.com
Front cover image courtesy Buffalo Courier-Express Archive, E.H. Butler Library, State University of New York, College at Buffalo

Library of Congress Control Number 2014937603

Joey 22/Matt Gryta. -- 1st ed.
ISBN 978-0-9911057-0-0

To all of the victims of Joseph G. Christopher,

Known and unknown,

May they rest in peace;

And to Four Horsemen of Justice:

Edward C. Cosgrove,
Leo J. Donovan,
Albert M. Ranni, and
Raymond P. "Sam" Slade

Prologue

Joseph G. Christopher had all of New York – and indeed much of the nation – in a panic for the entire duration of his wrenching, five-month murder campaign against black men in 1980. Christopher's killing spree came at a time when the nation was terrorized by a wave of hate-motivated killings of blacks, committed as some speculated, by a single racist maniac. Conspicuous groupings of murders took place in the Western New York cities of Buffalo, Niagara Falls, Rochester, as well as in New York City, Atlanta, Oklahoma City, Indianapolis, Cincinnati, Johnstown, Pennsylvania and Salt Lake City. Even children did not escape the rampage: the South was plagued by the Atlanta Child Murders, which resulted in the deaths of nearly 30 black children between 1979 and 1981. Buffalo, New York was overwhelmed by Christopher's rash of atrocious killings, which came one-after-another, beginning on September 22, 1980 with the shot of a .22 caliber weapon.

The national media turned its attention towards Buffalo during the events. Just weeks after the Buffalo murders started, Newsweek magazine ran a story entitled "The Fears of Black America." The article addressed the growing anxiety in the national black community sparked by what appeared to be racially-motivated slayings taking place nationwide. Some lawmen suspected that all of these atrocities were being carried out by, according to authorities quoted in the article, "the same white sniper whom the FBI would like to question about the shooting of black leader Vernon Jordan" in Fort Wayne, Indiana on May 29, 1980. Joseph Paul Franklin, a true American serial killer with a pathological hatred of African Americans and Jews, was acquitted in 1982 of the Jordan shooting, but admitted in 1996 that his motivation stemmed from seeing Jordan in the presence of a white woman. Underneath the surface and above it, in the post-Civil Rights era, racial relations were indeed fragile.

The Newsweek article cited a Buffalo television station's mid-October 1980 survey which revealed that sixty percent of black respondents feared for their safety on the streets of Buffalo. The article cited reports of Buffalo black women calling the police if their husbands were a few minutes late coming home from work. The situation made others fear the possibility of riots or even the eruption of race warfare, a concern that was only exacerbated by malicious events, such as the car-load of white supremacists who callously hurled slurs and bigoted hate speech at mourners during the funeral of the youngest of the Buffalo killer's victims.

The area's clergy, black and white, banded together in an attempt to stem a festering undercurrent of racial tension in the community, an undercurrent which was deliberately worsened by an anti-black rally organized by white supremacist Karl H. Hand in December 1980. On one of the coldest days of the decade for Buffalo, clergymen staged a mass counter-rally for unity in front of City Hall that was attended by thousands. Even so, tensions heightened.

Before the murderer was put to a stop, anxiety built in the City of Buffalo. Although a 185-person task force, comprised of top local, state and FBI law enforcement officials, was rapidly established for the investigation, some local lawmen felt so desperate for answers that they even resorted to hypnotism and psychics in their efforts to track down the killer. In an effort to lure a suspect, plainclothes black police officers drove around the streets of Buffalo incognito with an armed aide hiding in the back seat. Others in the community, perceiving a slow or stalled investigative effort, took matters into their own hands. Some intrepid black men purposefully lingered at night around bus stops to see if they could bait the killer still on the rampage – some with the goal of dishing out their own form of justice.

For months, dogged District Attorney Edward C. Cosgrove and his fleet of investigators labored to put a stop to the madness. As a young newspaper reporter, your author covered the story and all of its bizarre turns. Even John W. Hinckley, the would-be presidential assassin, was actively considered a suspect in the Western New York killings. Around the same age as the killer, Hinckley had used a similar firearm to shoot President Reagan on March 30, 1981, just days before a telephone call from a Fort Benning, Georgia military policeman about a peculiar, jailed Buffalonian they had in custody there, Joey G. Christopher. This man would come to be known as the .22 Caliber Killer. He hated to be called Joey.

This is Joey's story.

CHAPTER ONE

Bullets Begin

A dropout from Buffalo's central city Burgard High School, Joey didn't have much going for him other than his hobby, which he took very seriously. After the death of his father, Joey joined the Bisonette Gun Club. Joey's beloved father had been a member. After 120 hours of instruction, Joey passed a rigorous firearms course. He was certified as a firearms instructor at age 24. For months, Joey joined with other volunteer instructors at the club in training hundreds of area residents on safe gun handling techniques. He also taught a preparatory course for obtaining a pistol permit. At the time, the Bisonette was using the firing range on the Main Street campus of Buffalo's Canisius College, a local Jesuit institution, where Joey had also gotten a night maintenance job in February 1978. At the time, he still lived with his widowed mother on Weber Street in Buffalo's East Side, which was nearing the end of a demographic transformation into a largely minority community.

Joey's behavioral shortcomings became apparent to his fellow club members after some time in the organization. His periodic flashes of anger upon missing a bullseye were disturbing to many club members. Joey's already-lacking reputation took a serious dive after he lost his bid for the club presidency to a black man in 1979. Club administrators grew increasingly concerned about his bizarre behavior while holding loaded weapons. They opted to cancel his membership, citing his increasingly frequent outbursts on the firing range. John Hemphill, the middle-aged black guard at the Erie County government's County Correctional Facility who beat out Joey for the club presidency, later explained to the Buffalo Courier-Express newspaper in May 1981 that Joey was "eased out" of the club due to his "short fuse."

"We kind of discouraged him from participating" in club activities, Hemphill was quoted as saying.

"He didn't like me either, after he wanted to be president and I was appointed president instead."

Joey was fired from his job college maintenance job in March 1979. He had only managed to hold onto that position, which he actually really liked, for around 13 months. His dismissal came some time after a black coworker turned Joey in to college administrators for his habit of carrying a handgun on campus. He ostensibly used it on the campus firing range. Joey was confronted by the college administration in the summer of 1978 about his gun-toting. Administrators warned that it was illegal for him to have firearms on campus for any reason. But Joey didn't lose his job over his weapons. He was fired in March 1979 for sleeping on the job, having been discovered a third and final time catching zzz's during his shift.

Soon after these events, Joey's Erie County pistol permit was revoked. Joey dutifully reported misplacing one of the more than half dozen firearms his father had left him. By law, the revocation required Joey to sell off his beloved arsenal. However, Joey would secret away his father's .22 caliber rifle along with numerous hunting knives, in the basement of the family's Weber Street home.

Something snapped within Joey in the months after his firing and lost bid for the gun club presidency. His first violent strike took place sometime in 1980. According to reports, Christopher may have hesitated somewhat in a first attack on an unknown male. The story is that that man either slugged his attacker and fought him off, or successfully fled in panic as he saw Joey coming at him with a hunting knife.

Apparently frustrated at being bested once again by a black man, Joey took a few days after that failed attempt to plan a more serious endeavor, making use of his Bisonette Gun Club training. For this task, he selected his late father's cherished .22 caliber Sturm-Ruger 10-22 semi-automatic rifle, the barrel of which he shaved down so as to carry it on the streets inconspicuously. He left the house under cover of darkness, launching his campaign by killing four black males over a 35-and-one-quarter-hour period between 10 p.m. September 22, 1980 and 9:15 a.m. September 24, 1980.

NUMBER ONE

Glenn Dunn, a 14-year-old rookie car thief, picked the wrong place to park just hours after he stole his first and, apparently only, vehicle. Weeks before his death, Glenn Dunn, one of eight children, had enrolled at the city's Kensington High School. The athletically-gifted boy, a football wide-receiver and schoolyard basketball guard, had hoped to make the varsity squads there. But on September 22,

Joey's target practice site. Photo courtesy Buffalo Courier-Express Archive, E. H. Butler Library, SUNY College at Buffalo

1980, the teenager made what proved to be the fatal mistake of pulling into the parking lot of the Tops supermarket on Genesee Street near Schiller Park. He made the stop shortly before 9:30 p.m. as a favor to his passenger, Larry Robinson, who needed to cash a check. Motivated by his first unsuccessful attempt to "punish" a black man days before, Joey decided that night to escalate his campaign. He tucked his shortened rifle into a grocery back to avoid detection as he prowled the streets looking for potential victims.

With the increasing minority makeup of his own neighborhood, Joey early on opted for victims of last minute choice rather than targeting blacks with whom he had an association. That way, he figured, he would not have to fear some grieving neighborhood resident telling police about the strange white boy who lived on Weber Street with his mother.

Dunn parked his stolen car about 100 feet from the supermarket entrance. Joey had walked to the Tops parking lot from his own home just blocks away. Spotting the Dunn youth sitting in the stolen car, Joey blithely ignored the presence of a teenage boy and a clear-eyed former psychiatric nurse doing her weekly shopping. Wearing a hooded sweatshirt, Joey shuffled over to the stolen car with his trademark awkward gait. Pointing his weapon through the open driver's side window, Joey pumped three bullets into the fourteen-year-old driver.

Dunn was pronounced dead only eight hours after he – and possibly accomplices – stole a $10,000 blue Buick Century from the Paul Batt Buick dealership on Walden Avenue in the Buffalo suburb of Cheektowaga. Trauma doctors at the then-county-government-owned Erie County Medical Center on Grider Street would find gunshot wounds on the left side of Dunn's head and in his chest.

The 30-year-old Larry Robinson, who had talked Dunn into stopping at the supermarket, told authorities he had known the young murder victim for years but was unaware of his exact age. Robinson also told authorities that Dunn had not revealed that the car they were in was stolen until about an hour before the shooting.

Barbara Wozniak, a Floss Street housewife, told authorities she heard what she described as the sound of firecrackers as she was walking into the supermarket entrance just as Joey unloaded the barrel of his weapon into Dunn. But, she never saw the shooter's face. Madonna Gorney, a 30-year-old former psychiatric nurse, told investigators she got an arms-length view of Joey's face in the supermarket parking lot and saw him standing near the Dunn car moments before the shooting. Mrs. Gorney told police that when she walked past Joey as he sat outside the supermarket entrance, he had a rather "dull or blank" look on his face.

Another witness had a more direct line of sight – and also some direct knowledge about the identity of the shooter. Robert S. Oddo could see flames coming out of the weapon as the shooter repeatedly fired his gun at the driver of the vehicle. Oddo also knew the man firing it. He had grown up in the same East Side Buffalo neighborhood as Joey. Oddo, a Buffalo high school dropout-turned-laborer, had briefly dated one of Joey's three sisters. He had first noticed Joey sitting on a bench near the store entrance with a grocery bag next to him. Joey had likely sat on that bench for some time as he waited to spot his victim.

After witnessing the violent display, Oddo saw Joey flee the parking lot onto Floss Street heading north, right past Oddo's own Floss Street home and in the right direction to get to Joey's Weber Street home, which was only two blocks from the scene. Yet, Oddo told police on the night of the Dunn killing that he could only provide a general description of the killer. Later, he deliberately misled a grand jury by claiming that the killer had blonde hair, instead of brown, like Joey's. Oddo foolishly thought he could get a big cash reward for his knowledge, so he hid what he knew. He was the only actual eyewitness with the ability to identify the killer. It's reasonable to speculate that, had he not concealed his knowledge, many lives could have been saved.

As cruel evidence of the festering thread of racial hatred very much still alive at the time, the September 27, 1980 funeral of Glenn Dunn was marred by a terrible racist display. Two vehicles full of white males screamed out racist slurs as they drove past the standing-room-only crowd that had gathered outside St. Paul's Missionary Baptist Church on Kingsley Street during the late morning service. Horrified mourners told police some of these white males flew past the scene in a brown pick-up truck and the others followed in a blue compact car, which bore a grotesque display of a mannequin's head mounted on the hood. The funeral had attracted about 500 people to pay their last respects to a boy many hadn't even known, but who had tragically ended up the first of the four black victims shot that week in Buffalo and Niagara Falls. Because the Kingsley Street church was small, many had to stand outside for the service which had started at about 10 a.m. A number of the mourners reported to police that those foul-mouthed white men had smeared themselves with red paint and had drawn facsimile bullet holes on their bare upper bodies to further their denigration of the funeral service. Distracted by their grief, the mourners failed to take down the license plate numbers of the two vehicles. Unfortunately, no one was ever arrested for that vicious prank, which brought only more tears to the eyes of the many mourners at the service.

Joey apparently became energized by the success of his "hit" on Glenn Dunn. While authorities were ultimately certain he had nothing to do with the desecration of the boy's funeral, the second victim came not long after the first.

NUMBER TWO

About 14 hours after Dunn was murdered, Harold Green was fatally shot less than a block away from a Genesee Street church, also while sitting calmly in a car. Green was a 32-year-old honorably discharged U.S. Air Force veteran, who had been slowly working his way up the corporate ladder as an industrial engineer. At the time, Green was using his GI Bill funds and personal savings to continue studying for a bachelor's degree in engineering from the State University of New York College at Buffalo. He was munching on a sandwich during his lunch break in the parking lot of a Burger King restaurant in the 2000 block of Union Road in Cheektowaga when Christopher lumbered up to his parked car and shot him twice in the left side of his head about 12:40 p.m. on September 23, 1980. The brazen attack took place in broad daylight, not even a day after Dunn was killed.

Green, who had been promoted only a month earlier to an assistant engineering job at the Moog Valve Corporation, just blocks away from his murder scene, was pronounced dead at Cheektowaga's St. Joseph Intercommunity Hospital on September 28, 1980 after five days in a coma. Considered a technical wizard even before he graduated from Buffalo's Hutchinson Central Technical High School, one of the area's top public secondary schools, Green studied engineering at Buffalo's Erie Community College before going into the Air Force. During his four-year tour of duty, Green applied his engineering talents towards repairing bombers, even earning an award for outstanding service to his country. At the time of his murder, he was studying for his undergraduate degree in engineering while holding down a full time, well-paying job at the Cheektowaga manufacturing concern.

Sitting in the St. Joseph's hospital waiting room hours after her brother's shooting, Green's sister Debbie Tucker told a Buffalo Courier-Express reporter that, growing up on the city's East Side, her "truly brilliant" and now-dying brother had mastered the art of photography and played the saxophone. He had even built the stereo components in his home. Ms. Tucker told the reporter that her dying brother was their family's "earthly guardian angel," always following the straight and narrow path. Mary Tucker, another of Green's sisters, told the reporter in the hospital waiting room, that their brother, who had things breaking his way both professionally and personally at the time of the shooting, "was not a pompous person and he just took what was given him in stride."

"I think that's the thing that troubles us," Mary Tucker told the reporter. "If he was the kind of guy who was looking for trouble, maybe we could understand it. But, he was serious, hardworking, kept to himself, nothing but his family. He shunned trouble."

Though the Burger King parking lot was crowded during Green's lunch time shooting, police got somewhat confusing descriptions of the killer from a number of persons who claimed that they had seen someone lumbering away from Green's vehicle. Linda Snyder, a New York State Thruway Authority secretary, told authorities she heard what sounded like firecrackers as Green was shot. However, she could not identify the face of the shooter, who had plodded away from the scene with an odd gait.

NUMBER THREE

Emmanuel Thomas, a 31-year-old unemployed painter, was crossing East Ferry Street near his Zenner Street home with his buddy Franchoine "Frenchy" Cook at about 11:30 p.m. on September 23, 1980 when he was stopped in his tracks. He was trying to get back to Dorothy, his beloved wife of ten years, and his two young daughters, Sonia and Kimberly, when Joey walked behind him and yelled, "Hey, you!" That cry prompted Thomas to pivot around just as Joey fired three shots from his sawed-off rifle. Anthony Szymanski had been standing with some friends at the corner of East Ferry and Zenner when he heard Cook yell out to Thomas "everybody duck!"

Only one of the three bullets hit Thomas, but that bullet pierced his left temple and killed him instantly. Joey just lumbered away. According to what Mrs. Thomas later told authorities, a boy came to her door about 11:30 p.m. to tell her about the shooting at the intersection.

This was the third murder of a black man in about 24 hours. However, investigators sought possible motives and suspects in many unrelated arenas. Thomas and his wife had been scheduled, some eleven or twelve hours or so, after his murder, to testify at a Buffalo City Court proceeding on a reckless endangerment complaint against a neighbor. Mrs. Thomas and her husband had been slated to go to Buffalo City Court for a hearing on a complaint they had filed against Leslie Coleman, who lived two doors away from them on Zenner. Mrs. Thomas said Coleman had fired his rifle over her head during a neighborhood scuffle on August 24, 1980. Despite this dispute, Mrs. Thomas gave no indication that the unruly neighbor made any physical threats against her husband.

The investigation established that Thomas had returned to his drug-using, despite assurances to his wife that he was remaining clean. Mrs. Thomas strongly challenged the autopsy on her spouse that gave some indication he had returned to illicit drug use. To investigators, this opened possible lines of investigation about drug-related dealings. At this stage, law enforcement officials were not yet treating the killings as related.

But after Harold Green, Joey's second victim, was declared dead, investigators told the media that ballistic tests proved that the same weapon had been used to murder all of the black victims killed in Buffalo that week. Still, there was little immediate concern amongst law enforcement about a racist serial killing spree being underway. This was in part due to the fact that certain witnesses in the Burger King parking said they recalled the shooter as being an older man and wearing a hat, which prevented them from seeing the color of his hair. Two witnesses to Dunn's murder had described a youngish killer. And witnesses to the murder of Emmanuel Thomas, the third of Joey's shooting victim's, would speak of a gunman with shoulder-length blond hair. Also complicating the investigation, a teenaged Bailey Avenue car wash worker, Anthony Szymanski, also Burgard High dropout like Joey, insisted the gunman who killed Thomas had shoulder-length blond hair and a bald spot on the back of his head. Investigators told the news media they could not rule out the possibility that several racist attackers were using the same weapon to attack black men in Western New York. Cheektowaga Police Detective Dan Greene told the Buffalo Courier-Express, "Maybe its two guys working together or maybe our composite's wrong; maybe people just saw the guy differently."

Authorities learned from Mrs. Thomas and friends of the family, that even though Emmanuel had recently been out of work, he had been slated to return to employment within a week of his murder. His mother, Clara, tearfully lamented to a Courier-Express reporter: "So many times he'd come over here to use the phone – call people for a job, ask 'em, beg 'em. Why would anyone in the world kill him? Why? I will never know." Thomas, who had recently joined the choir at Buffalo's New Macedonian Church of God, had worked on the painting of the Peace Bridge linking Buffalo with Fort Erie, Ontario and on the new Buffalo Hilton hotel. Instead of a 32nd birthday celebration, which would have happened four days after the date of the killing, a funeral was held.

Widowed at the age of 29 with two young daughters, Mrs. Thomas moved off Zenner Street as quickly as she could. She also resumed the job search she had abandoned while her husband was working as a painter. Mrs. Thomas later told a Courier-Express reporter she had wanted to move "anywhere, just off Zenner Street."

"I'm really catching hell. I'm trying to get a job. My children are getting Social Security because of their father's death, but that's not enough for us to live on. I've always stayed home with the kids and when my husband was alive that was no problem, but now . . ." she said with tears in her eyes, trailing off.

During that Courier-Express interview, Mrs. Thomas said her 11-year-old daughter, Kimberly, was the subject of teasing by classmates at Buffalo's School II. She said that, with the cruelty that children can sometimes unfortunately display, classmates had nastily taunted Kimberly that, "Your father's dead and my daddy's alive." Kimberly's grades dropped amidst the constant hurtful remarks. While her teacher felt she had a strong intellectual ability to do good school work, Mrs. Thomas told the reporter her daughter seemed to have "some sort of mental block."

"I know what that's about – she's thinking about her father," the widow added. Mrs. Thomas said her 12-year-old daughter Sonya seemed to be free of such emotional problems at school, Buffalo's School 68.

"But," she stressed to the Courier reporter, "this summer I know they'll be thinking of their daddy. They were so attached to him. He used to take them on outings. I know they'll be sitting on that front porch waiting for him to come take them out."

Many months would pass before Joey was identified as a suspect. Families would spend what felt like an eternity with no sign of closure, and the black community raised concerns that the police were not doing enough to investigate the deaths of the black victims.

Joey was pleased to no end about the confusion over the gunman or gunmen. He was closely following news reports of the killings.

The spree continued unabated.

NUMBER FOUR

Joe Louis McCoy, 43, a lifelong bachelor, died seconds after Joey walked up to him at Niagara Falls' 11th and Cleveland streets at about 9 a.m. September 24, 1980 as he was returning to his Pierce Avenue home after his daily stroll. Joey, with his sawed-off .22 in a grocery bag, twisted McCoy in a hammerlock as he stuck the grocery bag to his head and shot him twice before waddling away in broad daylight with witnesses present. Witnesses told Niagara Falls police that the shooter had light-colored or blond hair. But none of those witnesses were able to make a positive identification of any potential suspects.

(BF1B-Oct. ⊕)SHOOTING VICTIMS--Four Buffalo-area men are victims of the lone gunman known as the ".22-caliber killer." They include (top): Glen Dunn, 14, Buffalo, and Harold Green, 32, Buffalo, and (bottom) Emanuel Thomas, 31, Buffalo, and Joseph McCoy, 43, Niagara Falls. Identities run left to right. (AP Laserphoto) (mr61750c-x fls) 1980
(Eds: This is a 1980 Courier-Express file picture)

Joey's four first victims. Photo courtesy Buffalo Courier-Express Archive, E.H. Butler Library, SUNY College at Buffalo

McCoy, who was known to have had a drinking problem and a minor criminal record, but no recent troubles, had last worked in a custodian's job at a Niagara Falls community center. He had obtained that job as a result of the federal Comprehensive Employment and Training Act (CETA) program, one of the federal government's many dollar-losing work training programs heavy in bureaucracy and low in long-term job creations in the late 20th century. At the time of his death, McCoy had been out of work.

McCoy was one of seven siblings. Robert McCoy, the victim's oldest brother, told the Buffalo Courier-Express after the shooting that his brother was, "just minding his own business, taking a walk like he does every day," when the gunman struck. McCoy told police and the news media that his brother had no known enemies and was likely just a random victim. He did not think that his brother had any white friends or associates whom he could have angered.

"Joe didn't have anything that anyone would want," Robert McCoy told a Courier reporter, adding, "He had no enemies. It was just senseless."

According to witnesses to the brazen daylight killing, McCoy never had a chance because, "when he turned, the gun was right there."

The victim's mother, Alberta McCoy, told the Buffalo Courier-Express, "Every day that goes by it hurts a little more."

"There are so many things I never got to say to Joe before he died. I'm just hurt," she added.

The killings coming so close together had prompted frustrated lawmen to turn to some unconventional methods for guidance. On October 3, 1980, District Attorney Cosgrove found himself entertaining a New York State Police plan to have a state trooper, who also happened to be a trained hypnotist, address one of the witnesses to Harold Green's daylight murder in Cheektowaga. Capt. Henry F. Williams, commander of the State Police Bureau of Criminal Investigation in Western New York and a dear friend and professional colleague of Cosgrove, had arranged to have trooper-hypnotist Robert Narrigan come from across the state to work on a man Cheektowaga police considered – wrongly – to be one of the best witnesses to the Green murder. But, Cosgrove quickly quashed that idea.

It turned out later that the alleged eyewitness had personally suggested to troopers that he might be able to remember more details of the Green killing under hypnosis. However, Cosgrove's decision not to use a hypnotist didn't prevent the resourceful Buffalo Homicide Chief Donovan from spending five hours with an astrologer and a psychic on October 6th in an effort to get more information about the killer. As it turned out, neither the astrologer nor the psychic warned Donovan that two Buffalo cab drivers were about to become the victims of two of Joey's more grisly attacks.

HEARTS OF DARKNESS

After the murder of four black males over that frightening 35 and ¼ hour period, a University of Buffalo psychologist who specialized in profiling dangerous criminal behavior correctly predicted that the then-unidentified killer would strike again.

On September 29, 1980, Dr. Norman Solkoff, of UB's Psychiatric Department, told a Buffalo Courier-Express reporter it would be reasonable to expect the violent killer, who made sure he shot all four victims on the left side of their faces – even forcibly turning one of the victim's head to ensure a left-side shot – would strike again.

"One of the best predictors of dangerous violent behavior is previous violence," Solkoff said.

"In view of the fact that four murders have been committed, more murders would have to be predicted," he added.

Solkoff's comments came ten days before Joey used a hatchet to kill two Buffalo taxicab drivers, 71-year-old Army vet and widower Parlor W. Edwards and 40-year-old Ernest "Shorty" Jones. Both victims worked nights on the city's East Side. They frequently catered to drunks, prostitutes and other colorful characters, who were also frequently very good tippers. Joey struck down Edwards on October 8, 1980. The very next night, Joey used a hammer and a sharp knife to murder "Shorty" Jones. Joey horribly dismembered both of those victims by crudely cutting out each of their hearts, just as had done when gutting the innards of deer after hunting with his father.

Due to the volume of news coverage that his spree was generating, Joey had rethought his homicidal methods. He employed a blow torch to melt down his beloved .22 caliber rifle before he set out in search of his next victims. This act both eliminated the weapon as evidence and demonstrated Joey's alertness to local news developments. Before leaving the house, Joey put his hatchet in a brown grocery bag, the same type of bag he had used to tote his now-destroyed rifle. He also brought another tool specially crafted for the events – a set of sharp wooden stakes.

Flagging Edwards down a short time after midnight on October 8, 1980, Joey asked to be driven to an industrial park off Sugg Road in Cheektowaga near the Greater Buffalo International Airport. After he had Edwards pull into a deserted business parking lot on Sugg Road, Edwards must have gotten a little suspicious. All of the businesses in the park were closed. Before Edwards could inquire, Joey whacked him with a hatchet from the back seat. But Joey did not strike a very good first blow. Edwards hurled himself out of the cab, but not before grabbing an iron bar he kept with him for just such encounters. Edwards, a well-conditioned 5 feet 10 inch, 180 lb. father of six, struggled with his attacker for about five minutes before Joey managed to knock him unconscious with the blunt end of the hatchet. Edwards fell to the ground. Joey kept pounding him on the head with the hatchet until he stopped breathing.

Feeling "crazy" and "strong, too," according to his later admissions, Joey then used the hunting knife to carve out the taxi driver's heart. He then drove one of the wooden stakes through the severed, blood-soaked organ. After wiping away blood from his face with the dead cabbie's own clothing, Joey stuffed him in the trunk of his cab and walked off. He discarded the heart in a field close to the airport. There, it was assumed that animals consumed it as if it were carrion.

The next night, also just after midnight, the methodical Joey, grocery bag in hand, flagged down "Shorty" Jones and had him drive him to a boat-launching ramp in another Buffalo suburb, Tonawanda. Unlike the feisty Edwards, who had fought for his life, Jones died without a struggle after being hit on the back of his head with a hammer. After crudely cutting out Jones' heart, Joey ceremoniously impaled it on a foot-long wooden stake. To guarantee Jones was dead, Joey slashed his throat and left him bleeding on the boat ramp. He discarded the blood-soaked heart in a field off Sheridan Drive after carrying it for some time in the grocery bag he brought with him. Again, animal vermin quickly consumed the second cabbie's heart. Authorities never recovered any bits of either organ.

Dr. Catherine Lloyd, Erie County's chief medical examiner, performed autopsies on the 145 lb. Jones and the 180 lb. Edwards hours after their bodies were found. She cited the cause of both their deaths as "exsanguination [severe blood loss] due to multiple injuries." In the Edwards case, Dr. Lloyd cited "multiple injuries to the head and chest." Because of the mounting intensity of the probe for the Western New York murderer, Dr. Michael Baden, the famed New York City pathologist, left a ball in the Big Apple and was flown to Buffalo still dressed in his tuxedo, and still smelling of sweat and alcohol. Baden agreed with Dr. Lloyd's findings.

Shortly after the mutilation murders, one of Edwards' daughters, who spoke on the condition that the news media never release her name, told Buffalo Evening News reporter Lonnie Hudkins that she couldn't understand why anyone would want to kill her father. Calling her father "a good man," who "didn't have any enemy in the world," Edwards' daughter said he only drove a cab at night because "he liked the work."

The two murders prompted the FBI to send evidence teams to Buffalo in the days after those attacks. They also prompted never-identified white supremacists to set fire to a large wooden cross, Ku Klux Klan-style, on a street corner on Buffalo's Jefferson Avenue in the heart of the black community hours after "Shorty" Jones body was discovered. Street-seasoned Buffalo police officers quickly doused that cross and continued to patrol amidst what they described to the news media as a "tense" atmosphere throughout the city.

RECRUITED

The unemployed Christopher and law enforcement officials – for vastly different reasons – benefited from the rush by the nation's armed services to refill their ranks after the military cutbacks Congress imposed after the nation abandoned Vietnam to the communist-supported forces of Ho Chi Minh in the mid-1970s.

Joey was bothered by his inability to hold a steady job. The army could fix that. Unaware of Christopher's bizarre hatred of black men and eager to boost her recruitment numbers, Sgt. Paulette Ratcliff, a U.S. Army recruiter, spent what she later described as "hours" with Joey after he first showed up at her recruitment office at the Federal Building on West Huron Street in downtown Buffalo on September 16, 1980, six days before his killing spree began. Sergeant Ratcliff considered Joey a "hot item" in terms of recruits because he came to her office the first time in what she later called, "such short hair I thought he was in the military already."

The Army recruiter was glad to learn that the only thing Joey needed before she could "get him into boots" was a physical. She expressed satisfaction at the fact that he had passed a military aptitude test in 1979 during an earlier attempt at enlistment, one that would be foiled by a hernia. During this second attempt, Joey apparently gave no indication and no records existed that might have indicated that Joey, of average intelligence, was really a slowly-smoldering homicidal racist.

At that time, the U.S. military was not being too selective about the various psychological issues that could affect a recruit's performance. Ratcliff told authorities she drove Joey back and forth from his Weber Street home several times before he was officially enlisted into the Army. One of those trips home was even to correct Joey's medical records after he belatedly disclosed that he had experimented with marijuana. The recruiter told authorities that she formally enlisted Joey into the Army six days before the Dunn murder. She would always contend that published police sketches of the suspected killer looked nothing like the clean-cut individual she first met on September 16, 1980.

CHAPTER TWO

The Task Force

The four so-called ".22 caliber killings" of four black men in Buffalo, and its northern neighbor Niagara Falls, in less than 36 hours between September 22, 1980 and September 24, 1980 sparked a fast-moving police investigation. The common racial theme and forensic similarities in those four homicides prompted Edward C. Cosgrove, the Erie County District Attorney, to take a closer-than-normal look at the killings long before his prosecutorial staff could begin to seek a conviction for any of them. The unique nature of those four killings quickly convinced Cosgrove, a former FBI special agent, that despite the good initial police work underway in both Buffalo and Niagara Falls, a more coordinated investigation was justified.

It was at 4:30 a.m. on October 9, 1980, that Buffalo Police Homicide Bureau got a call about the discovery at the foot of Sheridan Avenue of what proved to be the body of "Shorty" Jones, along with a knife, a trail of blood and a watch, near the mutilated corpse. Cosgrove had been formulating an overall investigative strategy to handle the initial four killings, but the gruesome killings of two black Buffalo cabbies on October 8th and 9th, kicked the investigation into high gear. He quickly called New York State Governor Hugh L. Carey to get his permission to set up what became known as the Major Homicide Task Force. Governor Carey was a personal friend of Cosgrove's.

Cosgrove speaks to the media. Photo courtesy Buffalo Courier-Express Archive, E.H Butler Library, SUNY College at Buffalo

In a successful effort to prevent news leaks on the work of what quickly grew into a 185-member task force, Cosgrove insisted on being its only public spokesman. This decision caused him to become the target of complaints by many local black community leaders who were unsatisfied with the amount of time the probe was taking to produce any results.

Enlisting the aid of veteran investigators from eight New York law enforcement agencies, Cosgrove selected as his Task Force "field commanders" Captain Henry F. Williams, then head of Western New York operations of the New York State Police Bureau of Criminal Investigation, and Leo J. Donovan, the chief of the Buffalo Police Homicide Bureau, both near-legendary Western New York lawmen. Cosgrove kept the FBI fully informed on all aspects of the work, given the potential implications of the random continuing attacks on black men.

A command post was set up for the Major Homicide Task Force in Cosgrove's downtown Buffalo prosecutorial office. Within its first 24 hours of operation, the task force had its own dedicated telephone lines, office equipment and a hotline for tips. Cosgrove had several inner walls in his 100-person prosecutor's office torn down in order to consolidate operations in a single section of his sprawling, multi-floor operation at the Erie County government building at 25 Delaware Avenue.

In the first two weeks of the task force's operation, Cosgrove handled over two hundred telephone calls from news agencies as far west as Los Angeles, as far north as Toronto and as far south as Atlanta, which since 1979 had been enduring the agony of the similar killings of young black children in what became known as the Atlanta Child Murders. All three national television networks had crews monitoring developments in the Buffalo attacks. Both the New York Times and Newsweek magazine assigned staffers to Buffalo to keep watch. Cosgrove defended his role as the sole spokesman for the homicide task force as his effort to minimize the possibility of inaccurate or potentially inflammatory information being passed on to the news media and the public. To some, this may have constituted a news blackout. However, tensions would repeatedly to spark between the press and law enforcement agencies for the duration of the investigation and proceedings.

On October 10, 1980, Dr. Michael Baden, the nationally-renowned forensic pathologist, and the University of New Mexico's Dr. Homer Campbell, a noted forensic odontologist skilled in examining dental structures, had flown into Buffalo to examine the corpses of the two slain cabbies. An FBI artist was also brought to Buffalo to develop artistic renderings of possible suspects. Those renderings, later criticized for looking nothing like Joey, were disseminated nationwide.

The Major Homicide Task Force was hard at work in "Phase I" of the investigation during the last three months of 1980. Ballistics testing of shell casings and slugs from all four fatal shootings confirmed that they had come from a sawed-off .22 caliber Sturm Ruger rifle. Local and national media quickly seized upon these facts, christening the unknown assailant as the .22 Caliber Killer. Task force members developed early computer software to accommodate the more than 175,000 bits of information that had been gathered in the investigation. The 24-hour-a-day continent-wide investigation generated some 5,018 tips and ultimately lead to investigations of 7500 vehicles, 11,000 possible murder weapons, and 2000 possible suspects – none of them Joey.

AND THAT'S THE WAY IT WASN'T

In October 1980, Walter Cronkite, for decades regarded as the predominant news voice in America and affectionately known as "Uncle Walter" to millions, erroneously announced to the nation on the CBS Evening News, his throne to his immortality, that Buffalo police had put at the top of their list of suspects in Joey's march to kill black men, an individual whom Uncle Walter said was wanted in at least six other states for questioning in connection with a series of shootings. Hours after the broadcast of that statement, Leo J. Donovan, the near-legendary chief of the Buffalo Police homicide bureau, told the local news media the Cronkite report was, "just not true."

Donovan accurately stated that lawmen were convinced the killer was from the Buffalo area. The chief also theorized that it would have been too risky for an out-of-town killer to stage the Buffalo-area shootings because of his unfamiliarity with the area and slim knowledge of possible escape routes. On October 3, 1980, Donovan stated – rather prophetically – that he was inclined to believe that one white man with a hatred of blacks and who lived in the Buffalo area had been committing the murders.

With that, Donovan may have short-circuited the strategically-gifted Erie County District Attorney Edward C. Cosgrove's attempt to impose a news blackout on the still-unsuccessful search for the racist killer of Buffalo-area black men. Though Donovan, always the cagey master investigator, did not air any grievances publicly, sources within the task force told the Buffalo Courier-Express that Donovan had disagreed with Cosgrove during a closed-door strategy session about the media blackout plan. Sources told the Buffalo Courier-Express that during an October 2, 1980 meeting in Cosgrove's downtown Buffalo office, Donovan had objected to the news blackout order, believing that it would actually hamper investigative efforts. Donovan had apparently stressed during that strategy session that he had already personally investigated over 1,000 homicides. His team of detectives had an excellent solution and conviction record. If he felt that the release of some information would help solve the murder campaign, he would see to it that the public learned of that information some way or other. On October 3, 1980, due in large part to Donovan's objections behind closed doors the day before, District Attorney Cosgrove rescinded his news blackout order.

Chief Donovan, who without intending to, had publicly disgraced "Uncle Walter," and stopped Cosgrove from turning the local news media into a possible enemy of the murder investigation with a news blackout. He was ultimately awarded a place of honor at Joey's eventual Buffalo murder indictment.

UNLUCKY NUMBER SEVEN

Two days after his last very strenuous run-in with a feisty, but ultimately murdered cab driver, Joey decided to change his tactics and try his luck at a Buffalo hospital where he and his family had gone for treatment. Dressed to not call too much attention to himself, Joey awkwardly stalked the halls of the Erie County Medical Center on Buffalo's Grider Street for several hours searching for his next victim. Appearing to be visiting some patient in the very busy, county-run hospital catering to the city's poor, Joey stumbled upon a frail Collin Cole, a 37-year-old male prostitute only recently paroled from prison. He was drying out in the hospital's seventh floor detoxification unit. Cole was the only black patient on that floor.

Joey didn't know Cole's background – he had a lengthy history of prostitution and vice charges, accumulated over many years spent strolling along the city's then sexually-debauched Chippewa Street,

passing as a "good-looking" female. Cole was now in the detoxification unit receiving treatment for a barbiturate overdose. He had
been paroled from the infamous Attica Correctional Facility east of
Buffalo after serving almost two years on a grand larceny conviction
from a May 1, 1977 $50 mugging of an 86-year-old man who had
been walking to an East Side senior citizens center for a hot lunch.
A year before the mugging, Cole, who had a history of vice arrests in
the 1960s and 1970s, served a four-month term at the Erie County
Correctional Facility east of Buffalo for forging a stolen check and
paying himself $122 from a closed bank account.

To Joey, who was still energized by his macabre attack on the
two cabbies, Cole was just an ailing black man unlikely to give him
any trouble. Knowing there was usually a flurry of movement, as
well as a supply of unattended patients, during mid-afternoon shift
change, Joey chose to enter the hospital at about 3 p.m. The attacker
began prowling the halls until he got to the seventh floor.

Joey closed the door to the two-patient Room 752 where Cole
lied alone in the bed closest to the window. Right as Joey began
strangling the ailing and uncombative Cole, a nurse walked by. That
nurse later told police that she had remembered leaving the door to
Cole's room open – she found it curious to see it closed. Following
her intuition, she entered the room. Startled, Joey quickly yelled
out, "He's fallen and hurt himself," and scuttled out of the way. The
nurse, who had apparently not seen Joey nearly choke Cole to death,
came to the aid of the "fallen" patient. Joey quickly left the room,
caught a nearby elevator and quickly fled the television-monitored
hospital without discovery or apprehension. Afterwards, officials
claimed a security guard had stopped Joey as he was fleeing and for
some reason claimed he was allowed through because he showed the
guard a security card.

No one will ever know how Joey made it, unfilmed and unstopped, out of that hospital crowded with patients, visitors and staff. District Attorney Cosgrove told the news media that the nurse and three other hospital workers had identified the would-be hospital killer as likely to be the same white serial killer running amok in the city, despite the fact that current descriptions pegged him as having dirty blond or light-colored hair. The witness descriptions available at the time didn't focus anywhere near Joey's true look.

Cole had to be taken to surgery for an emergency tracheotomy due to the severe neck injury. Joey had managed to inflict a crushed larynx before the nurse opened the door. The nurse had quickly sprinted to get medical aid and security guards. When guards flooded into Cole's room, the seriously injured patient told them, just before lapsing into unconsciousness, that his attacker said only: "I hate niggers!" Joey would never be charged with that October 10, 1980 hospital room attack.

Because of the two cabbie mutilation murders, the manhunt for a racist psychopath had grown to the point where black Erie County sheriff's deputies and New York State troopers were pretending to be taxi drivers looking for fares during late night drives through Buffalo's largely-minority East Side. By mid-October 1980, the task force was also directed to keep surveillance on any and all Ku Klux Klan-related activities in northwestern Pennsylvania, just south of western New York. That included reports on the various groups that the task force was told might show up to demonstrate against the Klan at a meeting scheduled for Fayette County, Pennsylvania on October 25, 1980. Such was the intensity of the search for the then unknown killer.

The seventh attack on a black man in Western New York prompted Assistant U.S. Attorney Drew S. Days III, chief of the Justice Department's Civil Rights Division, to come to Buffalo late in October 1980 to confer with Cosgrove and U.S. Attorney Richard J. Arcara. Days also met with about 30 area religious, civic, educational and law enforcement leaders during his brief fact-finding mission. In November 1980, Cosgrove and his task force also began corresponding with Atlanta Mayor Maynard Jackson and that city's Special Task Force on Missing Children, which was dealing with the horrors of serial killer Wayne Williams' systematic killings of up to 29 black youths and two adults beginning in 1979. Cosgrove's task force members met with prosecutors and investigators from the office of Fulton County, Georgia District Attorney Lewis Slaton to compare technical investigative issues. In a similar twist, Williams, who was a 23-year-old freelance photographer, also failed to resemble police artist sketches put out during the frantic search. Cosgrove stressed to Slaton's staff that they should emphasize to the news media that an artist's sketch was not supposed to represent the subject in the same manner that a photograph would. The task force instructed that individuals examining the artist's sketch should look to see if it prompted a recognition of someone with the same general features, and not necessarily an identical match.

CHAPTER THREE

Black Voices

S hortly after the four .22 caliber victims were shot and just days before the second victim Harold Green died on September 28, 1980, Henry D. Locke Jr., a Courier-Express newspaper reporter and columnist, interviewed a series of individuals from Buffalo's black community. Responses ranged from outrage at the slowness of the investigation and fear for personal safety, to speculation on the cause of the killings, and, for some, to a melancholic inurement to urban violence and a lack of police response.

Locke found that most of the black men he interviewed in the Buffalo area indicated they were more vigilant about their movements in public. James C. Speller, an artist, said to Locke: "The shootings have made me more cautious because two of the incidents occurred in an area which I frequent quite often. I don't have a car and, by walking, it makes me more vulnerable when a lot of nonsense is going on. I stay off the streets as much as possible."

Charles Grey, an East Side Buffalo property manager, told Locke: "I'm not really looking over my shoulders even if some nut is out there shooting people. I don't have that many enemies, but if the Son of Sam was out there, I would be concerned." The Courier reporter was told by Kenneth Echols, the Buffalo Board of Education's coordinator of integration: "Based on the increasing number of shootings in the last two days I guess I should be more concerned. It also may be wise for persons to avoid being in cars alone or walking down dark streets until the culprit is captured."

Locke was told by Jimmy Mobley, a retired automobile plant worker, that the shootings were the result of the area's high unemployment rate, combined with problems of runaway inflation and efforts to integrate local schools. Rev. James F. Banks, pastor of the Pleasant Grove Baptist Church at 225 Cedar Street, told Locke such incidents frequently take place in large cities around the country. "Drinking and the use of dope also may have had something to do with the shootings," the minister said. "I have reasons to be alarmed, but I haven't started looking back over my shoulders to see whether I'm being followed."

East Side tavern worker Eddie "Baldy" Barnes told Locke, "Shootings are an everyday thing with me, so I'm always overly cautious to avoid being a victim of some nut. The person doing the shooting is the type of animal I would like to run into because he would learn he would be dealing with an animal himself. I deal with psychos everyday so one more nut will be nothing new to me."

Another undercurrent was expressed by J. Carl Bland, a Buffalo machinist and community organizer. He told Locke: "The shootings have raised my concerns, but I'm always concerned when some innocent person has been murdered. When such incidents happen, I find myself asking why. Answers are difficult to come about." James

Tatum, who worked for Goodwill Industries, told the Courier reporter: "It could be some type of a conspiracy going on against black men. But I always make it a practice of looking over my shoulder when I walk the streets. I always check the streets before I leave my apartment."

An October 1980 Newsweek article also quoted Rev. Bennett Smith as expressing what the magazine described as "the most dominant view" of the attacks on blacks when he said, "There is no doubt the killer is mentally deranged, that premeditation is involved and that the killings are racially motivated." Erie County District Attorney Cosgrove was quoted as saying he thought, "[O]ne killer may be responsible for all six," of the Western New York attacks.

The Newsweek piece also painted a picture of unity, which may possibly have been more geared towards assuaging white fears of riots. "So far patience has prevailed . . . aided by gestures of support from the white community," including an official proclamation of a 21-day period of mourning for the six black victims and a "biracial Unity Day" rally held on the steps of Buffalo City Hall on October 19, 1980. Newsweek quoted Edward Tisdale, a 71-year-old Buffalonian, as saying "We're not going to go out hurting innocent people. What happened in Miami won't happen here either. We learned in the '60s not to take our anger out on ourselves and burn up our homes." Tisdale was referring to the three days of rioting, looting and burning in black neighborhoods after an all-white jury on May 17, 1980 acquitted white Miami-Dade police officers involved in the high speed chase that ended in the death of black motorcyclist Arthur McDuffie in December 1979. The Miami Riot of 1980, as it came to be known, was the first major race riot since the late 1960s. It wasn't halted until the Florida National Guard came to the aid of the Miami-Dade police force. Order was restored in that city on May 20, 1980 after ten blacks and eight whites died in the rioting. The four days of rioting resulted in the arrests of more than 800 people and property damage estimated to be well in excess of $80 million.

In a column that ran in the Courier-Express the day Harold Green died, which hit the streets hours before his death, Locke noted that some black officials and community activists speculated whether the .22 caliber shootings were racially motivated at all. Did Buffalo inherit a "Son of Sam" like David Berkowitz, who randomly killed young women and terrorized the New York City area from July 1976 until August 1977?

Certainly, the implications of a series of racially-motivated killings on forward progress and race relations were potentially very serious. In that September 28, 1980 column, Locke quoted Donald R. Lee, a Buffalo executive who was a former president of the New York State Conference of the NAACP, as saying that one of, "[T]he sad things about the questions being raised is that the murderer's actions could possibly trigger some negative reactions between black and white citizens, when in reality it is only some nut out there blowing people away."

"If his actions go unchecked, more and more people will become paranoid and may start arming themselves to guard against the attacker," Lee said. "In other words, they will go on the offensive, rather than the defensive. It will be sort of like a person buying a hunting license that he is not planning to use, but having it in case he needs it," he added. John Mose, minority enterprise coordinator for the Niagara Frontier Transportation Authority, a major Western New York government agency, said to Locke: "I'm not overly concerned about my safety, but I am concerned about the safety of my family. If someone attempts to harm me, I think I will be able to harm him. I will meet force with force."

Dr. Winton J. Hardiman, a former Western Region director of the state NAACP and a retired official of both the U.S. Department of Housing and Urban Development and the New York State Department of Labor, told Locke, "During an era when racial tensions may be running high because of the spiraling inflation and a high unemployment rate," Hardiman said, "the murderer's actions have sent cold waves throughout the black community and probably throughout the area." Community organizer J. Carl Bland told Locke, "No sane person, black or white, would be killing people indiscriminately. He has to be a psychotic who may have a grudge against black men that could be related to the civil rights movement or a racial incident that may have involved him years ago and he has now taken the cowardly way of fighting back."

Lebanon Arrington, a psychological counselor at the State University of New York College at Buffalo and the director of its student judicial system, told Locke that an overlooked theory was the possibility that the killer's actions were orchestrated by the "underworld" or some group that promoted racial hatred in a bid to slow the progress of blacks. But Arrington also told Locke that no matter what motivated the killings, they had sent shock waves in the black community and left it terrorized.

The .22 Caliber Killer so impacted Buffalo's black community that BUILD (Build Unity, Independence, Liberty and Dignity), a major civil rights organization active in the city, held a public forum at its Town Hall meeting at 1420 Main Street on October 7, 1980. BUILD's executive director, Rev. Charley H. Fisher III, called on all Buffalo's leaders and interested citizens to attend the meeting. To begin, Fischer declared, "We must put an end to this killer before more innocent bystanders meet with violent deaths."

He continued, "Since the murders began I have received several complaints from black citizens who said they were harassed by groups of white thugs along Bailey Avenue in the Kensington and Fillmore area. This type of harassment must be stopped immediately to prevent racial violence and further polarization of the various races here," Fisher said.

He told reporter Locke that BUILD invited police agencies, community groups, civil rights organizations, and religious groups to the meeting and also opened it up to anyone interested in bringing the killer to justice.

"The killer's actions that have created a wave of fear throughout the black community; already have made some citizens prisoners in their own homes," Fisher told Locke.

"We have received complaints that some elderly people are afraid to leave their homes out of fear of being killed," he said.

"In addition, the harassment of mourners at a funeral of one of the murder victims last Saturday [Glenn Dunn] has created additional fear among black citizens," Fisher said. "Things are pretty bad when an event as sacred as a funeral cannot be held without being interrupted by persons promoting racial hate," he added. Fisher also told Locke that BUILD was supporting the efforts of other area religious and civil rights organizations including Operation PUSH and the NAACP, which met with Buffalo Police Commissioner James B. Cunningham earlier in the week to discuss the crisis. BUILD joined those groups in calling on the FBI to get involved in the Buffalo investigation.

As weeks progressed without answers, others in the black community became more vocal with their disdain about the investigation's slow progress. William Maddox, described in the Newsweek article as a Buffalo-area drug counselor, was plainly stated, "If the killer was a black man, he'd be caught." With the Western New York black community, in Cosgrove's words, "understandably restive" over the attacks, Cosgrove met with a number of black community leaders and groups almost two dozen times during the first months of the investigation. One of his first meetings was with the nationally renowned civil rights leader Rev. Jesse L. Jackson, then executive director of the national organization, Operation PUSH. During that meeting, Jackson, a spell-binding speaker, remained silent, but Rev. Bennett Smith, one of the most vocal of the Buffalo black leaders critical of the law enforcement efforts, would not stop talking until Cosgrove gently kicked the sole of the clergyman's shoe. Cosgrove's tactic to quiet Smith so he could explain his strategy mortified his assistants in the room. But, as Rev. Jackson was leaving, he quietly quipped to one of Cosgrove's top aides that Cosgrove, who had spoken during the session about how his retired father had spoken publicly about the value of Martin Luther King Jr. to the nation, "had a good speech writer." As the investigation continued into spring 1981 without a suspect, Cosgrove admitted that the black community "became more vocal" in its criticism of the task force operation.

Tensions in Buffalo's black community worsened when a bus driver taking 43 members of the United Voices Choir of St. John the Baptist Church, one the city's major black institutions, was injured when a metal object thrown from the side of the New York State Thruway east of Rochester shattered the driver's window and cut him. The incident came only minutes after a car traveling with other choir members was nearly run off the road in the same area by an automobile carrying three Caucasian individuals giving the white power salute. The injured bus driver was treated at a hospital in Syracuse and was quickly released, but the Thruway incidents worsened morale in Buffalo's black community, coming as close as they did to the killings.

Officials and community leaders took responsive action in the face of the mounting unrest. Cash rewards for the capture of the killer started piling up within days of the first murders. The United Auto Workers labor union and its 25 Western New York chapters joined with the Buffalo Evening News, WKBW-TV, the Buffalo Police Benevolent Association, the Erie County Legislature and students, faculty and staff at the Erie County Community College's City Campus in seeking public donations for either the arrest of the killer or in aid of his victims' families. By the end of October 1980, the amount of awards outstanding for the killer's capture and conviction stood at almost $100,000. This included $75,000 pledged by the City of Buffalo and Erie County governments in cooperation with the Buffalo Area Chamber of Commerce. In addition to police and state troopers driving around Buffalo's East Side late at night in January 1981 hoping to lure the killer, reports began circulating of black men arming themselves and hanging around bus stops. Most of those men hoped to entrap the killer and end his reign of terror on the community, while some others simply hoped to collect the increasing amount of reward money being offered for information leading to the killer's capture.

By December 1980, community tensions continued to rise from all sides, without any leads in sight. A series of planned public demonstrations from both white and black power players contributed to fears of riots breaking out. On December 16, 1980, task force members received a memo ordering them to, "gather any intelligence concerning the planned demonstration by the American Nazi

Party in front of City Hall on January 15, 1981," and ordering them to submit a report on that demonstration no later than January 5, 1981. Also in December 1980, the task force obtained copies of posters advertising: "Wanted 1000 Black Men with Guns." The poster was linked to a planned January 15, 1981 rally at Buffalo City Hall that was allegedly being planned by a group known as "The New Black Knights." Adding to the angst of task force leadership about the upcoming convergence of potentially volatile events, Cosgrove received a January 11, 1981 Western Union telegram from a number of nationally-known civil rights attorneys including William Kunstler and Ramsey Clark formally protesting reports they had received about Buffalo Mayor Jimmy Griffin and Buffalo Police Commissioner Cunningham's alleged plan of "illegal and unconstitutional" actions to interfere with a planned Martin Luther King memorial rally slated for that same cold January day.

NEW YORK, NEW YORK

Joey reported for active duty as a U.S Army enlistee on November 13, 1980 and was sent to Fort Benning, Georgia. There he started basic training with the 197th infantry training brigade, a racially mixed unit that would play a major role in his downfall. With a Christmastime break from basic training and an accumulation of unfulfilled urges, Joey splurged on a bus ticket for a December 19, 1980 joyride to New York City. He arrived there the next day. On December 21, 1980, he bought himself a present at the famous Macy's Department Store – a 10-inch kitchen knife.

The next day he created a lot of overtime pay for several hundred uniformed New York police, plainclothesmen and detectives, as he staged an eight-hour murder and attack spree that became known as the "Midtown Slasher" attacks. This spree left four men, including a dark-skinned Hispanic, dead. The first of the "Midtown Slasher" killings commenced at about 3:30 p.m. December 22, 1980. However, Joey launched a practice round or two with his newly-purchased present at the 14th Street subway station at 11:30 a.m., when he stabbed and seriously wounded a 25-year-old black man, before fleeing unmolested. Then, at about 1:25 p.m., Ivan Frazer, a 32-year-old cook from the Bronx was attacked at the subway station at 53rd Street and Third Avenue. Police later said Frazer probably saved his own life by raising his hand and fending off Joey's knife thrust that otherwise would have struck him in mid-chest. He ended up with a nasty knife cut to the hand, but survived and provided valuable trial testimony.

Louis Rodriguez, a 19-year-old messenger, wasn't so lucky. The first and only Hispanic victim, Rodriquez didn't see his attacker coming. He was fatally stabbed in the chest as he was walking down Madison Avenue between 40th and 41st streets about 3:30 p.m. that afternoon. Joey fatally stabbed his second victim, a 30-year-old black man, on 37th Street near Seventh Avenue at 6:45 p.m.; his third – a 20-year-old black man – on 49th Street between Broadway and Seventh Avenue at 10:40 p.m.; and the fourth – a black "John Doe" never formally identified, at about 11:55 p.m., just outside Penn Station on 33rd Street near Madison Square Garden.

Killing time on Christmas Eve as he waited for his bus to Buffalo, Joey tried to stab Stuckey Anderson, a 38-year-old from the Bronx. But, when he came at Anderson outside the subway entrance on Park Avenue near 41st and 42nd streets, Anderson turned the tables. He grabbed Joey and pushed him down the subway steps, fleeing to report the incident. But, the attacker somehow managed to escape. The sometimes talkative Joey – a trait that would put him on his way to a New York State prison – said nothing to any of his Manhattan victims.

HOME FOR THE HOLIDAYS

Upon his return to Buffalo from his New York City holiday, Joey took a brief Christmas break. He resumed his crusade on December 29, 1980, killing Roger Adams, a 31-year-old Gibbons Street man waiting for a bus at the corner of Buffalo's Broadway Avenue and Beck Street at s7:30 a.m. to get to his job as a word processor for the National Fuel utility company. Joey cut Adams' jugular and stabbed him in the chest.

Seemingly inspired by his New York City excursion, Joey departed for a short jaunt to the nearby city of Rochester, New York. After taking a one-hour bus ride to the Flower City, Joey rammed a knife into the heart of Wendell Barnes, 26, at about 7:40 a.m. as he stood at a bus stop along with several persons from Winnipeg, Manitoba, who were in Rochester attending a church function. Though rushed to a hospital, Barnes died about 35 minutes after Joey stuck him. The horrified Canadians told Rochester detectives, correctly, that the physically awkward Joey had a peculiar gait and "ran funny," but they were never able to identify him from police photographs sent to their far western Canadian hometown two months later. Despite Cosgrove's theories about the connection, on March 21, 1981, Major Anthony Fantigrossi, chief of the Rochester Police detective bureau, made the bold claim that, "There's no way we can establish him [Joey] at the scene of the crime."

Having taken the short bus trip back to Buffalo on December 31, 1980, Joey, hoping to repeat his successful Rochester stunt, walked up to Albert Menefee Jr., a 38-year-old Army combat veteran of the Vietnam War and a decorated paratrooper, outside a drugstore at Main Street and Utica Street shortly after 4 p.m. and asked him for the time. When the congenial Menefee, a General Motors plant worker, replied "4:04," Joey thanked him by sticking a knife into his heart and twisting it. Menefee did not initially realize he had been stabbed. But, when he began feeling blood inside his shirt he quickly gasped, "Get that guy, he stabbed me!" The official task force report based on witness and Menefee testimony, noted that Menefee, "staggered back into the drugstore and collapsed." He was rushed to Buffalo General Hospital, where doctors found his heart had been "nicked" in the stabbing. His condition was initially listed as critical.

A clerk in the drug store told the task force that he witnessed the attack. He said it had been staged by a clean-shaven white man in a green fatigue jacket with its hood down. The attacker, the investigators were told, was wearing a dark red or maroon knit hat and fled west onto Utica Avenue and then headed north on Linwood Avenue, lined with stately, Queen Anne mansions. A woman at the bus shelter was unable to provide any description of Menefee's attacker. She complicated the investigation by claiming the attacker had long straggly hair, unlike the short-haired attacker lawmen thought that they were looking to arrest. Even with his awkward gait, Joey had continued down Linwood and managed to duck for cover once he got near Millard Fillmore Hospital. Army basic training had clearly paid off physically for Joey.

Surgeons at Buffalo General Hospital managed to repair Menefee's heart during emergency surgery despite the large amount of blood he had lost. He lived another 29 years. As a result of his experiences in the Vietnam War, Menefee, after the stabbing, worked for years at Buffalo City Hall for the Veterans Helping Veterans organization. Though hampered by declining mobility as he grew older, Menefee died in his own Buffalo home on May 15, 2009 at the age of 66. After her father's death, D-Nitha M. Maddox, Menefee's daughter, told The Buffalo News that she recalled being an 11-year-old when she saw the story about her father's stabbing on the front page of the newspaper and, "boo-hooing my eyes out." Ms. Maddox said that as her father grew older, he began expressing a lot of emotion whenever someone mentioned Joey's name to him. "He tried not to have a hardened heart," she told The News, continuing, "He was a fighter. He was just determined he would not let that keep him down."

Without slowing down, Joey celebrated New Year's Day by attempting to stab 23-year-old Calvin Crippen. An assistant manager at a fast-food restaurant, Crippen was waiting for a bus at Niagara Street and Hertel Avenue at about 2:50 p.m. The solidly-built Crippen managed to turn just as Joey swore at him from behind. Out of the corner of his eye, he spotted the hunting knife Joey was about to plunge into his chest. Crippen grabbed Joey and they both fell to the ground. Crippen got up quickly and peeled away, remarking to police later that day, "I just wanted to get out of there."

Interestingly, the ultimately ill-fated Crippen would be linked to a string of sordid side-bar tales, including that of his eventual murderer's judge. Crippen, who survived the January 1, 1981 attack, which Joey denied committing to his dying day because it had been an abject failure, ended up being sentenced to a 13-month federal prison term on his guilty plea to a cocaine trafficking charge in 1993. Following a brief investigation, FBI agents arrested Crippen and charged him with being the middleman in a drug trafficking deal. Crippen pleaded guilty to a single count of distributing cocaine. After spending 13 months behind bars, Crippen was released from federal prison on January 3, 1995. Yet, he was dead some 15 months later at the hands of someone else.

Having survived Joey and federal prison, the lure of easy money in the drug trade was a habit Crippen couldn't seem to break – that is, until Marvin "Kenny" Barber, one of his drug customers, took matters into his own hands. Having gotten into a dispute with Crippen over a drug debt, Barber invited him over to the 24-hour day care center the Barber family operated on Buffalo's Hazelwood Avenue. Having donned a bulletproof vest for the occasion, Barber shot his guest twice, the second time in the back of the head as he lay on the childcare center's floor. Barber wrapped Crippen's body in blankets and dumped the corpse behind concrete barriers on A Street in the Buffalo suburb of Lackawanna. It was found less than 24 hours after the murder. Lackawanna police also discovered and seized the .38 caliber revolver murder weapon at the Lackawanna Housing Authority apartment occupied by Barber's estranged wife. Already on state parole on both burglary and drug cases, and under indictment in a separate federal case, Barber cooked his own goose by talking on the phone with a friend about Crippen's murder, which led to his indictment in July 1996.

After two trials for the Crippen murder, the then 40-year-old Barber was sentenced by State Supreme Court Justice Ronald H. Tills of Buffalo to the maximum allowable 25-year-to-life term on December 29, 2000. As Tills sentenced him the second time for the Crippen murder, Barber insisted he had to shoot Crippen because their dispute over his drug money debt "came to the point where it was him or me." As a result, Barber was still serving the possible life term at New York State's Attica Prison into the second decade of the 21st century.

As if to prove conclusively that truth is stranger than fiction, the judge who gave Barber the life sentence wound up sentenced to 18 months in federal prison on August 7, 2009, for his September 2008 guilty plea to a federal felony charge of transporting prostitutes across state lines. By then retired and 74 years old, Tills, who had earned a reputation as a hard-sentencing judge, admitted he had recruited prostitutes for a number of weekend outings of the Royal Order of Jesters, an all-male, 22,000-member-strong fraternal group dedicated solely to the pursuit of "mirth." The Jesters group was a division of the Freemasons. Tills, a former Republican member of the New York State Assembly who had retired as a judge in 2005, got into hot water after a massage parlor in Niagara County was raided. That seedy establishment employed undocumented, and likely trafficked, women as prostitutes. Federal agents learned Tills was among its customers. Tills' crime involved him taking one of those women across state lines to serve as a prostitute at a Jesters convention in Kentucky. At his sentencing in the federal courthouse in Buffalo, Tills told the packed courtroom: "I will never forgive myself for the possible harm I've caused to the victims in this case. I'm embarrassed and I feel terrible about the shame I've brought to the bench and the bar." Reporting to federal prison on October 1, 2009, Tills celebrated his 76th birthday behind bars and was finally released from prison on January 24, 2011.

ATTEMPT ON LARRY LITTLE

Before Joey returned to basic training at Fort Benning, he tried to slash Larry Little, a Buffalo car wash owner, in front of Little's own Monroe Street house at about 6:30 a.m. on January 2, 1981. As he began running away, he fell into the snow, only to have Joey pin him down. The two struggled briefly before Little bit Joey in the leg and the attacker fled. Little would complicate the Buffalo investigation by telling police he thought his attacker cried out "my sister, my sister" before plunging the knife and missing his mark.

Following Joey's Manhattan knife attacks that left four men dead, Cosgrove redoubled his efforts amidst law enforcement push-back and growing voices of criticism from the black community. During Christmas week that year, checks and food baskets were given to the six victims' families during ceremonies at Buffalo's Bethel African Methodist Episcopal Church at 1525 Michigan Avenue in the heart of the city's black community. During that same December 23, 1980 church ceremony, bags of food were given to 75 needy Buffalo families under the church's annual Christmas basket program. Many black community leaders had such little confidence in the quality of the investigation that they called for a Christmas boycott of downtown stores as a way to try to pressure law enforcement authorities to track down a suspect. On January 1, 1981 the Black Leadership Forum, meeting at the Gethsemane Baptist Church, adopted a resolution saying, "It is the unanimous feeling of the group that the district attorney is either unable or unwilling to adequately investigate this case and bring it to a successful conclusion."

Cosgrove pressed onward. He launched an effort to get more direct involvement of the U.S. Department of Justice in the Buffalo investigation, but this attempt proved unsuccessful. In addition to weathering complaints from the Western New York black community, Cosgrove's belief in the related nature of the attacks in Western New York and Manhattan was being publicly panned by investigators in both the New York City and Rochester police departments. However, when witness descriptions of the NYC attacker started to match some of those associated with Joey's earlier crimes, cooperative links finally began developing across jurisdictions.

Cosgrove started planning in late December 1980 to roll out what he termed as Phase II of the investigation. He described how this stage of the investigation would involve assigning all-new law enforcement personnel to the task force, so that fresh sets of eyes could take a look at all the information that had been assembled in a still-growing collection of files. The district attorney ordered all information assembled in the five-month-long probe to be cross-indexed and entered into computers to help investigators zero in on a pivotal license plate, vehicle, or weapon owner – any clue with the potential to crack open the case. By early 1981, Phase II of the investigation was in full effect, with new teams of seasoned detectives reworking each file in concert with available scientific, ballistic and forensic tests, even though, unbeknownst to investigators, Joey was already under arrest at Fort Benning, Georgia.

Investigators reviewed every tip, no matter how unlikely the relevance. Periodically, the Major Homicide Task Force received help from concerned citizens. On March 10, 1981, Cosgrove received a signed letter from a man in Little Falls, New York claiming that he saw a white wrestler choke a "negro" wrestler on a broadcast from a Utica, New York television station and that. this white wrestler might be "the same person at large in Buffalo." The earnest letter-writer was so certain he had found the Western New York attacker that he had his signature on the letter notarized before he mailed it.

They considered leads no matter how small – or how large. On March 31, 1980, U.S. President Ronald Reagan was shot in Washington, D.C. by a 25-year-old named John Warnock Hinckley Jr. With no other serious leads in view, the presidential assassin was treated as a suspect in the Western New York attacks. Hinckley, who used a .22 caliber handgun, was in the same age bracket as Joey. He also stood 5 feet 10 inches tall and had blue eyes and blond hair, a profile similar to several eye witness reports in the Buffalo killings. New York State Police Investigator Jacob Williams reported to news media that Hinckley was considered an official person of interest in the Buffalo area .22 caliber killings.

Continuing to receive criticism from Buffalo area black leaders about the failures of the investigation, Cosgrove on April 1, 1981 rolled out Phase III. This effort involved a reinvigorated continent-wide plea for information about assaults by whites on blacks anywhere in the United States or Canada. He hoped to drum up some similarity somewhere that would propel the stalled investigation forward.

As the Major Homicide Task Force labored away, Buffalo's black leadership became angrier and angrier at what many were perceiving as the investigation's complete and utter failure. Black leaders in the Buffalo area made a serious attempt to get Erie County District Attorney Edward C. Cosgrove removed as head of the .22 Caliber Killer investigation only days before a major break in the case. During an April 27, 1981 meeting in Albany, Gov. Hugh L. Carey turned down a request for the appointment of a special prosecutor to take over the investigation. This inquiry was made by Arthur O. Eve, the

Deputy Speaker of the New York State Assembly and a Buffalo Democrat. That demand letter was also signed by Sheila Nickson of the Buffalo Leadership Forum. Eve and Nickson argued that the Buffalo black community, "[H]as lost confidence," in Cosgrove's handling of the investigation. As it just so happened, a few days earlier, down at Fort Benning, a colleague of Army Sergeant Thomas Carr of the fort's Criminal Investigation Division Command reminded him of that strange white guy from Buffalo in the base stockade who had recently started talking about attacking blacks up north.

CHAPTER FOUR

I've Killed

D id you know I was a mass murderer in Buffalo?" Joey asked his guard at in the psychiatric ward of Fort Benning's Martin Army Community Hospital in March 1981. Specialist Corwin said that as he was standing guard, Joey calmly awoke, lifted his head and with "a distant smile" began making statements about committing serious crimes. Officials had sent Joey to the hospital's B-4 psychiatric ward on suicide watch after he tried to slice off his penis while imprisoned in the base stockade.

"Private Corwin, it is true," he said Joey told him. "I've killed seven people in Buffalo and I've killed some people in New York."

Corwin had been watching Joey in the hospital ward for about a month before his disturbing announcements. Up until this time, Joey had been withdrawn and uncommunicative. Joey continued on with his monologue, saying that he committed these acts because, "I just wanted to." Corwin reported the patient's alarming unsolicited comments to medical officials.

Joey had returned to Fort Benning late on January 2, 1981 after his Christmas break from basic training. He quickly became unraveled. Within his first weeks back, he stabbed a black fellow recruit in the chest with a paring knife. Pvt. Leonard Coles, 25, of Danville, Virginia, was in the barracks minding his own business on January 18, 1981, when Joey lashed out. According to later reports, Joey mistakenly thought he heard Coles (no relation to his Buffalo hospital victim) call him a faggot. Coles managed to wrestle Joey to the barracks floor until others came to his aid and called for military police. Joey was locked up in the Fort Benning stockade. Not long after his confinement, Joey made another attempt on a black prison guard.

Joey was transferred between the stockade and the psychiatric ward of the Martin Community Hospital at Fort Benning twice during a three months period before April 14, 1981. The prisoner was first transferred to the hospital psychiatric ward because he had attempted to slice his penis off with a razor blade while on a five-week prison hunger strike. Joey had refused to eat his stockade mess because he was sure he was being drugged or poisoned. That strike caused Joey to drop almost 30 pounds over a two-month period. Joey spent most of his psychiatric ward stay in bed, despite having walking privileges within the ward. According to Fort Benning hospital staffers, Joey would periodically sit up in his bed or lie down in bed and shake his head and hands and say to himself, "Christopher, Christopher, Christopher."

Private Corwin wasn't the only person Joey spoke to at Fort Benning between mid-January 1981 and his return to Buffalo. Captains Dorothy A. Anderson and Bernard J. Burgess, two of the psychiatric nurses who ministered to Joey in the base hospital, also took part in conversations. Burgess said Joey complained about how fellow soldiers were constantly taunting him about his masculinity. A March 6, 1981 nursing report made out by the psychiatric staff detailed Joey's statements about regular harassment throughout his 3 ½ month-long Army career. "I'm usually not bothered by things," Joey is quoted in that hospital report, "But since I've been in the Army it seems as if everybody is trying to beat me down. I am a man. I don't like it when people insinuate that I'm not a man."

On April 10, 1981 at the base hospital, Burgess said, as he was asking Joey some routine questions about medications, Joey blurted out that he had killed 13 people.

"He asked me if I was aware of the killings that took place in Buffalo that had been in the newspapers and on television," Burgess later said. "I said I hadn't heard of them and he then told me how he killed some people [with a .22 caliber weapon]," Burgess stated.

Similar confessional language emanated to others. Capt. Anderson, who was black, said Joey came up to her at a nurses' station at the base hospital on April 13, 1981 and rather casually announced, "I murdered some people." Anderson said, "I asked how many and he said he didn't know. He said they were all males. I asked him why and he said there were 'signs' and that it was something he had to do."

Anderson later testified that she felt Joey had talked to her about attacking a black hospital patient in Buffalo as, "a possible vehicle for getting back to Buffalo." Capt. Anderson said that Joey committed an act of self-mutilation in the stockade because he "was tired of confinement." She quoted Joey as telling her, "I wasn't thinking what I did."

Sgt. Richard C. Morganstern, a stockade guard at Fort Benning, said that on April 26, 1981, he heard Joey speak of his murder spree.

According to Morganstern, Joey plainly uttered, "I did it. I did what they said I did in Buffalo."

Joey also shared some of his sentiments with a Roman Catholic chaplain, who also happened to be a Buffalo native. Father Michael Freeman had several talks with Christopher in the stockade after another chaplain told him a fellow Buffalonian was jailed there. Freeman said Joey, ". . . [F]elt he was being harassed in the training brigade and was angered and depressed," because blacks in his training unit referred to him as "faggot" and "wimp." The priest later testified that Joey told him that he was depressed and wanted to see a psychiatrist. Freeman assured Joey he would pass on his concerns to Fort Benning military police officials.

A sister of Cosgrove who was a Roman Catholic nun must have been praying quite fervently for her brother because on the afternoon of April 14, 1981, Sgt. Thomas Carr of the Fort Benning Criminal Investigation Division Command opted to call the Buffalo Police homicide squad after Corwin reminded him about the patient who kept making references to Buffalo killings. The long distance telephone call put the recent theory that John Hinckley could be the .22 Caliber Killer into the waste basket of Western New York law enforcement history. Carr's phone call kicked the Buffalo investigation into high alert, activating what Cosgrove later described as an, "intense round-the-clock" efforts centered on the newly identified suspect. On April 23, 1981 Buffalo Police Commissioner James B. Cunningham spoke to the news media about Carr's call. He described it as, "the hottest lead we've had yet."

Joey was hospitalized in the base hospital from March 6, 1981 to April 3, 1981 and again from April 10, 1981 to April 22, 1981, seven days before an Erie County grand jury in Buffalo, N.Y. handed up the first murder indictment against him. A second indictment would be lodged by a Manhattan grand jury weeks later. If the mild medications he was administered hadn't loosened his lips, all Joey would have faced would have been a court martial for his January 18, 1981 attack on Pvt. Cole in the barracks. After a few years in the stockade, he would have been shipped back to Buffalo by the mid-1980s, which could have paved the way for additional killings.

CHAPTER FIVE

Home Again

Six days after the fateful call from Fort Benning, W.J. "Joe" Cooley, a senior New York State Police investigator and a key member of the task force, interviewed David Martin Robinson, a Decker Street neighbor of the Christopher family. He was also Joey's best friend for about a decade before his entry into the U.S. Army. Cooley also interviewed Geraldine Lysarz, Joey's steady girlfriend until she broke off relations with him in November 1978.

Both Robinson and Lysarz told the investigator that the death of Joey's father, Nicholas Joseph Christopher, on May 21, 1976, had a profoundly negative effect on him. Robinson told Cooley that after Joey's father died, he began showing "extreme guilty feelings about the bad manner in which he treated his father while alive." Lysarz agreed with Robinson's assessment of the "deep guilt feelings" that Joey exhibited about the way he had treated his father. She told Cooley that Joey, "would go and sit for hours at his father's grave" at the Mount Calvary Cemetery on Harlem Road in Cheektowaga, New York.

Lysarz told the investigator that Joey was fired from his maintenance job at Buffalo's Canisius College in March 1979 for toting a loaded handgun on the urban college campus, reflecting a discrepancy from other reports about the reason for his termination. Cooley learned that a black maintenance co-worker named Ernie, whom Joey had befriended at the college, had reported his pistol-packing to school authorities. Lysarz told Cooley that Joey "came to hate" the black co-worker for that action and she thought it was what led to his firing. Lysarz also told Cooley that she used to shoot with Joey at his basement firing range and at the Christopher family hunting lodge. Evidently, Joey's mental state worsened after the breakup with Lysarz. Robinson told Cooley he had "noticed a marked change in Christopher's personality" following his breakup with her in November 1978. He said Joey, after the breakup, "appeared to withdraw into himself and would not talk to anyone."

Robinson, who last saw Joey while he was home on Christmas leave, described how Joey had to give up the rifles and pistols he had inherited from his late father upon reporting to Erie County gun officials that he could no longer locate a Beretta handgun that was included in his permit. Robinson told the investigator that Joey was convinced the handgun had been stolen by a black utility company meter reader who had come to his house. Joey blamed the loss of his family heirloom gun collection on that man, Robinson told Cooley. Lysarz added that Joey sold the gun collection to one of his cousins, Buffalo Police Officer Eugene Molinaro, after his gun permit was canceled. She said Joey came to despise Molinaro after he sold off some of the beloved collection.

On April 21, 1981, almost two dozen investigators armed with a search warrant spent four hours at Joey's family home at 89 Weber Street on the city's East Side. Cosgrove and the task force had obtained from Justice Theodore J. Kasler three search warrants: one for Joey's home, another for a tool shed at that site, and another for his family's hunting lodge at 28 Mile Creek Road in the town of Ellington in Chautauqua County, some 60 miles south of Buffalo.

Joey's Weber Street home in Buffalo, New York. Photo courtesy Buffalo Courier-Express Archive, E.H. Butler Library, SUNY College at Buffalo

That afternoon, Cosgrove, joined by New York State Police Lt. Raymond P. "Sam" Slade and about a half dozen members of the task force, showed up at Joey's Weber Street home and politely told Joey's widowed mother, Therese Christopher, she would have to sit in the kitchen with the district attorney and Slade while task force members searched every inch of her house for possible evidence. Mrs. Christopher, a nurse at Buffalo's Mount Mercy Hospital, recognized Cosgrove as the district attorney when she opened her front door. When investigators told her that the impending search of the properties she owned on Weber Street and in Ellington were due to her son's alleged activities, tears welled up in her eyes. Obediently, she let the team into her home. Investigators found a firing range in the basement of the Weber Street home with a bullet trap that collected fired rounds. At about 5 p.m., one of Mrs. Christopher's married daughters came to the kitchen door asking for money to buy medication her young daughter needed for an ear infection. While the team picked up a great deal of incriminating evidence, they failed to find a .22 caliber murder weapon.

On April 22nd, two homicide investigators, one from the New York State Police and one from Buffalo Police, were flown down to Georgia to get background information about Joey. Buffalo Homicide Detective Melvin G. Lobbett and State Police Investigator Thomas Rash arrived at the Georgia military base early on the morning of April 23, 1981 to attempt a chat with the suspect. Joey actually agreed to talk to the two Buffalo lawmen, but lawyers blocked that meeting. The two detectives were allowed by Army officials to seize as evidence a number of Joey's possessions, all obtained under another search warrant the two veteran homicide investigators picked up before leaving Buffalo.

Back in Buffalo, the task force got Joey's Erie County pistol permit and related records from Nicholas G. Baich, the county's pistol permit administrator. The task force learned Joey's pistol permit had allowed him to carry firearms of various calibers for target practice and hunting trips only. Baich confirmed that Joey's permit was revoked in 1979 after Buffalo police informed him that Joey had lost one of the weapons.

The Kasler search warrants ultimately led to the seizure of a number of spent .22 caliber casings, knives, some other weapons and clothing that seemed to match what some witnesses said the assailant wore. Ballistics tests in Buffalo also linked all four .22 caliber killings to the same weapon and confirmed that that weapon had been fired at Joey's hunting lodge. Some crime scene casings were also linked a misfired bullet found at Joey's Buffalo home. On April 24, 1981, Cosgrove got a court sealing order to prevent a premature public disclosure of the items sought in the warrants, in order to keep a lid on the sensitive investigation he was overseeing.

Based on a hunch by Sam Slade, a legendary criminal investigator and hunter, the investigators also picked up incriminating evidence in the form of twenty-two .22 caliber bullet casings and similar material at the Christopher family's hunting camp in Chautauqua County.

Like the standard criminal, Joey made a rather common planning error – the kind law enforcement officials at all levels of government rely on even the craftiest of felons to make. He forgot to clear his hunting lodge firing range and the grounds and trees surrounding it, as well as his Buffalo home basement, of shell casings and bullets. Law enforcement and court documents later made public disclosed that the court-approved searches led to the seizure of cartridges, gun stocks, empty bullet shells and the sawed-off barrel tip of the .22 caliber rifle Joey had likely used in his nearly-36-hour September 1980 killing spree.

Cosgrove also arranged, on the day of the search warrant action, for Army Captains Dorothy A. Anderson and Bernard J. Burgess to fly to Buffalo to tell a grand jury about Joey's bragging about his northern killing spree to psychiatric nurses and hospital guards. Kevin M. Dillon, the lawyer hired by Joey's mother, and Mark J. Mahoney, the equally talented criminal defense lawyer Dillon got to join him in the case, tried to block the grand jury testimony of the two Army nurses as being a violation of a hospitalized patient's "privileged communication." However, State Supreme Court Justice Samuel L. Green denied their motion. Cosgrove and the Major Homicide Task Force got an Erie County grand jury to indict Joey for the three Buffalo-area killings of Glenn Dunn, Harold Green and Emmanuel Thomas on April 29, 1981. A suspect was finally charged.

With all of this action, two previously skeptical New York City police detectives in late April 1981 were inspired to travel to the Georgia military facility and then stop in Buffalo to confer with investigators. Cosgrove noted that Joey's January 18, 1981 barracks attack on a black recruit bore similarities to the knife attacks in Manhattan, Rochester and Buffalo. His theories about statewide linkages were finally starting to be taken seriously. Up in Niagara Falls, Niagara County District Attorney Peter Broderick said on April 29, 1981 that he was meeting Niagara Falls police officials and other task force members about the killing of the fourth .22 caliber victim, Joseph Louis McCoy, in that city. "I will review the evidence they have gathered and decide whether it warrants grand jury action," Broderick told the Buffalo Courier-Express. Joey was indicted for the Niagara Falls .22 caliber killing soon after.

The indictments triggered the interstate extradition process. On May 1, 1981 New York Governor Hugh Carey signed an extradition request that Cosgrove had rushed to the governor's Albany, New York office. A New York State Police trooper delivered Carey's signed request to the office of Georgia Governor George Busbee the very next day. Governor Busbee honored the Carey request and signed Joey's extradition paperwork on May 2, 1981. The document was then rushed to Muscogee County Sheriff Gene Hodge, who had custody of the Army private. Down in a courtroom outside Fort Benning, Georgia Superior Court Judge John Land held an extradition hearing. Judge Land approved Joey's transfer back to Buffalo, but barred any questioning of him by the task force members until they were out of Georgia. During the extradition hearing in the Georgia courtroom, Joey had sat in a cell in the same building as his widowed mother, Therese, who had flown down to Georgia to be near her son for the hearing. After Judge Land's order, Christopher's attorney Dillon walked out of his courtroom saying he still questioned the identification process that lawmen had used to link Joey to the .22 caliber killings in Western New York.

All that fast-moving action in Western New York and Georgia had prompted Richard Nicastro, deputy chief of the New York City police detectives bureau, to tell the New York Times on May 7, 1981 that Joey was then "the top suspect" in the December 22, 1980 Manhattan stabbings, which appeared to have a racial link.

"No one else is being actively investigated," Nicastro told the New York Times. However, he said New York authorities still had "yet to determine" if Joey was actually in New York City that day. Joey's presence there was subsequently confirmed by checks with the U.S. Army, as well as transportation and hotel concerns.

Governor Carey ordered a state-owned plane to secretly fly Joey back to Buffalo for a series of May 1981 lineups planned at police headquarters. Buffalo Homicide Chief Leo J. Donovan and Lt. Sam Slade flew down to Columbus, Georgia and on May 8, 1981 took custody of Joey from Sheriff Hodge. The Buffalo lineups were held for witnesses to the various shootings and knifings in Buffalo, Rochester, Niagara Falls and New York City. After the plane from Georgia landed at the Air Force base in Niagara Falls, Joey was taken by a closely-guarded police motorcade to the Erie County Holding Center in downtown Buffalo to prepare him for the lineups at police headquarters. He was forced to wear a ski mask when brought into the downtown lockup after 9 p.m. that night.

The next step was arraignment to formally notify the accused of the charges and afford him the opportunity to enter a plea of guilty or not guilty. The May 11, 1981 court arraignment was held before Justice Samuel L. Green, the Buffalo court system's chief criminal term judge and ultimately one of New York State's most-revered and honored black appellate judges. The proceeding was held up about two and a half hours until Donovan could get to the courthouse. Before flashing cameras, Donovan led the ski-masked Joey and his many uniformed escorts into Green's second-floor courtroom at Buffalo's Erie County Hall, which once housed the office of Grover Cleveland when that future U.S. President was mayor of Buffalo.

Joey immediately insisted upon acting as his own lawyer. "I don't feel they have anything against me," Joey told the judge.

"I don't feel I need a lawyer," Joey told Justice Green.

"Do you feel you can represent yourself?" the judge asked him.

"Yes, sir," Joey quickly responded.

That answer prompted the Green to order a psychiatric examination that defense attorneys Dillon and Mahoney had been seeking to determine if Joey was mentally competent to stand trial and aid in his own defense. The judge's decision led the visibly irritated Joey to protest:

"I understand what the charges are, and I don't want to see any doctors. I'm not going to communicate with any doctors!"

During the 45-minute arraignment, Dillon and Mahoney tried unsuccessfully to quiet Joey. After being informed by the judge that he had a right to an attorney even if he could not afford to pay for one, Joey asked the judge:

"Do I need an attorney?"

"You should have an attorney," the judge responded.

"I don't want an attorney," Joey told the judge, continuing, "Do you have evidence against me?"

Joey's lawyers Dillon and Mahoney. Photo courtesy Buffalo Courier-Express Archive, E.H. Butler Library, SUNY College at Buffalo

Justice Green had arrived at the bench after a successful career as one of Buffalo's top black defense attorneys. His subsequent judicial career included a later appointment to the appellate court in neighboring Rochester. He was frequently mentioned under a string of governors as a possible appointee to the State Court of Appeals, the state's high court in Albany. Justice Green told Joey:

"Don't you understand the law is very technical? How will you be able to defend yourself?"

"I will represent myself," Joey responded. "You ask me a question and I'll answer it."

Mahoney was permitted to speak off the record with Joey, but the judge denied Joey's request to speak to his mother. After this exchange, Justice Green ordered a brief recess. When back on the bench, Green ruled that Joey could represent himself, but Dillon and Mahoney would be retained as his legal advisers during what proved to be the first of a bevy of court-ordered psychiatric examinations in Buffalo and New York City over the next few years. He entered his plea of not guilty.

Hours after Joey was arraigned, New York State Supreme Court Justice William J. Flynn was named to handle all pretrial and trial proceedings in Joey's case. The evidence against Joey mounted.

Based on what Erie County District Attorney Edward C. Cosgrove called additional "scientific and testimonial" evidence, Joey was charged on May 28, 1981 in a superseding indictment with the three Buffalo-area .22 caliber killings, the attempted murders in Buffalo of Albert Menefee the prior New Year's Eve and the New Year's Day attempt on the life of Calvin Crippen. The superseding indictment folded these other charges into those already confirmed in the first proceeding.

On May 29, 1981 an unmasked Joey was arraigned on that new indictment before Justice William J. Flynn. During the 10-minute session, a clean-shaven Joey, dressed in a light blue pullover sweater, a Navy blue blazer and jeans, merely responded, "Yes, sir," after attorney Mark J. Mahoney entered innocent pleas on his behalf.

CITY OF GOOD NEIGHBORS

Joey's arraignment as the alleged .22 Caliber Killer shocked the Weber Street neighbors who had always known him as a "good kid" who helped them with home improvement projects, cut their grass for what they all thought were unduly low prices, and who went to

Roman Catholic Mass every Sunday. On April 29, 1981, the day Joey's first indictment was made public, 81-year-old Weber Avenue neighbor, Mrs. Edward Schroeder, told the Courier-Express's Celia Viggo that she sympathized with Joey's mother, whom she called "a good person." Mrs. Schroeder discussed how Mrs. Christopher sang in the church choir. She also described how she had been barraged by so many alleged media types since Joey's name had become public that she simply stopped answering her door unless she was expecting a visitor. "I'm so sick of these callers," Mrs. Schroeder told Viggo. "They pester you, they call up on the phone. I can't tell them anything. I know the [Christopher] family and I can't say nothing bad about them."

Another Weber Avenue woman who refused to give Viggo her name said she felt like going to nearby Police Precinct 12 and asking for police protection from all the intruders who had been disturbing the narrow, tree-lined street filled with modest brick and frame homes with postage-stamp front lawns. The quiet block housed many elderly longtime residents and a few young families. Susan Stefaniak, 33, told Viggo that Weber Avenue had become "like a superhighway at times," filled with random persons coming just to gawk at the Christopher house and peer into its windows. Ms. Stefaniak said that parents on the street were not letting their children leave their own yards because of all the curiosity-seekers. Ruth Even, 58, the Christophers' next door neighbor, said she had asked Joey to clean up her yard the previous summer and he only charged her $30. "That seemed too little, I figured it was worth a lot more," Ms. Even told Viggo. "But he told me, no, that was more than enough."

Linda Janiszewski told Viggo that Joey was "a person who just helped everybody." She said many of the neighbors, especially the senior citizens on the street, "were kind of heartbroken," to hear of Joey's arrest. Ms. Janiszewski also told Viggo it was just "disappointing" to see newspaper, radio and television reporters "hanging on the doorsteps" as people left for church.

NO COMFORT

Joey's neighbors were not the only ones affected by the news of the charges. After Joey was indicted, Joseph McCoy's mother, Alberta McCoy, told the Buffalo Courier-Express she had found "no comfort" in his pending prosecution. The wife of Emmanuel Thomas told a reporter she planned to be in the Buffalo courtroom when her husband's murderer was brought in.

"I'm gonna be there," she said. "I know I probably won't be able to take it, but I want to look at him. I just want to see him," Thomas told a Buffalo Courier-Express reporter.

"All I can say is that I'm glad [that someone had finally been charged]." She told the reporter she had stopped reading the newspapers and looking at television in the months before the arrest.

"My nerves are shot. Every time they said there was nothing new, I'd start to cry," she added.

William and Betty Dunn kept a picture of their slain son above their Fougeron Street living room mantle along with those of their other seven children. After Joey was formally charged, Mrs. Dunn told a Courier-Express reporter that when she heard news reports of Joey's indictment, she said, "Thank you, Jesus, but it wasn't quick enough . . . I read the 23rd Psalm and I go to church on Sunday. I know the Lord said 'vengeance is mine.' I know the Bible says we shouldn't hate. But, Lord help me, I hate him! I hate him! I hate him!" She told the reporter she was glad two Army psychiatric nurses from Fort Benning, Georgia "came forward" and told the grand jury about Joey's boasts about killing blacks in Buffalo. Mr. Dunn joined his wife in telling that reporter "no words" were sufficient to convey the emotional trauma he endured after the killing of his young son. Indicating he feared the white killer might be exonerated by a court jury or judges, Mr. Dunn also said "I just hope to God the man does some time."

Mrs. Dunn recollected the emotions she felt when the race-based pattern of the Buffalo area killings became apparent in October 1980: "At first I wanted to go out and get revenge on every white person I saw. But I know I can't blame all white people for what one did."

"It took them [investigators] seven months to get into this thing," Mrs. Dunn continued.

"Now that they've caught him, my son can rest in peace. I'm glad they caught him and I hope he gets what he deserves. It had gotten to the point where I couldn't sit in a car without worrying," she added in reference to the fact that her son was killed while calmly sitting in a car. Mrs. Dunn told the Courier-Express reporter that her bitterness over what she considered to have been the slow speed of the murder investigation was finally diminishing with the arrest and indictment of Joey. However, she added that, "if seven white men had been killed, they would have been grabbing any black man off the street. Seven months . . . that really hurt me."

Mrs. Dunn said she also understood the shock that Joey's former neighbors had expressed to the news media after his arrest. But, she did not fail to note that ". . . [H]is family has got two lawyers. Their son is 25 and alive. My baby wasn't but 14 and he died."

A TORRENT OF CHARGES

Indictments and arraignments rained down from courtrooms across the state from Buffalo, to Niagara Falls, all the way to New York City and Rochester. The same week that Joey was indicted in Buffalo, a Manhattan grand jury also indicted Joey for one murder and one attempted murder for the other stabbings he pulled off there on December 22, 1980.

However, Rochester law enforcement had a tougher time moving forward. Ten days after Joey's arraignment in Buffalo, Rochester officials admitted that the investigation linked to a fatal stabbing of a black man there the previous December 30th had reached a "dead end." Maj. Anthony Fantigrossi, chief of detectives for the Rochester Police Department, said witnesses to the fatal stabbing of Windell Barnes at a Rochester bus stop who hailed from Winnipeg, Manitoba were unable to identify Joey as the attacker when shown a group of police mug shots. The Canadians who had been in Rochester for a church function were unable to attend lineups held in Buffalo in the spring of 1981, Fantigrossi said.

"There's no way we can establish him [Joey] at the scene of the crime," given the lack of eyewitness identification and any physical evidence, Fantigrossi told the news media.

Despite some successful indictments, questions swirled about Joey's mental competence to stand trial. In the first installment of what proved to be a continuing series of court-ordered mental examinations in Buffalo and Manhattan for the next few years, Joey was examined by Dr. John M. Wadsworth and Dr. George Molnar, two psychiatrists serving as consultants for the Erie County Forensic

Mental Health Service. Despite Mahoney complaining about the two psychiatrists having met Joey "just once," the trial judge ruled that the two mental health experts had found Joey not incapacitated, meaning he was not "one who as a result of mental disease or defect lacks capacity to understand the proceedings against him or assist in his own defense." On June 2, 1981, Justice Flynn officially declared Joey legally competent to stand trial.

A minor press controversy erupted on June 9, 1981, when The Buffalo Evening News ran a story quoting unnamed sources in the Erie County District Attorney's office claiming that the "best way" to resolve Joey's pending criminal charges would be through a mental illness plea on his part. The next day, an angry District Attorney Edward C. Cosgrove was quoted by the rival Buffalo Courier-Express saying Joey would be "prosecuted as fully and as firmly as the law allows," categorically denying any prosecution wish for a quick insanity plea.

"There is no such consideration and the only person who makes that kind of decision is me," Cosgrove asserted, according to the Courier story. Joey's lawyers Dillon and Mahoney also rebuked The Buffalo Evening News story. Mahoney told the Courier that the prosecution claim was ". . . [N]ews to me. Right now we have no commitment of bringing on an insanity plea. Things can change down the road but right now the plea is not guilty." Dillon said, "We don't want a plea. We haven't even considered the possibility of a plea. Our intention is to proceed through trial and acquittal."

On June 29, 1981, a Niagara County, N.Y., grand jury handed up a one-count indictment charging Joey with second-degree murder in the killing of Joseph Louis McCoy the previous September 24th. Joey was brought from Erie County under heavy guard to Lockport, N.Y. hours after the grand jury action. He was escorted out of the

Erie County Holding Center about 1:10 p.m. on June 29, 1981 for the ride to Lockport and arraignment before Niagara County Judge Aldo L. DiFlorio. Attorney Kevin M. Dillon entered a not guilty plea for the silent defendant before Judge DiFlorio. The judge assigned Mark J. Mahoney and the Niagara County Public Defender's Office to represent Joey at that trial. The Niagara County grand jury's action closed the book on the last of the criminal charges ever to be lodged against Joey there. This was due to evidence problems and prosecutorial decisions not to seek an extra pound or two of flesh for all the other largely evidence-uncorroborated racial attacks by the forlorn suspect, who was, to seasoned lawmen, highly likely to end up dying in prison anyway. Several of the witnesses who testified against him before the Niagara County grand jury failed to identify Joey during a Buffalo police lineup about all four .22 caliber murders in May 1981. Niagara County prosecutors did not want to risk losing the case in the long run. Joey would never be tried for the McCoy killing.

Joey was initially due for arraignment in a Manhattan courtroom on July 13, 1981 on the indictment for the December 22nd murder of one man and the stabbing of another. But Joey's fourth arraignment for the Manhattan charges had to be postponed because commercial airlines refused to fly the dangerous suspect across the state. This time Governor Carey refused deploy his personal jet to bring Joey to Manhattan. His staff cited scheduling problems. Amid the refusal of commercial airlines to fly Joey to Manhattan for his murder arraignment there, the Manhattan District Attorney's office ultimately paid Cord-Air, a private carrier based in Batavia, New York, to fly Joey to New York City in a six-passenger, twin-engine plane for a July 20, 1981 arraignment.

Accompanied to court in Manhattan by attorney Mahoney, Joey calmly answered, "Not guilty," when New York State Supreme Court Justice Myriam Altman asked him how he stood on the indictment handed up to her two months earlier by a New York grand jury. Just as he had done in Buffalo, Joey asked the Manhattan judge if he could represent himself in that case. The Manhattan judge reminded him he was not a lawyer. During the 10-minute arraignment, Justice Altman named Frank A. Bress, a well-known Manhattan criminal attorney, to serve as co-counsel with Mahoney on the Manhattan indictment.

Upon his return to Buffalo, Joey went into what jail sources called an emotional and behavioral "shell" at the Erie County Holding Center. Joey was kept on a 24-hour watch both because of his Fort Benning stunt and the large number of black inmates housed in the facility. He refused to talk to anyone. When brought up to the jail's rooftop recreation area, instead of working out or playing basketball with other inmates, Joey just sat forlornly in the middle of the recreation area until he was returned to his cell. That July, optimistic local and state court officials scheduled what they expected to be the start of jury selection at Joey's first murder trial for September 8, 1981. Yet, they had no inkling of the number of mental and psychiatric evaluations that Joey would be ordered to undergo before any evidence was presented against him.

NEWS MEDIA ATTACK

Within a week of Joey's indictment, his lawyers, Kevin M. Dillon and Mark J. Mahoney, launched a two-state court fight designed to keep the media out of the courtroom. They first moved for Muscogee County Superior Court Judge John Land to block the release of affidavits used in mid-April as the basis to search for evidence at the Christopher home in Buffalo and the family's hunting cabin. That act prompted attorneys for Buffalo news media outlets to run to Justice Theodore S. Kasler, who had approved the search warrants, to argue for their rights to them. This began a series of challenges by the local news media, who wished to preserve their access to what was one of the most significant crime stories in decades. They would take their fight all the way to the nation's highest court.

The media mouthpieces succeeded in getting the search warrant reports made public in New York. Henry W. Killeen, who represented The Buffalo Evening News in the affidavit fight, argued to Kasler that the gist of the affidavits was already public knowledge and sealing the documents would be the same as, "barring the door after the horses have left the barn." H. Kenneth Schroeder, who represented WIVB-TV in Buffalo, told the judge that Christopher's attorneys concerns about prejudicing the eventual murder trial – then expected to be a jury trial – was, "a highly speculative claim that at this point is premature." Courier-Express attorney Alexander C. Cordes argued that the search warrant affidavits were "presumably public records" and in sealing them, "the only person who gets hurt is the public." They prevailed on that matter, but that was only the beginning of their crusade.

Attorneys representing the media urged trial judge, State Supreme Court Justice William J. Flynn, to allow all pretrial hearings in the case to be open to the public. However, on July 22, 1981, Justice Flynn shut the courtroom door on the news media and public, ruling that all pretrial evidence hearings in the three Buffalo killings would be conducted in private. According to Flynn, "The court finds that there are no reasonably available alternative means to insure a fair trial except to close the pretrial hearings."

Flynn's ruling prompted an afternoon legal road race between the trial and appellate levels of the New York State court system. Moments after the trial judge's noontime ruling, attorneys for local news media rushed to the chambers of New York State Appellate Justice John J. Callahan across Delaware Avenue from Flynn's courtroom and a short block away from Joey's downtown jail. When the media attorneys asked Callahan, a former Buffalo trial court judge who, like all members of his appellate court traveled to Rochester about 90 miles east of Buffalo to conduct appellate hearings, to stay the scheduled start the next day of the pretrial session, he cut them off, noting Joey's attorneys were not present. After the media attorneys withdrew their request for an appellate stay of the hearings, Flynn had both sides reargue their positions during a closed-door afternoon hearing in Erie County Hall, only to stand firm on his decision that the pretrial proceedings would be closed to the public and the news media.

The actual start of the pretrial hearings was briefly delayed by New York State Court of Appeals Judge Matthew J. Jasen who wanted a chance to hear arguments by attorneys for the news media pressing for open hearings. After hearing arguments on July 27, 1981, Jasen also refused to halt the closed-door proceedings. They had staked their claim on the unsuccessful argument that the public had a First Amendment right to know what was going on in court based on preserving the defendant's Sixth Amendment to a fair trial.

Paul J. Cambria, a noted Buffalo First Amendment attorney, who would famously represent publisher Larry Flynt, and who, at the time, served as the national chairman of the First Amendment Trial Lawyers Association, agreed with the judges: "There is no burning need for the public to know at this stage," Cambria told Michelle Williams of the Buffalo Courier-Express, stressing that the information about the case was only being delayed, not permanently kept from the public.

"The defendant's right to a fair trial may be irreparably injured if the information is revealed now. But the public is not irreparably injured if there is a delay of the information," Cambria said. "I'm totally against it never being revealed, but I'm not opposed to the delay," he added.

Behind a newly installed steel fence, spectators and news media representatives stood as Joey's closed court pretrial hearings began shortly after 2 p.m. on July 23, 1981. Joey was brought to Flynn's third-floor courtroom at Erie County Hall on Franklin Street through a tunnel that led to the County Holding Center on Delaware Avenue. The tunnel was first installed to protect U.S. President McKinley's killer, Leon Czolgosz, from the angry mobs that assembled outside the courthouse after he shot the president at the Temple of Music at the Pan-American Exposition on September 6, 1901.

At the pretrial sessions, five witnesses from Fort Benning, local law enforcement officials and several surviving assault victims testified before Flynn about incriminating statements Joey allegedly made at Fort Benning and identification of him at crime scenes. On August 12, 1981, the pretrial session was adjourned to give both sides a chance to contact possible witnesses who were out of town or otherwise unavailable for testimony. Flynn scheduled the start of the multiple-murder trial for September 30, 1981.

The press continued to fight for access. On August 17, 1981, Presiding Judge Michael F. Dillon of the Rochester-based Fourth Department State Appellate Court formally disqualified himself from a September 1st court hearing on the media issue. Michael Dillon, the former district attorney for Erie County, New York, was the father of attorney Kevin M. Dillon (who would become a future Erie County district attorney, as well).

The Buffalo area news media pressed U.S. Supreme Court Justice Thurgood Marshall, who oversaw the New York courts for the nation's top court, and the full New York State Court of Appeals, the state's high court, to open the Christopher pretrial proceedings to the press and the public. On August 28, 1981, the full U.S. Supreme Court in Washington, D.C., refused to halt the closed hearings, volleying the matter back to the state court. In a 7-1 vote, with only Justice William J. Brennan backing the news media, the nation's high court rejected arguments by the attorneys for the news media that the closed session infringed improperly on the First Amendment right of freedom of the press.

Thus, the media's fight was remanded to the state's higher courts. At the request of New York State Attorney General Robert Abrams, whose office defended Justice Flynn on his closed-hearing order, the state appellate court in Rochester conducted a closed hearing September 1st on the news media bid to force the opening of the court hearings. On September 11, 1981 the Rochester state appellate court unanimously upheld Flynn's decision to conduct closed-door hearings to protect Christopher's right to a fair trial. The Rochester court, headed by Justice Richard J. Cardamone since Presiding Judge Dillon had stepped away from the case, held in a one-page ruling that Flynn had "responded satisfactorily" to higher court holdings on the issue of closed-court hearings and that "exclusion of the press constituted a proper exercise of discretion" on Flynn's part.

Separately, on September 11, 1981, Justice Flynn pushed the start of the murder trial to October 7, 1981 to give Joey's attorneys the additional time they said they needed to prepare for trial. On September 21st, Justice Flynn – learning that Christopher's widowed mother had spent about $10,000 of her slim finances on her son's defense – formally ordered state taxpayers to foot the bill for the legal fees of Dillon and Mahoney, retroactive to September 1, 1981.

To accommodate the public and the news media, as well as for improved security reasons, state court officials on September 29th moved the murder trial from Justice Flynn's third-floor courtroom at Erie County Hall in Buffalo to a larger second-floor courtroom there.

Jail guards told local news media that, in the first five months Joey spent under 24-hour guard at the downtown lockup, he hadn't read, smoked or watched the television placed in his isolated cell. Guards revealed to Michelle Williams of the Courier-Express that Joey ate alone and never saw the general inmate population at the jail. He slept "most of the time" and physically had to be forced out of his cell to attend rooftop exercise sessions, during which he would mostly sit in the middle of the rooftop area. The guards told Williams that Joey rarely talked to any of them but did complain about his legal "rights" whenever he was strip-searched after visits from family members or his two attorneys.

In preparing for the expected start of a jury trial, Erie County Sheriff Kenneth J. Braun ordered more courthouse security than was used during recent trials of prison inmates indicted after the historic 1971 Attica Prison riot, which took place in the region. Braun told Courier reporter Michelle Williams on October 3, 1981, "I'm not taking any chances as far as security is concerned." Braun ordered a partition set up behind the wrought-iron fence that had been installed on the second-floor of the Franklin Street courthouse for the earlier Attica riot trials. This would shield Joey from both news cameras and the public as he was escorted into the courtroom daily after emerging through the underground alley connecting the holding center to the courthouse. The sheriff also ordered armed deputies to be positioned at various spots in that tunnel and outside the courtroom.

Despite all of the build-up, momentum slowed in early October. On October 7, 1981, the start of jury selection was postponed for one week. On October 14th, it was delayed again until October 19th as a result of the New York State Court of Appeals one-sentence decision denying efforts by the news media to reopen pre-trial proceedings and get transcripts of all testimony. The highest state court had ruled that, "no substantial constitutional question is involved," in summarily rejecting the news media request.

The start of jury selection was put off again until October 20th as Joey's attorneys pressed for prosecution material that might be favorable to their client's defense during the expected jury trial. At that time, it was estimated that it would take between one-to-four weeks to select the twelve members of the jury and would then involve about an additional month of actual testimony. But, a timely rendering of justice would not arrive for Joey's victims and their families.

JOEY THROWS A LEGAL WRENCH

As jury selection began on October 20, 1981, Joey wore a dark-colored jacket, blue jeans and an open-collared sports shirt. He came to court in handcuffs, a bullet-proof vest and leg irons, which were all removed in the courtroom on orders of the judge. But, as the proceeding was about to begin, Joey stunned the packed courtroom by announcing to Justice Flynn that he wanted *him* and not a jury of 12 citizens to decide his fate.

"I feel you are an educated man, you know the law and you are the judge," Joey told Flynn that morning, prompting defense attorney Mark J. Mahoney to exasperatedly exclaim, "I don't approve of this!" Flynn proceeded to tell Joey that he would be required to sign a waiver of a jury trial. The court would also have to determine whether Joey understood the consequences of his decision.

"I'm not signing nothing!" Joey told the judge. "Just put on the record I'm waiving a jury!"

"Then I'll have to decline your waiver and proceed to jury trial," Flynn firmly responded. Somewhat theatrically, the judge ordered prospective jurors to be brought into the courtroom. Twelve individuals, including nine women, two of whom were black, and three men, were seated in the jury box for a first round of questions. Joey ignored them and stared straight ahead until Flynn asked each of them their backgrounds. At that point, Joey began staring intently at the prospective jurors.

After a brief initial round of questions, the judge asked the first set of possible jurors to leave the courtroom. Joey had changed his mind. He decided to sign the waiver, telling the judge the jury trial waiver was the "only" legal privilege he intended to give up in the case. Flynn approved the waiver over the vehement objections of defense attorneys Dillon and Mahoney. Mahoney demanded a hearing to determine if Joey really understood the consequences of his trial decision. Flynn responded, "It's very clear he does not want a jury. I have no discretion," noting Joey had already been determined competent.

That got an agitated Joey to ask the judge: "Am I on trial against my attorneys or am I on trial against an indictment?"

Mahoney insisted he and Dillon were sure Joey was "not doing this knowingly," continuing, "We ask a hearing to determine if the defendant is capable of knowingly waiving a jury." Mahoney told the judge the jury waiver was "almost equivalent to a plea."

The judge responded bluntly, "I've made my ruling and that's all there is to it."

After the morning court session ended, Mahoney told reporters he might bring a motion demanding that Flynn disqualify himself as trial judge, because he had already been exposed during the closed pretrial hearing to information that might not be admissible as trial evidence. He suggested Flynn voluntarily excuse himself from the case.

Mahoney felt confident Joey would have done much better before a jury. "I view it as a more acceptable task to sway 12 jurors than one judge with trial experience," Mahoney told The Buffalo Evening News during the lunchtime break. Mahoney conceded his only recourse would be to include the jury waiver issue on any appeal stemming from an eventual conviction in the case. But Dillon told reporters he doubted the jury waiver issue would cause problems, stating "I don't think it will make it any more difficult."

With Joey's attorneys, particularly Mark J. Mahoney, tangling with both the judge and prosecutors, Justice Flynn refused to reconsider his decision the next day. Though Mahoney argued that the records of the case were "insufficient to support the supposition that the defendant knowingly and intelligently waived his right to trial by jury," the judge disputed his argument.

"It would be intolerable to force the defendant into a jury trial when he said he doesn't want it," Flynn said from the bench. Mahoney argued that Christopher had recently been "diagnosed as psychotic." With this claim, Joey stood from his chair at the defense table and asked the judge if he could "approach the bench."

"I'd rather Mr. Mahoney not finish," Joey told the judge. From the bench Flynn assured Joey, "You have made it clear you want to waive a jury."

After Mahoney finished his argument, the judge warned him to keep his courtroom comments proper. The obviously-aggravated attorney had complained about some prospective jurors having been reading the newspaper in court in violation of court orders.

"If potential jurors can disobey, why can't I?" Mahoney contended.

Mahoney and Dillon urged the judge to investigate why possible jurors were disobeying his orders. But Flynn reminded them that his admonitions to jurors became moot when he approved a non-jury trial.

After the October 21st court session, Dillon said he was still considering asking Flynn to disqualify himself as judge in the case, but added, "We'll have to look at the ramifications and the defendant's feelings first. What if my client wants Justice Flynn to hear his case?"

Flynn did order a series of psychiatric tests to try to resolve the continuing dispute on whether Joey had the mental capacity to knowingly give up his right to a jury trial. The decision indefinitely postponed the start of the now-26-year-old Army private's trial. Mahoney and Dillon continued to press Flynn to step down as judge. Despite the fight about Joey's mental capacity on this issue, his attorneys said they were not considering an insanity defense at that time. "I'm more concerned about his waiver of a jury trial," Mahoney told Courier-Express reporter Greg Faherty on October 26th.

Mahoney also said that, should Joey change his mind and agree to a jury trial, he and Dillon would withdraw their bid to get Flynn to step down.

CHAPTER SIX

Hearing After Hearing

J oey's agitation with the mental health testing that both the court and his own attorneys forced him to undergo increased in the autumn of 1981. Even though two psychiatrists had declared him mentally fit for trial in June, one of those psychiatrists would change his mind upon conferring with defense counsel.

Mahoney and Dillon persisted in raising their doubts about Joey's mental state as trial approached. As a result, Flynn ordered a second round of mental competency tests, which took place on October 28, 1981 at the Erie County Holding Center. Dr. Wadsworth and Dr. Molnar conducted the second set of forensic examinations. It was during the second round of examinations that Wadsworth and Molnar arrived at conflicting opinions on Joey's mental state. Justice Flynn was left with no choice but to order a third round of tests on November 5th.. A psychiatrist selected by Joey's attorneys was also permitted to observe the examinations.

The third set of exams irritated Erie County District Attorney Edward C. Cosgrove, whose team of prosecutors had opposed the judge's order. Cosgrove told The Buffalo Evening News that it was simply time for the prosecution of Joey to "move forward." After the November 5th court session, defense attorneys Mahoney and Dillon remarked that the third round of testing, which the judge had ordered to be expedited, would finally give Flynn a "complete" view of Joey's mental state. The third round was conducted between November 10th and 11th by Dr. Brian Joseph and Dr. Harry Rubenstein.

But on November 13th, they, too, submitted what court officials would only describe as "conflicting" psychiatric conclusions as to Joey's mental competence. This finding represented the second disagreement between psychiatrists in only two weeks. Justice Flynn did not immediately comment on the newest reports. An angry District Attorney Cosgrove demanded a "full public airing" of all the psychiatric reports filed so far. He stressed the resolution of Joey's mental state the previous May. Cosgrove said he intended to make sure the judge understood the critical importance of keeping the various test reports secret. He denounced the latest court-ordered psychiatric tests as an unwarranted delay of the start of the multiple murder trial. Because of the conflict between Drs. Joseph and Rubenstein, the judge ordered yet another psychiatrist to examine Joey on November 18, 1981.

"There should be a full understanding on the part of the public of all that's taken place since the case was ordered to trial and jury selection began on October 20," Cosgrove told The Courier-Express' Greg Faherty on November 13th. This comment came after Justice Flynn that day blithely announced to the press that he had "nothing to report," as he had yet to review the latest psychiatric reports.

Meanwhile, costs were racking up. That same day William J. Diggins, head of the Erie County program to aid indigent prisoners, reported that since Justice Flynn on September 1, 1981 granted Joey indigent status, the county government had paid out $2,481 for investigative services and stenographic records ordered by the two defense attorneys, who had not yet submitted fees for their own services. Diggins said that Joey's widowed mother, Therese Christopher, who paid out more than $10,000 in court-related fees since her son was formally arrested in the spring of 1981, "was not legally bound," to pay for any of her son's defense costs because he was an adult. Joey had been granted taxpayer-funded legal representation on his pending murder and attempted murder case in Manhattan, as well. Diggins said that Mrs. Christopher, in nearly bankrupting herself to help her only son, "saved the taxpayers considerable money." At the time, Diggins was overseeing annual payments of about $1 million in Erie County taxpayer funds for attorneys assigned to represent about 4,600 indigent Erie County criminal suspects.

'A hearing was held on the competency issue on November 24th. Amid defense attorneys' complaints about the hearing being conducted in an open courtroom, Justice Flynn cited a 1979 ruling by the state's high court, the Court of Appeals in Albany that disputes over the mental competency of a criminal suspect must be conducted in open court.

At the hearing, Dr. George Molnar, a Canadian psychiatrist who was then clinical director of the Department of Psychiatry at the Erie County Medical Center, said that Joey was "a disturbed person" suffering from "a severe paranoid personality disorder." Molnar reported that he did not find Joey suffering from a psychosis or major mental disorder, that he was of "average intelligence," and that he thought rationally.

As Judge Flynn was ending the first day of the mental competency hearing, Joey tried to cross-examine Dr. Molnar.

"Your honor, before we leave, can I ask Dr. Molnar a couple of questions?" Joey asked the judge. When the Flynn told him he should instead confer with his two lawyers who were actually fighting his demand for a non-jury trial, Joey said, "I don't want to consult with counsel, I want to ask him [Molnar] a couple of questions." The judge shut him down.

Prosecutor Duane M. Stamp complained to the judge that day about what he called defense attorney Mahoney's continuing efforts to influence the findings of the court-ordered psychiatrists who had examined Joey. Though prosecutors had been denied permission to attend those jailhouse examinations, Mahoney had been present every time. Stamp accused Mahoney of overstepping his "observer" status during those sessions and engaging in what Stamp called, "gross salesmanship and lobbying of the worst sort," based on what he had heard from the psychiatrists who believed Joey to be mentally competent. Prosecutor Stamp also questioned the sincerity of Mahoney's demand for closed hearings on mental competency issues to protect Joey's right to a fair trial, reminding the judge that Mahoney called Joey "psychotic" in open court.

As the hearing proceeded, Dr. Molnar repeated his professional assessment that Joey was fit to stand trial, even though the subject did display feelings of suspicion, reclusiveness, of being threatened and "hypersensitiveness" about the behavior of everyone around him – classic marks of a paranoid personality. Molnar conceded under both prosecution and defense attorney questions that Joey, at his examination on October 28th, refused to answer any questions about his feelings toward other people or his exact reasons for wanting a non-jury homicide trial. Molnar contended Joey was "less willing to talk" during this examination because of the dispute over the type of trial he would be having with his own attorneys. Molnar testified that during the recent examination, Joey "skillfully parried or sidetracked" all questions about his personal motivations and, in general "any intimate feeling or thought that he had." Molnar told the judge Joey refused to talk to him about his relationship with his late father, his reasons for joining the Army or "his views on race."

Prosecutor Stamp periodically complained to the judge about Mahoney's "dueling" with Dr. Molnar to try to force the doctor to agree with him that Joey was psychotic. As Molnar was pressed by Mahoney, the general picture of the still-sealed reports of the two Army psychiatrists who examined Joey at Fort Benning (Matthew Levine and Eleanor Law), came out. It was disclosed that Lt. Col. Levine found Joey to be a paranoid schizophrenic, while Maj. Law found symptoms of either schizophrenia or the less severe paranoid personality disorder that Dr. Molnar diagnosed.

Throughout Dr. Molnar's oft-times esoteric discussion of the field of psychiatry and how it dealt with a subject like Joey, he stressed that Joey failed to exhibit symptoms of incoherence, hallucinations or delusions that typically accompany schizophrenia. Dr. Molnar, in response to questions from prosecutor Stamp, said that as a Canadian psychiatrist, he found that American psychiatrists have a tendency to "overdiagnose" schizophrenia. He also said he found that Joey's refusal to answer many questions about emotions was to be expected given Joey's "guarded" paranoid personality which drove him to "stonewall" whenever he could.

During the November 24th proceedings, Mahoney touched briefly on what he told the judge were the "litany" of problems he and Dillon were having in trying to get Joey to accept their legal advice. He said Joey would not accept their suggestion that he try to keep his hair cut the length it was at the time of the .22 caliber rampage. Likewise, he refused to wear "appropriate" clothing to court rather than the Army boots, blue jeans and blue corduroy jacket he regularly donned. Toward the end of Molnar's day-long testimony, Joey, not seeming to be talking to anyone in particular, loudly declared from the defense table, "You can say anything you want, but I won't cooperate."

Joey's anger at suggestions that he was foolish not to follow his attorneys' advice and his increasing annoyance at all the mental testing he had undergone, came to light in testimony by Dr. Harry Rubenstein. The second of the five psychiatrists who had assessed Joey, Dr. Rubenstein testified on the third day of the second mental competency hearing, that Joey told him on November 11th that, "He'd seen enough psychiatrists." Rubenstein, head of the intensive treatment unit handling violent mental patients at the Buffalo Psychiatric Center, testified on November 27th that he agreed with Dr. Molnar that Joey could understand court proceedings and was mentally capable of assisting in his own defense, though unwilling at times.

Rubenstein said that when he began his examination of Joey, the suspect was initially friendly, but quickly became suspicious and guarded in his response to questions. He said Joey, "got a little angry," when he told him he was being a "damned fool" and "very silly" in not following his attorneys' defense strategy. Three times in a rapid succession Joey responded to that by saying "So I'm a damn fool, huh?" Rubenstein told the judge.

During the Rubenstein examination, Joey said he would only answer non-emotional questions. Joey told Rubenstein he would respond to further questions from psychiatrists by telling them to "look in the record," the psychiatrist testified. In response to a question from prosecutor William J. Knapp, Dr. Rubenstein testified that he found Joey's reactions to his session with him in the jail "appropriate," given the fact that he had already been jailed six months and undergone repeated psychiatric examinations.

"He has been incarcerated for six months in a sort of isolated area and he has held his cool, so to speak, but I think he's a frightened young man," Rubenstein said of Joey. Nevertheless, Rubenstein told the judge he found the continual smile Joey displayed during his November 11th examination to be inappropriate.

"I feel he uses this as a defense technique," Rubenstein testified. "I don't know if he realizes he's doing this or just does it unconsciously." As Mark Mahoney cross-examined Rubenstein, he asked him whether he considered the 35-minute session he had with Joey during which he admitted Joey failed to answer 90% of his questions to be a successful examination.

"I think I was successful in finding he was competent," Rubenstein responded, conceding that he came to no conclusive diagnosis.

"All I know is, he's competent. I think I was successful in finding he was competent." When Rubenstein stressed that Joey denied to him having any delusions or hallucinations, Mahoney pressed him on that issue. He asked him if someone suffering delusions or hallucinations typically realizes their problem.

"Sometimes they'll tell you, sometimes they won't," Rubenstein answered.

Conflicts between Rubenstein and the defense team arose. Rubenstein said he was told on November 11th by Dr. Michael Lynch, a psychiatrist hired by Joey's attorneys, that he believed Joey was a paranoid schizophrenic in need of treatment. Rubenstein also noted that Mahoney had previously told him that Joey would not receive his mother for visits. But Rubenstein reported to the judge that Joey told him that he got along well with his mother. In court the day before, Joey was seen conferring with his mother in the courtroom where she has been every court session. Rubenstein admitted on the stand that he found Joey to be, "difficult to relate to," but he found no reason to doubt Joey's description of his relationship with his mother.

As the second competency hearing entered its fifth day of testimony, Dr. Seung-Kyoto Park, the last of the five-assigned psychiatrists to examine Joey, testified that a "marked" deterioration in his personality began with the May 21, 1976 death of his father, Nicholas Joseph Christopher. Park, director of the psychiatric consultation service at the Erie County Medical Center, said he was convinced Joey was mentally ill because his inquiries had revealed that Joey became, "very despondent, religiously preoccupied," with his father's death. He reportedly expressed a death wish as he withdrew from friends following his maintenance-man father's death. For a time after his death, Joey made almost daily visits to his grave and he broke up with a girlfriend, the psychiatrist testified. Dr. Park told the judge he found Joey's "magical" thought processes were those of a paranoid schizophrenic who refused to submit to his own unacceptable wishes and feelings by projecting them onto others. His professional assessment was that Joey needed psychiatric treatment before trial.

Dr. Park told the judge he found that, at the Holding Center where he was kept in solitary confinement for his own protection, Joey regularly kept a white towel over his face while laying on his bed. At that moment, Joey interrupted the testimony and began asking Dr. Park a series of question about what Joey called his "symbolic" act of keeping a towel over his face in jail. Dr. Park contended that acts like this supported his diagnosis. The Korean-born psychiatrist told Justice Flynn that Joey's guarded nature, his suspicion of others, his refusal to cooperate with his lawyers and his apparent need to feel he is able to control everything happening around him were signs of his mental illness.

"Losing control means revelation of unacceptable wishes and feelings which paranoid people cannot stand," Dr. Park testified. But Prosecutor Stamp got Dr. Park to acknowledge that Joey's examination was only the second major court-ordered mental examination he had conducted since he began engaging in forensic psychiatry in January 1981.

As court began on November 30, 1981, prosecutors Stamp and Knapp attempted to get the judge to personally question Joey, arguing that New York State law and court precedent make a judge's own courtroom observations, coupled with a judge's own questioning, the "strongest" basis for determining whether a defendant is fit for trial before psychiatric treatment. On December 1, 1981, the competency hearing was adjourned due to the death of Justice Flynn's elderly mother.

District Attorney Cosgrove took the opportunity to publicly air his grievances about the Federal Law Enforcement Assistance Administration's apparent rejection of his request for $1.2 million in federal funds. Cosgrove said that to date the .22 Caliber Killer investigation had cost the New York State and Erie County governments more than $1.5 million and had consumed more than 150,000 staff hours. Cosgrove said the cost figures didn't include the as-yet untallied scientific, ballistic, computer and clerical expenses linked to the investigation. The district attorney reminded everyone that the murder task force he set up in October 1980 had studied 5,018 tips involving about 2,000 possible suspects, 7,500 vehicles and 11,000 weapons before the arrest. New York Senator Daniel P. Moynihan personally urged then-U.S. Attorney General William French Smith to approve Erie County's application for $1,234,664, noting that the federal government reimbursed Fulton County, Georgia for its costs in investigating the killings of black children in the Atlanta area. But, the denial of federal funds stood.

When the competency hearing resumed on December 7, 1981, Dr. Park disclosed that according to Dr. Brian Joseph, one of the five court-assigned psychiatrists who had examined Joey, the defendant had such severe mental problems that in the absence of treatment there would be an absolute barrier to his ability to stand trial fairly. Dr. Park told the judge that because Joey would not answer many of his questions during their 90-minute session, he could not pinpoint the exact reasons that Joey irrationally feared that unnamed persons were out to get him. Dr. Park did not respond when Joey asked him, "Is it peculiar to part your hair on one side or the other without giving a reason?" Joey continued, "Anything you do [can be considered peculiar] if you don't give a reason." Joey also questioned the doctor's contention that his refusal to respond to questions really supported a diagnosis of schizophrenia.

"If I had sat in my cell and looked at the wall and said nothing what analogy would you have made?" Joey asked the unresponsive doctor. A short time later Dr. Park told the judge he was convinced Joey had a desire to be found competent to stand trial.

Prosecutor Stamp contended that Joey's recent predicament made him understandably moody and uncommunicative, but not mentally ill. Dr. Park disagreed with Stamp's claim that Joey's recent "psycho-social" stresses were the result of his arrest and his continuing fight with his own attorneys about their trial strategy. Dr. Park insisted that, "there was a continuous consistency in his behavior," since long before he entered the Army that supported findings of mental illness.

After Dr. Park left the stand, prosecutors Stamp and Knapp argued to the judge that Dr. Park's conclusions about Joey lying on his jail cell bunk with a white towel over his head when he arrived for his 6 p.m. November 18th examination were erroneous. They contended it was typical for many inmates to use a towel to shield them from the constant bright lights in the downtown lockup.

"Many inmates put towels over their faces when they are trying to sleep in the well-lit jail," Knapp argued.

Dr. John M. Wadsworth, called to the stand by Joey's attorneys after Dr. Park, told the judge he agreed with Drs. Park and Joseph about the need to get mental treatment to deal with Joey's paranoid schizophrenia. That prompted Joey to ask Wadsworth if he had "anything to prove I'm not competent or is it just a matter of opinion?" Dr. Wadsworth, who in May said he found Joey competent for trial, but changed his mind after his second examination of him on October 28, 1981, admitted, "It's a matter of opinion." On Dr. Wadsworth's second day on the stand, he conceded that he had very likely misdiagnosed Joey that spring, insisting that his most recent examination of him convinced him Joey was psychotic.

"I suspect there are a number of bizarre things going on [in Joey's mind] that he absolutely refuses to allude to," Dr. Wadsworth testified. Under cross examination, the doctor admitted his reassessment of Joey was based in part on the same background material he had when he examined him back in May. But in reassessing Joey's mental condition, he said he reviewed "in somewhat more detail," the written findings of the Fort Benning, Army psychiatrists who examined him after he was hospitalized for his self-mutilation incident.

"In the past clearly he was psychotic; there isn't any doubt in my mind at all." Dr. Wadsworth testified, as he alluded to still-sealed documentation on Joey's pre-Army dealings with mental health workers. Joey spoke up when Dr. Wadsworth said that during the October 28th session Joey had been "fishing" for responses when he would ask him a series of questions.

"I did indeed," Joey said loudly. Joey told the judge he got angry when Wadsworth asked him what he called a "succession" of questions on the same subject during that jailhouse examination. Dr. Wadsworth told the judge that during his second jailhouse examination of Joey, the defendant was "more paranoid, more suspicious and laughed inappropriately" and made "inappropriate, almost bizarre smiles.

"He's not competent to waive a jury trial," Dr. Wadsworth testified, telling the judge Joey, "glibly refused to give a reason for his jury waiver. He was not competent to assist his defense." Under cross-examination, Prosecutor Knapp asked Dr. Wadsworth if Joey might not have talked about his reasons for waiving a jury trial because he felt no explanation would be acceptable. Dr. Wadsworth replied: "More likely he is a victim of his own psychotic process and this leads him not to comment."

Joey's frequent courtroom outbursts during testimony by defense-supported psychiatrists so exasperated attorney Mahoney that he finally told Dr. Wadsworth it appeared to him that Joey acting out his own version of Sherlock Holmes "to your Watson."

On December 8, 1981 Dr. Brian S. Joseph, the last court-assigned psychiatrist to examine Joey, told the judge that Joey's "bizarre" attempt at self-mutilation at Fort Benning was very likely another effort on his part to try to come to grips with his terror-filled consciousness. Called to the stand by Joey's attorneys, Dr. Joseph, director of Buffalo General Hospital's Community Mental Health Center, told the judge that his November 10th examination of Joey and his review of the still-secret documentation on his mental health, convinced him Joey was mentally ill and need of treatment.

As he was being cross-examined by prosecutor Stamp, Dr. Joseph admitted that his written report on the November 10th examination erroneously indicated Joey was suffering from mental retardation in addition to being mentally ill. Joey piped up again after Dr. Joseph told the judge that he found Joey's frequent laughing while remaining largely untalkative during the exam to be another sign of his mental disturbance. Joey told the judge that his laughter was simply an "irrelevance" and not significant of anything. Dr. Joseph told the judge that Army reports indicated that Joey, who was still fighting his two civilian attorneys' efforts to shape his defense, was even uncooperative with his Army lawyer after he was arrested for the attempted murder of a black fellow recruit last January.

"Much of what he does is calculated to make himself feel [he isn't mentally ill]," Dr. Joseph told the judge. He said that the defendant was, "very scared and very terrified," because he was intellectually aware of his powerlessness against the "malevolent forces" he feels are trying to harm him. Dr. Joseph also explained that based on what defense attorney Mahoney told him, Joey's hostility and open disdain for attorney Dillon, who his mother hired to defend him, may very well be a result of the murder suspect's hostile feelings toward his surviving parent. Under cross-examination by prosecutor Stamp, the psychiatrist said Joey's unwillingness to deal with Dillon could be an effort "to get back at his mother" for some imaged wrong against him.

Dr. Joseph testified that Joey's mental illness prevented him from developing a close rapport with anyone. Dr. Joseph told the judge he was convinced Joey's, "wish to relate to somebody," was at times for him, "just overwhelming." Joey's type of schizophrenia, Dr. Joseph told the judge, was similar to that of many patients he regularly dealt with and was marked by a "rigidity of thought, a conscientiousness and a protectiveness" concerning his emotions. He testified that such schizophrenics can "appear quite normal" and Joey was "not so disturbed that it would be immediately obvious." During a late afternoon private bench conference, Joey could be heard telling the judge: "Your honor, I made a decision and I'm going to stand by it."

Prosecutor Knapp openly accused defense attorney Mahoney and psychiatric consultant Lynch, one of the Buffalo area's most famed psychiatrists, of having tried to subtly influence the findings of the five court-assigned doctors during the discussions they acknowledged they had with each of them before they examined Joey at the Erie County Holding Center. Knapp also argued that while prosecutors had been barred from attending Joey's jailhouse mental examinations, even as his defense attorneys were allowed to attend them in an observer status, Mahoney had routinely violated that order of the judge by trying to persuade the examiners to side with him on the mental health issue.

That prompted Mahoney to complain to the judge about what he called the "personal attack" on him. Mahoney called it a sign that prosecutors had made a less-than-complete preparation for court proceedings throughout the case. Mahoney also insisted that Dr. Lydia Keitner, head of the Erie County Forensic Mental Health Service, who arranged the court-ordered jailhouse mental examinations, had permitted the defense team the pre-examination discussions with the psychiatrists. But Prosecutor Knapp insisted that those pre-examination talks provided the examiners a distorted view of Joey's mental state. Justice Flynn said he would take the prosecution complaints about the pre-exam defense lobbying efforts "into consideration" on reaching his own conclusions about Joey's mental state. He remarked that it was only due to a state legislative "oversight" that prosecutors were barred from attending such fitness to proceed mental examinations, except in the case of an insanity defense having been raised. Joey's lawyers had yet to invoke an insanity-related defense, which if they had, would have allowed prosecutors to be present for the examinations, the judge noted.

In closing arguments on December 10th, Mahoney insisted it would be "irresponsible" of him as a defense attorney to permit a mentally ill patient to jeopardize his own defense, noting that all five psychiatrists who examined Joey since last spring found him suffering from at least a "serious mental disturbance." Mahoney insisted Joey's refusal to tell anyone his thoughts on almost all subjects was linked to his mental illness. He said that, as a lawyer, he objected to the thought of "the defendant being able to direct the course of the proceedings when he is incapable of doing so." Mahoney declared that when fairly viewed, the competency finding of Dr. George Molnar was that Joey is a mentally "incapacitated person." Mahoney noted a flaw in the findings of Dr. Harry Rubenstein, who failed to offer a diagnosis of Joey's mental state.

"Dr. Rubenstein's evaluation is exceedingly colloquial and suffers in comparison with the other reports," Mahoney told the judge.

Prosecutor Stamp countered the defense attorney's lament, calling Dr. Rubenstein "the most believable, straight-forward witness" who testified at the hearing.

"I suggest that what sustained his common sense approach was his not having to engage in unsupported speculation," Stamp said of Dr. Rubenstein. Stamp contended that, on the other hand, the three court-assigned psychiatrists who disputed the prosecution's view, made "tremendous inferential leaps across factual voids." The prosecutor urged the judge to ignore the claims of the defense-backed psychiatrists that Joey's seemingly coherent courtroom remarks were really symptomatic of his alleged illness.

"The psychiatrists are telling the court you should disregard what your eyes see and your ears hear," Stamp told the judge. Joey demonstrated that he had a right to, "...remain the captain of his ship," through his own courtroom-questioning of the psychiatrists, said prosecutor Stamp. He contended defense attorneys Dillon and Mahoney merely wanted Joey "forcibly medicated" to make him "more compliant" with their wishes. Stressing that, in New York State, even diagnosed paranoid schizophrenics could be tried in criminal courts, Stamp argued the real issue in the second mental competency hearing was the defense attorneys' anger at Joey's unwillingness to wholeheartedly accept their legal advice.

Under state criminal procedure law, Flynn had to decide whether Joey was mentally competent to stand trial by being able to presently understand court proceedings and assist in his own defense. The judge did not say on December 10th when he would make his ruling. Joey's mother and the oldest of his three sisters, who had religiously attended every day of the competency hearing, declined comment as they left the downtown Buffalo courtroom that day.

But, on December 16, 1981, Justice Flynn ruled that Joey was too mentally ill to stand trial without hospital treatment. He said that the psychiatric testimony he had heard left him "no choice" but to order treatment. The judge ordered state mental health officials to treat Joey for up to six months with the goal of getting him returned to court for a murder trial "as soon as practicable." The judge ruled there was not enough evidence to support prosecution contentions he was presently clear-headed enough to understand what was going on around him in court and to consult with his lawyers "with a reasonable degree of rational understanding."

Under the judge's ruling, state law provided that Joey could be treated in a state mental hospital for up to one year before another court assessment of his mental state would have to be made. In a three-page ruling, Flynn said it was his personal opinion that Joey's psychiatric treatment should take only a short period of time, but he noted that under New York criminal law, the amount of time a criminal suspect could undergo treatment before trial was open-ended. The judge said his decision on treatment was an "exceedingly close" one for him because of the divergent psychiatric opinions he had heard expressed by the five psychiatrists. He said those five experts produced "no preponderance" of conclusive evidence as to Joey's actual current mental state, but prosecutors failed in their legal burden of proving that Joey was fit to stand trial. This left him no choice but to order treatment.

That same day, Mark Mahoney, the only attorney Joey would interact with, said he was skeptical of Flynn's estimate of a short hospital stay, but he said he was certain Joey would eventually be rendered fit to stand trial. Mahoney told The Buffalo Evening News that the length of Joey's hospitalization would, "...depend on the approach taken and the attitude of [state mental health officials]."

Under very tight security, Joey was driven from the downtown lockup in Buffalo, where he had occupied a cell in solitary confinement for 224 days under a constant suicide watch, to New York State's 300-bed Mid-Hudson Psychiatric Center for the criminally insane at 4 a.m. on December 17, 1981. Joey, who had become the subject of three anonymous telephone death threats hours after Flynn's ruling, was outfitted in a bullet-proof vest, leg irons and handcuffs as he was led from his cell. Ten plainclothes and uniformed deputy sheriffs stood guard as he was placed in a specially-equipped and protected car for the journey. The trip to Mid-Hudson, a heavily guarded facility in New Hampton, N.Y. in the Catskill Mountains, took about 6 ½ hours, with State Police vehicles accompanying the sheriff's vehicle all along the state Thruway. They worked in relays along the way, until Joey got to the psychiatric center.

Erie County Sheriff Kenneth J. Braun also ordered special security precautions for Justice Flynn, District Attorney Cosgrove and attorney Mahoney for days after the mental health ruling due to threats leveled against them.

Under the dictates of the New York State criminal code pertaining to mentally troubled persons accused of crimes, mental health officials could come back to court periodically to seek permission to keep treating Joey for up to two more years. After that, they would need further court orders to keep him in a secured facility like Mid-Hudson.

The holding marked the closing of a chapter for Erie County District Attorney Edward C. Cosgrove. He had opted not to seek a third four-year term in the grueling post and was stepping down as the county's chief law enforcement official on December 31st. About a week before the ruling, Cosgrove had prosecutors Stamp and Knapp produce a lengthy memorandum on all aspects of the case to make it easier for future prosecutors to pick up the case upon Joey's hopefully eventual return to the trial court. On the same day Flynn issued his ruling, Cosgrove officially closed down the 185-man Major Homicide Task Force. He had no public comment.

Naturally, the ruling had an effect on proceedings in other jurisdictions. Niagara County, NY, District Attorney Peter L. Broderick told The Buffalo Evening News he would abide by Justice Flynn's mental competency ruling and not force Joey to trial for the McCoy shooting until he was declared mentally competent. And while Joey was technically still facing attempted murder charges at Fort Benning for the stabbing of a black recruit in January 1981, Army officials had deferred to their civilian law enforcement counterparts. A spokesman for Manhattan District Attorney Robert Morgenthau, was more equivocal about what effect Flynn's ruling could have on the pending Manhattan case. Mary DeBourbon, a press spokesman for Morgenthau, told the Courier-Express and Buffalo News that, "the findings in the Buffalo case are not binding here." But she said "we haven't made a determination at this point as to what effect if any" Flynn's treatment order would have on the New York City prosecution. "But the findings in Buffalo will certainly be taken into account," DeBourbon said. The gears of justice ground to a halt.

Albert Menefee, one of Joey's few surviving victims, was not pleased with the court's decision. Hours after Flynn's order was made public, Menefee, who survived a knife wound to the heart the previous New Year's Eve, told The Buffalo Courier-Express that the ruling "just isn't fair."

"It just doesn't make any sense. There's no justice in the case," Menefee told the Courier.

"I lost everything. I'm still unable to work. I tried shoveling snow last week and got pains all through my chest. I signed up for my last unemployment check last week and after that I don't know what I'm going to do."

Menefee, who was hospitalized for 13 days after the open-heart surgery that saved his life, said "It appears I'm on a road of no return, but I'm not about to fall over and die. But when I heard that he is not fit to stand trial I couldn't believe my ears. He is going off to a hospital and all I can do is sit at home and babysit because that is the only job I can find. But I guess I'm better off than the families of the black men who died, because all they can do is sit at home and cry."

CHAPTER SEVEN

Reverberations

After New York State Supreme Court Justice William J. Flynn ordered Joey committed to a state mental facility, the Buffalo black community exploded with anger. The mental treatment order provoked outrage especially amongst Leadership Forum members. Members of the Forum, the year-old group of 20 local black politicians, clergymen, lawyers and community leaders that had formed to speak for the black community about the .22 Caliber Killings, openly denounced Justice Flynn's order. James W. Pitts, the Ellicott District Councilman on the Buffalo Common Council, told The Buffalo Evening News hours after the news broke that, "Something has to be done to make judges more accountable." Pitts condemned the ruling as a "cop-out" and told the newspaper, "This is a slap in the face, particularly to the black community and the City of Buffalo."

"If someone is not brought to justice for the killings, you are going to have a violent reaction from some sectors of the community," Pitts declared. On the same day, Masten District Councilman David

A. Collins said Flynn's ruling made it imperative that he and other members of the Leadership Forum launch an "immediate dialogue" with Richard J. Arcara, the former U.S. Attorney for Western New York, who would soon assume his new job as the newly-elected Erie County district attorney. Collins also told The Buffalo Evening News, "This guy [Christopher] is just as capable of standing trial as Gail Trait," a mentally disturbed young Buffalo black woman who was sentenced to 25 years-to-life for the 1978 murders of her four young children. Sent to prison at age 26 while still asking her jailers where her four children were, Trait spent ten years in prison before an appellate court overturned her multiple murder conviction. After that reversal, New York State Supreme Court Justice Theodore Kasler finally sent her to a state mental facility for the psychiatric treatment he said she had always needed. She spent ten more years in a mental hospital.

Daniel Acker, president of the Buffalo NAACP, told The Buffalo Evening News of the Flynn treatment order: "This is the kind of decision that causes more violence in our cities." Stressing the different court treatments of Trait and Christopher, Acker said the differences revealed the inherent racism in the local judicial system. Rev. Bennett W. Smith, of the influential black Buffalo church St. John the Baptist, told The Buffalo Evening News that day, Joey would never step foot in to another courtroom again.

"This is the last you'll hear of Joseph Christopher," Rev. Smith said. "Justice will never be done."

A day after Flynn's order, Jack Williams, the brother of a mentally-troubled Buffalo black man who was then serving a five-year prison term for an assault conviction, staged a protest outside of Erie County Hall, which housed Flynn's courtroom. Carrying a cardboard placard, Williams, 32, a coast-to-coast truck driver, told The

Buffalo Evening News that the Christopher ruling was a manifestation of both judicial racism and a double standard in the handling of
defendants of difference racial backgrounds. Williams said his imprisoned brother, Larry, 39, was mentally disturbed but didn't get
any treatment until he was imprisoned two years earlier.

"My brother has never been mentally stable," Williams told the
newspaper.

In a December 18, 1981 letter to Cosgrove during his waning
days as district attorney, Ellicott District Councilman James W. Pitts
said he found Justice Flynn's decision, "indeed disappointing." But
Pitts wrote that he found Cosgrove's decision to shut down the task
force "even more shocking."

"It is my opinion," Pitts wrote, "that the disposition of Joseph
Christopher has not provided any justice nor sound reasons for the
dismantling of the investigative efforts in solving the .22 Caliber
murders. As the outgoing District Attorney, I know it is much easier for you to take this position given the fact that your responsibility
for that matter ends when you leave office. However, many questions are unanswered and many concerns are being raised about the
fitness of such a decision."

"The Joseph Christopher case," Pitts' letter continued, "raises a
particular concern about what information was generated at the
pretrial hearings and subsequent deliberations which led to Justice
Flynn's decision. Why was there so much emphasis placed upon
Joseph Christopher's competency to stand trial? I know that you
would not be able to reveal or attempt to answer this question.
However, it seems to me that the decisions that you made, emphasize the importance of knowing the answer to that question. Also,
why did you, as the outgoing district attorney, choose to disband the
investigation and not recommend that the investigation continue;

especially considering the incoming district attorney's previous relationship with the investigation as a United States Attorney? Additionally, I would like to know if you would be willing to issue a report summarizing the investigation up to the time that you decided to disband it; e.g. How many man hours were spent, what information has been generated in terms of leads, the dispositions of the taxi cab murders, etc. To disband the investigation without answering these questions simply because one is in a lame duck position would be irresponsible."

"Finally," Pitts wrote, "I would like to know if you intend to make any specific recommendations to the incoming district attorney about Justice Flynn's decision surrounding Joseph Christopher. It seems to me that the seriousness and magnitude of the .22 Caliber Killings is something that cannot be pushed to a back burner. I would hope that you would give the courtesy of a response," Pitts ended.

In a letter to Pitts dated December 31, 1981 – Cosgrove's final day as district attorney – he assured the councilman that Joey's uncharged cases remained "in an active and pending status," being handled by the state police, the Buffalo police homicide squad and various other local police departments. In Cosgrove's letter, he stressed that the uncharged criminal cases linked to Joey remained open from an investigative standpoint. Cosgrove wrote that he closed the Major Homicide Task Force because the "great bulk of the investigative work has been accomplished" and the need for the district attorney's "presence at every investigative step has lessened considerably." Cosgrove stressed that "there is no statute of limitations in homicide cases" and that, "if sufficient legal evidence is obtained to charge any of the remaining cases, it will be presented to a grand jury for consideration." On the issue of Joey's mental health,

Cosgrove wrote the city councilman that the issue of competency to stand trial had been raised by Joey's team of attorneys and that "is the right of each defendant charged in New York State." Cosgrove also noted in his letter that the mental competency issue was initially, "resolved in the People's [prosecution] favor," but Joey's attorneys raised the issue again, even "when the defendant sought to waive his right to a jury trial," over the objection of his defense team.

The outgoing district attorney stressed in that letter that the trial judge took the issue of Joey's demand for a non-jury trial "very seriously" since it meant Joey "was attempting to waive a constitutionally guaranteed right." Flynn, Cosgrove wrote, conducted "a full hearing in open court" before determining Joey was mentally incapacitated. In the letter to Pitts, the outgoing district attorney assured the city lawmaker that once state psychiatric experts declared Joey mentally fit for trial, "he will be fully prosecuted by this office. Hopefully this will be soon." Cosgrove also assured Pitts that incoming District Attorney Arcara was familiar with all the work of the homicide task force and, "as a part of the orderly transition between administrations, he will be fully briefed on all aspects of the investigation." Cosgrove again noted that over a seven-month investigation, the Major Homicide Task Force investigated "over 5,000 tips, 2,000 persons, 7,500 motor vehicles and some 11,000 weapons." He also said "some 175,000 bits of information" on the investigation are preserved in government computers and the murders of the two black cabbies and Roger Adams, "remained uncharged but are being thoroughly investigated."

Cosgrove wrote to Pitts that he had personally assumed the role as sole spokesman for the task force "to minimize the possibility that inaccurate and inflammatory or contradictory information might be disseminated to the public." And he reminded the councilman that "as I advised you in our numerous conferences during the pendency of the investigation," he had set up the task force so his prosecutorial office, "could provide the coordination and the administrative framework for this most difficult inquiry."

At a three-hour December 19, 1981 meeting of the Black Leadership Forum at Buffalo's Gethsemane Baptist Church, the group called out, as its spokesmen told The Buffalo Evening News, to "all people of good will" to join them at a Buffalo Common Council session December 22, 1981. They aimed to publicly express their dissatisfaction with Judge Flynn's mental treatment ruling, to object to the Common Council's plan to honor outgoing District Attorney Cosgrove and to protest Cosgrove's recent disbanding of the special task force. The Forum voted at that meeting to present Cosgrove during the upcoming council session at Buffalo City Hall with a "citation of infamy" for what they considered his mishandling of the murder investigation. Its chairman, Rev. Herbert V. Reid, told The Buffalo Evening News, "The district attorney's decision to disband the special task force is in no way related to Christopher's 'incompetence' in light of the unsolved murders of blacks in Buffalo, Rochester and New York City all linked to the .22 Caliber attacks."

Rev. Reid, who was also president of the Southern Christian Leadership Conference's Erie County, N.Y. Chapter, told The Courier-Express that Cosgrove's decision to disband the 185-member task force on December 16, 1981, the same day as Flynn ordered Joey to be hospitalized, "may be a signal to him that the case is over, but for the black community it is not over. It will never be over until justice is done." Reid also said that after that December 19, 1981 meeting, that the Forum was on the verge of meeting with incoming District Attorney Arcara and would urge him to reconstitute the special task force "and continue an aggressive investigation into all of the unsolved murders of black males."

During its December 19th meeting, the Forum voted to circulate petitions across town demanding that Christopher be brought back from the state's Mid-Hudson Psychiatric Center, where he had been sent for treatment days earlier, to stand trial immediately. Members of the Forum told The Buffalo News they knew such petitions might have no tangible effect on the legal process in the case but, in the words of Ellicott District Councilman Pitts, the petitions would display the mass opposition in Buffalo for the court ruling and the disbanding of the task force. The Forum also agreed during that meeting to research public records to see how federal authorities or the New York State Attorney General's office could be brought in and possibly take over the prosecution of Joey.

At the December 22, 1981 Buffalo Common Council session, an estimated 200 or so black Buffalonians gathered in the council chambers to register their dissatisfaction with the manner in which the outgoing District Attorney was handling the investigation of the .22 Caliber Killings. The protest prompted South District Councilman James P. Keane to withdraw the resolution he had filed for the session lauding Cosgrove for his performance at the county's chief law enforcement official. When Masten Councilman David A. Collins began to try to speak about Keane's actions, Council President Delmar L. Mitchell quickly cut him off, saying "There's no discussion." Led by Rev. Reid, the crowd stood up in the council chambers and raised lighted candles as Keane formally withdrew his resolution from consideration. Mr. Reid later told the media that the candles were meant to symbolize the question – Has the light of justice gone out in Buffalo? When Mitchell gave Rev. Reid permission for remarks, even though Common Council long-standing rules forbade speeches from the audience at full council sessions, Keane, Lovejoy Councilman Norman M. Bakos, Fillmore Councilman Arthur Gospodarski and Delaware Councilman William L. Marcy Jr. all walked out of the council chamber, claiming the meeting had been disrupted.

In Rev. Reid's speech to the remaining councilmen he said, "We're calling on all people in the City of Buffalo – white and black – to unite and save Buffalo. But Buffalo cannot be saved until there is justice for all people." Reid also called the Keane resolution honoring Cosgrove an "insult to the black community."

"We do not appreciate being insulted, not only black people but all people of good will," Reid added. After the council session that day, Bakos told Buffalo Evening News reporter Carl Allen, "I left for the same reason I walked out of the meeting when the KKK was here. They should respect the council and its process." Marcy told Allen the Reid-led crowd, "showed a disrespect for law and this legislative body." Keane told the same News reporter he opted to withdraw the resolution to, "save Ed Cosgrove the embarrassment," of the boos he likely would have received had he showed up and been presented a copy of the resolution.

"It doesn't change the way I feel about Ed Cosgrove," Keane said. "The Irish-American community is insulted by these actions today. Highly insulted. Ed Cosgrove is a member of our community, South Buffalo."

Some of the blacks citizens who had come to the Common Council's 13th floor chambers for the session told reporter Allen they had come to show their disapproval of Cosgrove's disbanding of the special task force and Justice William J. Flynn's decision to send Joey to a guarded state psychiatric center for treatment. Leaving City Hall, Rev. Reid and almost two dozen black clergyman and protesters walked to the District Attorney's office several blocks away and delivered the "citation of infamy," only to be told by Erie County sheriff's deputies who routinely guarded the office that Cosgrove was not there. Outside the building, Rev. Reid said, "The message is that we want justice. It might be that Christopher is innocent...then let's let him go free. If he is guilty, let's punish him. But let's not cop out."

That Christmas Eve, Cosgrove told this author, then a Buffalo Evening News reporter, that despite the criticism of his handling of Joey's prosecution, he felt the caliber of the 185-man probe he headed had been unassailable.

"The fact that, during a time of national racial turmoil and violence, this investigation was initiated, conducted and concluded on the highest professional level has become a matter of record," Cosgrove said in making his first public comment about the criticism he had been receiving.

In the first weeks of 1982, Ellicott Councilman Pitts continued to press investigators on the status of the killings of the two Buffalo cabbies, Parlor Edwards and Ernest Jones, as well as the murders of Roger Adams of Buffalo and Windell Barnes of Rochester, crimes for which Joey would never be prosecuted. Despite Cosgrove's December 31, 1981 letter to Councilman Pitts early in January 1982, Pitts publicly denounced the former district attorney having made what he characterized as "incorrect" or inaccurate claims about the status of the continuing probe. Pitts also publicly vowed then that he would continue his push for arrests in those four unsolved murder cases.

Late that January new Erie County District Attorney Richard J. Arcara restarted the task force and joined with Rev. Reid, chair of the Black Leadership Forum and president of the Southern Christian

Leadership Conference in Erie County, in calling for the public to provide police with information about the unsolved killings. Reid told the news media after Arcara's announcement that, "We'll need all the help we can get." Pitts announced that a petition drive he had launched to get the task force back in business had collected more than 10,000 signatures in Buffalo and Niagara Falls.

On January 9, 1982, Rev. L.T. Boyce, then pastor of Buffalo's Calvary Baptist Church and a member of the Black Leadership Forum, telephoned Cosgrove at the then-private attorney's suburban Buffalo home and told him he found Cosgrove to be "one of the most courageous persons" he had met. Boyce also told Cosgrove that after reading Cosgrove's detailed 11-page long final summary of the work of the Major Homicide Task Force, he voiced praise for the murder task force's work. Though Cosgrove never publicly mentioned getting the call from Rev. Boyce, a former Memphis, Tennessee clergyman who was an active member of Dr. Martin Luther King Jr.'s civil rights crusade and a close friend of King for almost a decade, Cosgrove did tell close associates he would always treasure the black clergyman's insistence that he did not agree with the criticism of him by other members of the Black Leadership Forum.

In the midst of Joey's non-jury triple murder trial in April of 1982, Ty Jones, the son of Ernest "Shorty" Jones, released two poems he had written on the anniversary of his father's slaying. Jones told Gene Warner of The Buffalo Evening News in April 1982 that the pain of the grizzly slaying of his father had never been eased, even with Joey's indictment for four other murders:

"The first year [after his dad's killing] was really cold. We just turned people away. I couldn't talk to anyone about it. I was so frustrated. There were thoughts in my head that I had never put down. I was just lying in bed that night [the first anniversary] and thinking about my father. Everything was dead, my dad and the day." And so he wrote the poems. The first of his poems, was entitled "No Memory Fades." It read, in part:

> There are times to hide truths
>   camouflage lies
> And time to wish it would all fade away
> But it won't Not ever
> No memory fades

Jones told Warner that composing those poems eased his feelings because, "I had written it down. I had gotten it off my chest." Jones said he hoped his poems could ease some of the pain for the families of the other murder victims, none of which he ever met. He told Warner, "I have become part of another group. I'm a Buffalonian. I'm a New Yorker. Now I'm part of another group, the survivors of a massacre." Even though he doubted Joey killed his father, he said he felt through his poems "close" to those other mourners.

"I can't forget all the other victims, even though only my father's death affects me," he told the reporter. "I hurt for all the other mothers because my mother was hurt so much."

When Warner asked Jones how he felt about Christopher, unaware at that time that his father's murder would remain "unsolved" indefinitely, Jones carefully and in a soft-spoken voice said: "I'm not violent. I wouldn't attack him or anything. I can't say I don't have anything against him. I think justice should be done. I think he needs help. He doesn't need to be hanged or electrocuted. God will punish him anyway.

CHAPTER EIGHT

Habeas Corpus

After almost four weeks at the psychiatric center in New York's picturesque Catskills, Joey, after talking to other inmates, launched legal proceedings to get out of the hospital through the established channels at the New York State Mental Health Information Service. Joey's effort initiated a State Supreme Court hearing that would be conducted behind the walls of the maximum-security Mid-Hudson Center, 40 miles north of New York City. Robert Spoor, director of communications for the State Mental Health Information Service, told The Buffalo Evening News that Joey's self-initiated legal action was "not unusual for patients to do." Spoor said court sessions were routinely held behind the walls of that facility in an effort to protect the legal rights of patients. Spoor said attorneys for the State Mental Health Department would oppose Joey's bid for release during the court session, with a ruling expected in several weeks. Spoor said Joey asked the mental health information service "to file a petition for a writ of habeas corpus that he is not mentally incapacitated and should be released from our custody." Under a habeas corpus action, a person formally complains to the courts that he is being kept in a prison or other custodial situation without due process of law. "If he were to win in the hearing, it would prove that he is competent to stand trial," Spoor said. He said officials at the psychiatric facility "feel he still needs treatment. If we felt he didn't need treatment we would return him to the courts."

During the January 20, 1982 proceeding, Judge Albert Mishkin ordered testing of Joey by a psychiatrist not connected with the facility. Mishkin, a Family Court judge on temporary assignment at the psychiatric center that day, agreed to let Health Information Services officials select that independent psychiatrist who would assess Joey's claims that he was not in need of treatment. In a written statement Joey penned for that action, he claimed he was being illegally detained in the facility without the due process of law. He wrote: "I am not an incapacitated person and I am aware of the charges pending against me and am capable of assisting in my own defense."

Mishkin put off a ruling until February 17th, but in the meantime, Manhattan prosecutors convinced Justice Benjamin Altman of Manhattan that Joey's Buffalo lawyers and the three psychiatrists who supported them were correct. Altman formally ruled Joey incompetent to stand trial there prior to at least three more months of hospital treatment. But in the fast moving chain of events concerning Joey's mental health, psychiatrists at the Mid-Hudson Psychiatric Center, during a closed-door hearing on February 17th before Westchester County Judge Gerard Delaney (who was substituting for Mishkin that day), declared Joey legally fit to stand trial.

Barbara Wehmeyer, a spokeswoman for the State Mental Health Office in Albany, told The Buffalo Evening News later that day that Dr. Erdogan Tekben, director of the psychiatric center, had disclosed his staff's findings to Judge Delaney during that hearing. Wehmeyer said Erie County prosecutors would likely receive official word from the psychiatric center in "the next week or so" but plans for Joey's return to the Buffalo jail were launched that day.

Under tight security, several Erie County sheriffs' deputies drove to Mid-Hudson late on February 23rd to bring Joey back to Buffalo. The next day, as the team of deputy sheriffs was waiting at Mid-Hudson for Dr. Tekben to sign papers certifying Joey's competency, The Buffalo Evening News broke an exclusive story by Lee Coppola, then the top investigative reporter in Western New York and possibly the entire state: Fourteen days before the .22 caliber spree got underway, Joey had sought treatment at the Buffalo Psychiatric Center.

The Coppola exclusive revealed that Joey had checked in to the Buffalo psychiatric hospital, and registered complaints about being unable to keep a job and not getting along with people. During the September 8, 1980 psychiatric center visit, Joey told a doctor that he was depressed about his inability to find a job. That doctor determined Joey was then not an immediate danger to himself or others and scheduled him for further counseling. Staff scheduled Joey for an appointment at one of its community treatment facilities near his home in East Buffalo, but he never attended the appointment, even though the psychiatric center staff tried to contact him. Joey's visit to the psychiatric center on September 8, 1980 only came to light in February 1982, because center staffers had stumbled across his screening report as they were cleaning out records to be discarded.

The day the Coppola exclusive ran, District Attorney Richard J. Arcara put one of his top and most trusted aides, Deputy District Attorney Albert M. Ranni, who was already overseeing all prosecutorial matters in the busy office, on the Christopher prosecution team along with Stamp and Knapp.

Prosecutor Al Ranni. Photo courtesy Buffalo Courier-Express Archive, E. H. Butler Library, SUNY College at Buffalo

When Joey finally arrived at the Erie County Holding Center again at about 5 p.m. on February 24th, he unnerved some of the jail staff by showing up grinning and asking, "What's for dinner?" After being told that dinner would be macaroni and cheese, Joey was escorted to his cell in a high security area of the jail where he was assigned a white roommate. When reporters for the Courier-Express heard holding center superintendent Joe C. Foreman announce several days later that Joey had been placed with a white cellmate, reporters pressed him on that point. Foreman responded: "You expect me to put a black in with him?"

In addition to observing a dramatic change of attitude, the jail staff found that Joey had also picked up a new habit at the psychiatric center in the Catskills – smoking. Joey brought 10 packs of Marlboros and Winstons back to the downtown lockup. The deputies who brought him from the Mid-Hudson facility told Coppola that during the seven-hour ride back, Joey had talked openly and joked with them. One of the deputies, left unidentified in Coppola's exclusive because Sheriff Braun had banned talks with the media, said Joey was, "like a different person." Coppola wrote that as Joey was walking in untied Army boots through the tiled corridors of the downtown jail, he grinned and nodded to a number of the uniformed jail guards he had gotten to know during his first 224-day stay there. One of guards told him, "Welcome home."

Joey never read the Coppola scoop in The Buffalo Evening News. Nevertheless, he became angry about a Buffalo Courier-Express follow up story about that pre-spree psychiatric center visit that ran on February 25, 1982. Joey mistakenly thought the Courier had broken that story and wanted to set the record straight. Despite the best efforts of attorney Mahoney to dissuade him, Joey set up a February 26, 1982 jailhouse interview with Courier reporter G.M. Seal and its Metropolitan Editor Mark Francis.

The peculiar jailhouse interview had been arranged by Joey himself in a call to the Courier-Express at about 11:45 a.m. on February

25th. He told the Courier to send a reporter to the jail because he had a statement to give.

"I think you'll find it pretty interesting," Joey claimed during that brief call. When he was asked to give a hint of what his statement might be about, he refused and said "I think you can get a reporter down here pretty fast."

Attorney Mahoney had met at the jail with Joey for two hours on February 25th and again hours before the February 26th jailhouse interview in an effort to try to get him to cancel. Just as the two Courier representatives were entering the jail to talk to Joey, Mahoney told reporters, "If he wants to give an interview or make a statement it's up to him. I'm not going to stick around. I'm not going to be put in a position of being a potential witness" at the upcoming murder trial. Mahoney also told the media he would have no comment on any statement Joey gave the Courier because of "my ethics" as a lawyer.

In Courier reporter Seal's February 27th story about the 21-minute interview that he had with Joey the previous day, Seal disclosed that Joey handed them a written statement alleging he had been drugged while at the Fort Benning infirmary the previous spring. He then declined to answer their questions.

Seal wrote about how a smiling Joey readily shook hands with both Courier staffers after being brought into the first-floor library at the jail for the interview at 10:45 a.m. Joey came dressed in a blue and gray plaid flannel shirt over a navy blue dress shirt and a white T-shirt with green khaki trousers and white sweat socks but no shoes. Joey's hair had been allowed to grow until it curled down below his shirt collar. He refused to allow himself to be photographed during the jail interview – the first interview he granted to any media – and he barred the use of tape recorders during the session.

Before the brief interview began, Joey signed and dated two consent forms, releasing the jail from liability in connection with anything he might say during the interview. Seal reported Joey's eyes kept shifting regularly from his two interviewers to the table at which he sat and to the rows and rows of law books lining the walls of the jail.

"I'm not really going to answer any direct question to me," Seal reported Joey telling him as the interview began.

"I'm just going to show you a little comment I wrote." Joey pulled the folded piece of paper out of the chest pocket of his flannel shirt and he gave it to Francis and Seal. As the reporters were quick to note in their story, the spelling and punctuation in the note were Joey's:

"In regards to Wednesdays [sic] sensationalism, As for being sent to the hospital at Fort Benning, I was sent to the hospital as a result of my not eating in the stockaid [sic]. I was being slipped some kind of drug every time I ate. I went from 153 to 116. In the hospital I gained weight and was sent back to the stockaid [sic]. Again I was druged [sic]. I made a small slice in the skin on my penis and asked to go back to the hospital. At prior stay in the hospital the main topic of conversation was The Atlanta Case. I have just this comment for know. [sic] Joseph Christopher."

Joey told Seal and Francis they could copy his written statement. When they asked him, according to the Seal exclusive about the Coppola exclusive of February 24, Joey did not explain whether he read that story. He indicated he thought it had run in the Courier-Express. When Seal and Francis pressed Joey about his alleged homicidal admissions to nurses at the southern military base hospital,

Joey just said "I'm not making any more comments right now because you're going to print everything I say, so...." He never completed that thought, according to the Seal piece. Seal wrote that throughout the brief jailhouse interview, Joey appeared, "to be totally in control of the situation and of himself during the interview. He seemed coherent and rational and displayed few signs of stress." During the interview, Joey turned down a cigarette offered him by the Courier team but he admitted he recently started to, "smoke a few now and then."

As the Courier team pressed Joey politely during the jailhouse interview, Joey got upset, stood up and, in Seal's words, "spun counter-clockwise" to the green metal door behind him. He knocked for deputies and asked to be taken back to his cell. Seal reported that a deputy then told him to sit down until the halls of the holding center were cleared, as security in the jail was extremely tight for the interview. He reported that no other visitors were permitted to either enter or leave the nearby visiting area during the interview. Joey was heavily guarded as he moved to and from his cell. Commenting on Joey's "hazel eyes constantly shifting," Seal reported that Joey returned to his chair in the library and sat silently with his arms folded over his chest and his elbows resting on the table. He also wrote of the "ever-present half-smile and half-scowl" Joey wore until deputies came into the library and took him back to his room.

But, even as Joey was talking to the Courier staffers on February 26th, Coppola broke another story about how Joey claimed he had stopped eating food in the Fort Benning stockade and at the psychiatric ward of the base hospital because he felt he was being drugged. Coppola's February 26th piece disclosed that Joey was interested in trying to dispel perceptions that he was mentally unstable and that he had tried to dismember himself with a razor in the Fort Benning stockade early in 1981.

A day after the "exclusive" jailhouse interview ran in the Courier-Express, District Attorney Richard J. Arcara told The Buffalo Evening News that he and his staff would closely examine that interview to see if any of Joey's comments could be used against him at trial.

More or less telescoping his upcoming courtroom disagreements with the state psychiatrists, Defense Attorney Mahoney told The Buffalo Evening News that among the unresolved pre-trial issues in the case was whether Justice Flynn was legally bound to accept the competency finding of the Mid-Hudson Psychiatric experts. Following a closed-door meeting with both sides on March 9, 1982, Judge Flynn ordered yet another mental competency hearing. The judge said he was legally obligated to have another such hearing because Joey's attorneys were challenging the findings of the Mid-Hudson psychiatrists. After the closed-door session that day, Dillon explained to The Buffalo Evening News that he and Mahoney had pressed for another hearing, citing grounds in the state criminal procedure law.

"We aren't satisfied with the reports submitted by the Mid-Hudson Psychiatric Center" and Justice Flynn is still legally obligated to make the final call on the issue of Joey's mental readiness for trial, Dillon added.

Judge Flynn, on March 12, 1982, denied the request by Dillon and Mahoney for Joey to submit to more examinations from Buffalo-area psychiatrists before the next hearing. Flynn told The Buffalo Evening News that the upcoming competency hearing would deal only with the defense attorneys challenge to the sufficiency of Joey's recent hospitalized mental treatment at the Mid- Hudson facility – a narrow issue. The judge told The Buffalo Evening News that he had already informed the defense attorneys that, "I didn't intend to appoint any more psychiatrists," to examine Joey.

The start of the March 16, 1982 court session had been delayed while Erie County Sheriff Kenneth J. Braun himself had to personally coax Joey to agree to come to court that morning across Delaware Avenue from the Holding Center. As soon as Joey arrived in court that chilly March morning, he began complaining to the judge about his own lawyers' continuing efforts to have him ruled a paranoid schizophrenic, incapable of standing trial.

"The DA didn't ask for this hearing and I, not being incapacitated, didn't ask for the hearing either," Joey complained to the judge shortly after he was unshackled. "I don't feel they have a right to just keep asking for more hearings." Joey had also recently penned a letter to the judge complaining about his attorneys' demands for another competency hearing. Christopher also informed the judge about what he called the "definite preponderance of evidence" from Dr. Paul Chellappa and the other Mid-Hudson psychiatric team members supporting his mental competency.

During the March 16, 1982 court session, prosecutor Albert M. Ranni joined with Joey in protesting the need for more pre-trial mental competency proceedings. After Ranni began renewing the objections of prosecutors to the competency dispute, defense attorney Mahoney complained to the judge about what he described as a prosecution effort to drive "a wedge" between Joey and the defense team. And Joey complained to the judge about his attorneys' tactics, saying his case "should not be a contest between psychiatrists."

Once the hearing got underway, Justice Flynn discovered that the doctors at Mid-Hudson were all puzzled when Christopher had arrived there. Dr. Chellappa, one of those Mid-Hudson psychiatrists, testified that Joey had appeared "rational" when he arrived at the facility. Dr. Chellappa told Judge Flynn that Joey had been treated at Mid-Hudson for two months merely as a courtesy to the court.

Responding to questions from prosecutor Duane M. Stamp, Dr. Chellappa, who had personally overseen Joey's hospital treatment, told the judge that as far as he could tell from a review of all of Joey's records, his mental competency had been established during the first mental competency hearing months ago. Contending that from a professional standpoint, there had only been a "50-50" chance Joey actually needed any hospital mental care and treatment, Dr. Chellappa said it was his view that Justice Flynn's concern about the locally-divided professional opinions of Joey's mental health rather than any signs of an observable illness had prompted him to order Joey's institutionalization. Joey "appeared rational" the very first day he arrived at Mid-Hudson under heavy guard. After a brief stay in a private room, he was moved to an infirmary ward with other patients, Dr. Chellappa testified. He told the judge Joey was only kept at Mid-Hudson for two months because he had simply refused to talk to many of the professional staff there about his criminal case.

"I found him to be a stubborn person," Dr. Chellappa said of Joey.

Dr. Chellappa testified that Joey's treatment at his facility consisted mainly of talks with staff psychiatric specialists, rather than drug therapy. He told the judge Joey seemed to become more open in his responses the longer he was at the facility. By mid-January, Joey had begun to discuss his criminal case and indicated he was well-aware of the nature of the charges against him and that he faced a lengthy prison term if convicted. The state psychiatrist told the judge that Joey had spoken to him about his personal desire for a non-jury trial because he felt a judge could be fairer in assessing his fate than a jury of lay people. Joey felt a jury "might be swayed by what they hear or read" about his case and would not be prepared to determine his guilt or innocence based on the evidence presented in court, he added.

During a break in Chellappa's testimony, Mahoney told the news media outside the courtroom he and Dillon opted to challenge the Mid-Hudson diagnosis because that was in Joey's best interest from a legal standpoint.

"The defendant has attorneys who represent him and his interests and as long as we represent the defendant, we are obliged to make motions which are necessary to represent his best interests, as we would with any client," Mahoney said.

After a one-day delay caused by Justice Flynn's prior court commitments, the mental competency hearing resumed on March 18, 1982 and Joey resumed his boycott of the session. Reading from a prepared letter he had drafted in long-hand, Joey told the judge that his own reading of the New York State criminal procedure law, which Flynn had cited as the basis for his scheduling of the second mental competency hearing, did not contain any specific provisions for a second hearing in light of the findings of the psychiatrists who dealt with him at the Mid-Hudson facility. Using his own less-than-perfect grammatical style, Joey's hand-written note to the judge stated: "The reports of those tests [at Mid-Hudson] did not come back unanimous."

As Joey loudly complained again about the need for the hearing, Justice Flynn ordered him to be returned to the holding center. Joey was only in court for 10 minutes or so that morning. After Joey left, defense attorney Mahoney began to cross-examine Dr. Chellappa.

During a day-long round of cross-examination, some court observers concluded that, from the battery of questions Mahoney kept posing at the doctor, the state psychiatrist was as much a subject of that competency hearing as Joey. Mahoney openly questioned Dr. Chellappa's credentials and his motivations concerning Joey's situation. But the doctor insisted the Mid-Hudson staff rightfully concluded Joey was sent there for pre-trial treatment more to satisfy the judge's legal concerns than for any discernible signs of mental illness. Dr. Chellappa stressed that Joey was basically subject to fits of moodiness and inattentiveness. He also said he found Joey liked to "tease" authority figures. Dr. Chellappa said that, even though Joey had been sent to the state's only mental hospital treating criminal suspects awaiting trial, he displayed no sign of mental illness during his stay and was not treated for any diagnosed mental illnesses while he was there. Dr. Chellappa proffered an explanation that the psychiatrists who examined Joey and concluded he was a schizophrenic had done so because any perceived bullying would have likely prompted Joey to refuse to give those doctors an answer to their questions.

A native of India, Dr. Chellappa told the judge Joey became increasingly responsive to his own questions after he made it clear to Joey that he "respected" his feelings and wouldn't press him. He told the judge he believed the sensitivity he showed Joey enabled him to develop the first "meaningful relationship" that Joey had with any of the psychiatrists who have been examining him since January of 1981. Dr. Chellappa told the judge Joey denied to him that he had any complicity in any crimes and he acknowledged accurately his current legal predicament.

The state psychiatrist had also asked Joey, as he was preparing to leave Mid-Hudson on February 24, 1982, "Do you have anything against the blacks or dark-skinned people?" Dr. Chellappa admitted that his curiosity got the best of him, after having heard reports of Joey's supposed hatred of blacks and dark-skinned men. Joey said he had no grudges against anybody. Dr. Chellappa inquired, "Does that include the blacks?" Joey just responded again that he had nothing against anybody. When the doctor pressed him on that point and said to him, "Even the blacks?" Joey "just nodded and smiled.

"He didn't want me to have the satisfaction of hearing his own words," the doctor testified. Dr. Chellappa refused Mahoney's request for him to give a psychiatric interpretation of the nod and smile, saying it was only a magnification of Joey's personality traits.

"He might have something against blacks, he might not," Dr. Chellappa testified.

Mahoney attacked Dr. Chellappa's qualifications. The doctor, who in his testimony casually referred to fellow psychiatrists as "shrinks" and "head shrinkers," was forced by Mahoney to admit he had yet to receive certification from the American Board of Psychiatry. Mahoney also got Dr. Chellappa to admit he had failed the qualifying test for that important professional honor at least twice before the judge made Mahoney transition to a different set of questions. Mahoney reminded the judge that the three court-appointed psychiatrists who concluded that Joey was mentally ill one year earlier were all board-certified psychiatrists.

Under questioning from Mahoney, Dr. Chellappa admitted his first impressions of Joey's mental competence, or as Mahoney said "his supposed competence," came after only spending ten minutes reviewing Joey's medical records and his initial 15 to 20 minute meeting with Joey. A skilled inquisitor, Mahoney forced Dr. Chellappa to admit on the stand that Joey had refused to take almost all the different types of assessments the Mid-Hudson staff wanted to administer, including a urinalysis, psychological evaluations and brain wave tests. Yet, Dr. Chellappa somewhat incongruously insisted he still found Joey cooperative and helpful with the staff.

After Dr. Chellappa testified that he found Joey not to be "reclusive," as his accompanying medical reports had documented, Mahoney read reports from Mid-Hudson nurses attending to Joey which all suggested he was having "minimal interaction" with hospital staff and other patients. The nursing reports also indicated Joey spent long periods of time laying on his hospital bed and refusing to join other inmates in watching the Super Bowl on television or getting involved in other patient activities.

After Dr. Chellappa testified that he had concluded on January 18th that Joey was mentally competent, Mahoney produced a January 26th letter from one of Dr. Chellappa's superiors stating that the Mid-Hudson staff could not make an accurate psychological determination about Joey because Joey had refused to cooperate and agree to tests they wanted to administer. That prompted Dr. Chellappa to angrily insist that letter was not necessary because he felt he had the situation with Joey under control. He also said his superiors had not consulted with him before sending that letter to Justice Flynn.

Dr. Chellappa testified that he decided the judge had "had difficulty" assessing Joey's mental state last fall due to the "divergent" and yet "exceedingly close" psychiatric opinions he heard in court. He said Joey told him at Mid-Hudson that he was willing to deal with Mahoney in preparing for trial but harbored a "dislike" for Dillon, saying he only wanted Dillon working in a "clerical" capacity in preparing the defense case.

After Dr. Chellappa completed his second and final day on the stand in Buffalo, Justice Flynn denied motions by Dillon and Mahoney for a third round of psychiatric examinations of Joey. The judge derided that defense tactic as a "back door" bid to circumvent his decision that no further testing was required. The two defense attorneys, after a futile day-long attempt to force Dr. Chellappa to back off on his conclusions about Joey's mental health, told the judge they would personally finance re-examinations of Joey by Drs. John Wadsworth, Brian Joseph and Dr. Park, who agreed with the defense attorneys, and Dr. George Molnar, who found him fit for trial.

At Mahoney's request, the judge sealed from public view the affidavit the defense attorneys gave him a day earlier outlining the reasons they felt further psychiatric testing was justified. During a March 19, 1982 court session, both Mahoney and Dillon denounced Dr. Chellappa as a "quack" and a "charlatan" who reached a medical conclusion after only a cursory review of Joey's problems.

When Flynn again pressed Joey that day about his demand for a non-jury trial Joey told him:

"Your Honor, we have been over this on many occasions. You asked me, told me, I was going to come here this morning and you would pose the same question again, jury or non-jury. I'm here. I said non-jury trial. Your honor, I have been sitting here for I don't know how long, and I have made my decision and that's the way I'm going to stand."

The defense attorneys told Flynn that day, which constituted one of the nastiest court sessions so far in the case, that they would continue to vigorously represent Joey. Amid complaints about their courtroom tactics from the three prosecutors, Dillon and Mahoney told the judge the only way they would leave the case now is if he, as the trial judge, removed them. During the hearing, prosecutor Stamp had complained about the two defense attorneys having rendered the case "tightly wound around a psychiatric axis and ground to a halt." Flynn refused to comment from the bench on the defense attorneys' offer to pay personally for more testing. But he ordered them and the prosecutors back before him five days later for his decision on the mental health dispute.

Never one to mince words on the bench, Justice Flynn on March 23, 1982 ruled Joey mentally fit to stand trial and ordered a tentative April 6th start to the trial.

"The court is satisfied that the defendant is not an incapacitated person," Flynn ruled. "The court orders criminal action against the defendant to proceed."

Joey immediately told the judge he wanted to proceed with a non-jury trial as he had been demanding since late October.

"I'm going to stand with my decision," Joey told the judge, who nonetheless urged him to think about it again overnight. The judge also told Joey that if he really wants a non-jury trial because he expected him to be his judge, he might be disappointed. Justice Flynn told Joey he was still considering the motion of Dillon and Mahoney from last fall that he withdraw as judge in the case. Flynn also told Joey that he, as a judge, believed the best method for resolving the case would be with a jury trial, explaining that as the defendant, Joey would have a chance to select the members of the jury. Flynn told Joey he felt juries were better than judges at determining the truthfulness of witness testimony. And the requirement for a unanimous verdict virtually eliminated chances of a wrong-headed verdict.

During that court session, prosecutor Stamp told the judge he found the defense attorneys' continuing effort to have Joey stand trial before a jury, against Joey's own wishes, to be a stratagem designed to ensure the reversal on appeal of any possible non-jury trial conviction. Stamp also told the judge forcing Joey to unwillingly stand trial before a jury would likely be "constitutional error." Justice Flynn rejected efforts by Dillon and Mahoney for permission to ask Joey 75 questions they had prepared on the jury waiver issue. In reviewing the proposed questions, the judge said he found many of them too esoteric and dealing more with the attorney-client relationship than with a defendant's ability to intelligently give up his right to a jury trial. Dillon and Mahoney refused to provide the news media with copies of the 75 questions. Prosecutor Stamp told the judge he felt many of the proposed questions could only be intelligently answered "by a third-year law student."

Dillon said of the prosecutors: "I think that they'd be well advised to go back and do their homework on the prosecution of this matter rather than worrying about Joseph Christopher." Dillon also said he found it, "quite obvious that the prosecutors would like nothing better than to take on Mr. Christopher legally one-on-one. They want to try to minimize the participation of Mr. Mahoney and myself."

By then, black citizens and leaders were actively picketing outside the downtown Buffalo courthouse, protesting delays in the trial. As the judge was rendering his decision on the mental competency issue, two black men were issued appearance tickets on misdemeanor criminal contempt charges for picketing with cardboard signs within 200 feet of the courthouse advocating Justice Flynn's removal from the case.

On March 24, 1982, Joey's wish for a non-jury trial was granted and the judge made him sign a formal waiver of his right to a jury trial. As his two lawyers began to renew their request for Flynn to step down from the case, Joey abruptly walked toward the courtroom door. The judge told sheriff's deputies he could go back to the downtown jail.

After the hearing, Dillon and Mahoney told the news media they would abandon their attempt to press upon Joey the advisability of a jury trial, but they questioned the motives of the prosecutors in the case.

"We've made our position quite clear over the last six months and we will not raise the issue of a jury trial again," Dillon said.

They believed the prosecutors were deliberately trying to undermine Joey's right to a fair trial by playing on his superficial understanding of the law. Dillon said he and Mahoney found the constant courtroom expressions of concern by prosecutors about their handling of their argumentative client's case to be both "highly improper" and of questionable sincerity. In response, District Attorney Richard J. Arcara said he found Dillon and Mahoney's complaints about the conduct of his three prosecutors to be "highly improper."

"We are attempting to move this case to trial as quickly as possible," Arcara told The Buffalo Evening News. "We are advocates and we have a right to address the court on issues we think are pertinent and relevant."

Another heated closed-door meeting on April 2, 1982, between the judge, prosecutors and Dillon, led to another delay in the scheduled start of the first murder trial. After that ended, Justice Flynn confirmed that he moved back the start of the trial from April 6th to April 12th. Though neither Dillon, nor the main prosecutorial team would talk about the meeting, Justice Flynn confirmed that Dillon was complaining that prosecutors had yet to turn over to the defense team all the legal documents and evidence to which they were entitled. The judge also confirmed that he had yet to rule on the defense motion that he recuse himself from the case to relieve any public concerns about his ability to objectively reach a verdict, given his extensive history of involvement in the case.

Later that day, Dillon told The Buffalo Evening News that the effort to remove Flynn from the case was designed to prevent the public from harboring any suspicions that the non-jury proceedings were rigged in any way.

"What we essentially want is a fact-finder [judge] who would be in, at least arguably, the same position as prospective jurors, in that he knows no more about the case than what he has read in the news media," Dillon said.

"We think that that would be fair to all parties concerned and I'm sure the prosecution wants to make sure they aren't participant in any proceeding that has any appearance of taint or impropriety." Deputy District Attorney Albert M. Ranni, the lead prosecutor in the case, said the district attorney's office remained "very firm" as it had since the defense brought up the issue that there was no reason Justice Flynn had to disqualify himself from the case.

Dillon and Mahoney won that procedural fight. On April 5, 1982, Justice Flynn officially withdrew as the judge in the case. In announcing his decision, the judge said, "In the administration of justice it is important not only that a trial be impartially conducted but also that the appearance of impartiality be maintained."

"Because of the extraordinary scope and duration of pre-trial proceedings in which I was necessarily involved, the appearance of impartiality would best be served if the trial proceeded before another trial justice," Flynn added.

One of 21 state trial-level judges available in Western New York at that time, Flynn also recused himself as judge in the shooting death of Joseph McCoy, which was slated to go to trial in Niagara Falls, and for the knife attacks by Joey on Albert Menefee and Calvin Crippen in Buffalo. After Flynn's recusal announcement, State Supreme Court Justice James B. Kane, administrative judge for the entire eight-county Western New York area, said he and State Supreme Court Justice Theodore S. Kasher, the district's chief criminal court judge, would confer and expeditiously select a new trial judge. "We will appoint a judge who is available to begin handling the case immediately," Kane said shortly after Flynn announced he was stepping down.

Under New York State's Judiciary Law, the issue of a judge withdrawing from a case was up to the judge's own conscience. The only time a judge was legally obligated to drop out of a case was when the judge had family ties or a direct financial interest affected by the case or if the judge once been a litigant or a lawyer in the case. A judge was not even obligated to withdraw from a case even if the judge admitted to actual bias against any of the parties in the case. In such a situation, a judge would be expected to ensure that no one could detect "the slightest impression of judicial impropriety" through that judge's rulings and actions.

Defense attorney Dillon called Flynn's action the appropriate decision, vowing that he and Mark Mahoney would be ready to go with the trial on April 12th as then scheduled. Dillon also cautioned that he and his co-counsel did not, "anticipate making any more motions [that would delay the trial start]," adding, "but we've been in that position before."

CHAPTER NINE

New Judge, First Trial

After Justice Flynn recused himself following ten and a half months of exhaustive pretrial proceedings, Administrative Judge James B. Kane moved quickly to select a new judge. On April 6, 1982, he named State Supreme Court Justice Frederick M. Marshall to take over. Marshall, 62, was one of the district's most highly-esteemed judges Known as a workaholic, no-nonsense judge, Marshall already presided at some of Western New York's most important criminal trials of the latter half of the 20th Century. Marshall was known in local legal circles as a judge who ran a highly-efficient courtroom and strictly controlled the procedural maneuvering of attorneys. Off the bench, he loved gardening, golf and gourmet cooking. In announcing Marshall's selection, Justice Kane said he selected him because of his "ability and experience."

Marshall met with the attorneys on both sides of the case on April 8, 1982. Given the lack of an actual murder weapon – prosecutors counted on extensive ballistics evidence to make their case.

This evidence would be comprised of matching bullets and casings found at Joey's Buffalo home, his hunting lodge and at the three Buffalo murder scenes. Armed with court orders, investigators had seized .22-caliber ammunition and bullet casings from Joey's Weber Street home and at his Cherry Creek hunting lodge. The investigators searched the firing range set up there and also pried bullets from trees near the lodge. All the prosecution ballistics evidence was analyzed by FBI experts in Washington, D.C. Back in October 1981, defense attorneys Dillon and Mahoney had retained Chicago ballistics expert John Sadunas to examine and raise all possible questions about the prosecution ballistics evidence. In the spring of 1981, then-District Attorney Edward C. Cosgrove publically labeled that evidence "conclusive" proof of Joey's guilt.

Joey's trial begins. Photo courtesy Buffalo Courier-Express Archive, E.H. Butler Library, SUNY College at Buffalo

At 10:01 a.m. on April 12, 1982, a pudgy Joey walked into the
courtroom at Erie County Hall where Marshall would decide his
fate. He was dressed in his usual courtroom uniform, described by
observers as a "nondescript" dark-blue corduroy jacket, Army boots
and a white shirt. Joey's upper lip gave the suggestion he was beginning to grow a mustache, despite pleas from his two lawyers that he
remain clean-shaven. In his only apparent concessions to the requests of his lawyers, Joey had had his longish hair cut over the
weekend. He wore metal-framed glasses that gave him a studious
look.

So many news media organizations sought permission to send
representatives to the trial that only six of the 36 available courtroom seats were able to accommodate members of the general public, a number of whom had lined up outside the Franklin Street
courthouse hours before the scheduled start of the proceeding. Joey's widowed mother, Therese Christopher, was provided a seat in
the spectator area.

Deputy District Attorney Albert M. Ranni began his 44-minute
opening statement by methodically giving the dates, times and loca-
tions of the three murders involved in the trial. With Joey staring
onward with a static, unemotional expression, Ranni referred to him
as the "vacant and blank-looking man," who many alleged eyewitnesses said "looked dopey." The prosecutor said that the murderer
was wearing the same type of metal-framed glasses Joey was wearing
that day. Ranni told the judge the prosecution would prove that, at
Fort Benning, Joey "smugly bragged" to black Army nurses "how he
hates niggers," – in sum, that he was the masked murderer being
sought nationwide for the racially-motivated killings.

Each of the three victims was killed by an assailant armed with
the .22 caliber Ruger rifle lawmen found missing from the "treas-

ured" gun collection when the suspect's Buffalo home was searched in the spring of 1981, Ranni told the judge. Though Joey had always told friends he would never break up the gun collection his father had left him, when lawmen searched the Christopher Weber Street home in the spring of 1981, "one gun was missing...the Ruger," Ranni told the judge. The prosecutor stressed that Dunn was murdered only two blocks from Joey's Weber Street home and Thomas was killed about a mile from that location.

In a hint of a possible weakness in the prosecution case, Ranni openly scoffed during his opening statement at what he called the "silly" police sketches compiled early in the investigation. Instead, Ranni insisted that the "unique repetitive signature" that each rifle leaves on every bullet fired from it pointed to Joey's guilt. Ranni declared, "One gun killed three people. One person killed three people."

In contrast, Defense attorney Mahoney spent just five minutes in his opening remarks, complaining about what he called the "biased" nature of the prosecution case against his client. This was in spite of the fact that the court had made an earlier ruling in an effort to lessen any possibility of bias: Justice Marshall reaffirmed Justice Flynn's ruling of six months earlier that any prosecutorial cross-examination of Joey, should he take the stand, would be limited to evidence about the actual shootings and not expanded into his feelings about other people. Even with that ruling, Joey's attorneys refused to say whether they planned to put the defendant on the stand.

Outside the courtroom, Dillon and Mahoney disputed prosecutors' claims that eyewitnesses and ballistics evidence would conclusively link Joey to the first three murders. Mahoney said he and Dillon planned to prove to the judge that prosecutors "adjusted" the known facts and theories about the murders "to accommodate the defendant as a suspect" rather than objectively putting together the provable facts about each killing and developing theories to fit those facts.

The first prosecution witnesses on the stand described victims Emmanuel Thomas and Glenn Dunn as illicit drug users. Dr. Catherine Lloyd, the Erie County government pathologist who examined all three victims' remains, testified that Thomas had a fresh heroin track mark on his left arm at the time of his murder. She said he was also drunk at the time of death. Detective Joseph A. Judkiewicz, of the Buffalo Police Evidence United, testified that police found marijuana "roaches" or butts and airplane model glue apparently used for sniffing to get high in the stolen car in which Dunn was murdered.

The balance of the Judkiewicz testimony and the testimony of four nurses from St. Joseph's Intercommunity Hospital, where victim Harold Green was rushed after the shooting, constituted the standard showing by the prosecution team to confirm that ballistics evidence had been properly preserved and documented by police. Sister Emily Zuba and fellow St. Joseph's nurses Margaret Klass, Geraldine McGuire and Betty Pieczynski told the judge bullet fragments recovered from Green's brain were catalogued and turned over to police investigators. Though Green lived for six days after he was shot, Dunn and Thomas were both pronounced dead on arrival when they were rushed to Buffalo's Erie County Medical Center.

The seeming air-tight prosecution case linking Joey to all three Buffalo-area murders was thrown for a curve on the second day of the trial, as defense attorney Mahoney forced a prosecution homicide detective to admit that Robert Oddo, the 17-year-old East Side resident who allegedly witnessed the murder of Glenn Dunn, had told his own sister the gunman was blond, rather than brown-haired

like Joey. Just the day before, Ranni had established that Oddo had
gotten an "arms reach" view of Joey's face and then watched at some
distance as Joey allegedly shot Dunn three times in a Genesee Street
supermarket parking lot. Though Detective Alois G. Williams had
been called to the stand by prosecutors for some routine testimony
about his role in collecting bullet fragments that had been removed
from Dunn's brain, Mahoney extracted a reference to a blond killer
during his cross-examination. Mahoney got Williams to admit that
when he interviewed Robert Oddo's sister, Kathleen Oddo, several
days after the Dunn shooting, he wrote down in his investigative
notebook Miss Oddo's statement that "her brother told her the
shooter had blond hair."

Other fissures in the prosecution's case surfaced. On the second
day of testimony, Dorothy Thomas, the widow of victim Emmanuel
Thomas, took issue with claims that her husband was back on illicit
drugs the night he was killed. Mrs. Thomas testified that her husband was shot near their East Side home less than 12 hours before he
was to go to Buffalo City Court on a complaint he had lodged against
Leslie Coleman, a black man who lived two doors down from them
on Zenner Street. Mrs. Thomas told the judge she and her slain
husband had filed a reckless endangerment charge against Coleman
on August 24, 1980 shortly after Coleman had fired a rifle over her
head because he mistakenly believed she had beaten his young
daughter. All court records on the complaint against Coleman were
sealed at the request of the Erie County District Attorney's office
after the murder of Emmanuel Thomas.

The widow Thomas told the judge she did not believe police reports and earlier trial testimony that an autopsy disclosed her unemployed husband had returned to the drug habit that she insisted he
had kicked seven years before his murder. Admitting she had denied

authorities access to all her husband's belongings after his murder, Mrs. Thomas testified the her husband had been gone from their rental home at 70 Zenner about five minutes before a neighbor boy came to the house about 11:30 p.m. on September 23, 1980 and told her of the shooting. Justice Marshall also became irked at prosecutor Duane M. Stamp's effort to find out from Mrs. Thomas how much beer her husband had drunk the night of his murder.

"I don't know if it's going to help me decide guilt or innocence if he [Mr. Thomas] had a couple of beers, but go ahead," the judge told Stamp, overruling Dillon's objections about the relevancy of such questioning.

Under cross examination from Dillon, Thomas disclosed that, shortly before his murder, her husband had "squabbled" with their landlord, John Herko. Dillon worked to extract other potential killers. Thomas also stated that two white men were tenants of Leslie Coleman two doors away from her house in the predominantly black neighborhood where she lived. She said she knew those two white men only as "Billy" and "Joe" and admitted one of them had brown hair like Joey and had a build similar to Joey's.

But, the prosecution's case continued. On the second day of the trial, Cheektowaga gun dealer William Goetzmann told the judge that Joey's late father, Nicholas Joseph Christopher, visited his store, the Gun Center Inc. at 3385 Harlem Road, and had purchased what authorities contended was the missing murder weapon, a used semiautomatic .22 caliber Ruger rifle with a telescopic sight, on October 28, 1974 for $69. Goetzmann also confirmed that photographs introduced into the trial by prosecutors showed Joey holding that now-missing rifle during family outings.

During day-long prosecution testimony of police detectives from Buffalo and Cheektowaga in addition to Mrs. Thomas and

Goetzmann, the judge chided all three prosecutors for what he called their needlessly "laboring" over the questioning of the police witnesses by asking preparatory types of questions that were only really necessary when a jury was hearing a case. Justice Marshall, at one point, even admonished Stamp to get to the "nub" of what he wanted to elicit from witnesses.

Cross examination opportunities abounded for the defense team. Dillon and Mahoney got Cheektowaga Detective William Fenske to admit during cross-examination that authorities never followed up on fingerprint evidence of a number of suspects that he had obtained from the car of murder victim Green. Fenske was forced to admit to the judge that he found 12 sets of fingerprints on the outside of the driver's side door of the car Green was sitting in when shot twice in the head.

The prosecution case took a turn for the worse on the third day of testimony, as Joey's attorneys called the widow Thomas back to the stand. She testified that Frenchy Cook, who had been with her husband during his fatal shooting, told her afterward that police sketches of the killer were "a long way off" in terms of their accuracy. David Robinson, 26, a longtime friend of Joey, told the judge that same day that Joey had closely-cropped brown hair at the time of the .22 caliber killings, not long dirty-blond hair like that depicted in the police sketches. A self-employed building cleaner, Robinson told the judge that Joey had "rather short" hair at the time of those killings.

Robinson did admit that Joey maintained his father's extensive gun collection at the family's Weber Street home and was skilled in gun modification procedures. He also acknowledged that Joey had had possession of his late father's now-missing .22 caliber Ruger rifle. He said he last saw Joey with that rifle either in "late 1978 or early 1979." Robinson insisted that even though they saw each other after the four .22 caliber murders, he and Joey never discussed any such events. The judge sustained the defense attorneys' objections to prosecutor William J. Knapp's attempt to get Robinson to admit on the stand that around the time of those killings. Joey was behaving peculiarly.

But the next day, Rev. Michael Freeman, a Roman Catholic Army chaplain, testified that days after Joey was arrested at Fort Benning, he complained about having been "persecuted" by blacks since his high school days. Father Freeman testified that as Joey had spoken to him in the stockade dining hall several days after the January 18, 1981 barracks knife attack. According to the priest, Joey seemed severely depressed and spoke of having been the object of "name-calling" and "homosexual slurs" from black recruits whom he had been training with that month. Father Freeman told the judge that in the base stockade, Joey asked him to seek Army psychiatric help for him.

His testimony came after the Erie County Sheriff's Department increased court house security and redoubled daily bomb-search activity around the third floor courtroom based on what later was described as a prank telephone call to Buffalo police headquarters that morning about a bomb allegedly having been planted in the nearby court house. Hoax or not, Erie County Undersheriff Thomas F. Higgins told the news media that the courtroom and its environs were searched by what he called a reinforced court house security staff before and after each day's court proceedings and even during breaks in testimony.

Over the objections of Joey's attorneys, Father Freeman was allowed to take the stand and testify about one of the many talks he had in the stockade with Joey. The priest said Joey had released him from his vows of confessional confidentiality about one particular talk because Joey had said that he was depressed and wanted help in accessing a psychiatrist. The priest testified that Joey, whose mental condition had been a major pretrial legal issue, told him he "felt persecuted and could not find peace of mind in the stockade." He said Joey told him he had been struck by one of the guards shortly after his arrest. Father Freeman said Joey also told him one of the black soldiers in his basic training unit had "grabbed him in the seat of the pants and called him names with sexual overtones." He testified that Joey said "he felt he was being harassed in the training brigade and was angered and depressed," because blacks repeatedly called him, "faggot and wimp." But the priest told the judge Joey had given him no evidence that he had acted on that anger. Father Freeman said he felt that by disclosing what Joey told him in that one 20-minute stockade talk he could get him some psychiatric help. The Roman Catholic priest asserted that he was bound by the priest-penitent privilege and could not reveal any of his other stockade discussions with Joey late in January 1981.

Despite Father Freeman's vivid testimony, the prosecution was not getting any closer to meeting its burden of proof. As Erie County District Attorney Richard J. Arcara observed testimony from the spectator gallery, defense attorneys Dillon and Mahoney got two female prosecution witnesses to admit they did not know the sex, age or race of the suspect they claimed they each had seen fleeing from two of the murder scenes. Linda Snyder, a New York State Thruway Authority secretary, testified that she never saw the face of the suspect she claimed to have seen running from Harold Green's car in the parking lot of a fast-food restaurant on Cheektowaga's Union Road at about 12:30 p.m. on September 23, 1980. Snyder told the judge the shooter was wearing cream-colored clothing and a light-colored fishing hat. Barbara Wozniak, a Buffalo housewife from Floss Street, told the judge the suspect she saw fleeing from a supermarket parking lot at Genesee and Floss streets where Dunn was slain at about 9:45 p.m. on September 22, 1980 wore a dark-colored, hooded jacket and pants. She conceded she also never saw the face of that shooter. Both Ms. Snyder and Ms. Wozniak told the judge the fatal gunfire they heard sounded like exploding firecrackers, but they did not draw any similar conclusions about the killer's look.

But the next day was not so good for Joey's defense attorneys. Madonna Gorney, a former psychiatric nursing aide, said she got a "full face" view of Joey from about two feet away as he sat near the entrance of the supermarket at Genesee and Floss streets moments before Glenn Dunn was shot and killed. The 30-year-old mother of two became the first witness to publicly and positively place Joey at the scene of one of the .22 caliber murders.

When Mrs. Gorney pointed to Joey as he sat in the courtroom and identified him as the "slightly retarded" white man she saw sitting near the supermarket entrance the night of the Dunn shooting, Joey's mother, Therese Christopher, audibly gasped in shock. Joey displayed no emotional reaction, yet stared intently at Mrs. Gorney the entire time she was on the witness stand. Mrs. Gorney told the judge she also picked out Joey at the May 12, 1981 police lineup – the same lineup at which Oddo had claimed that he could not identify the shooter. Mrs. Gorney testified that she did not speak to Joey as she walked past him into the supermarket. Ironically, she told the judge she had been relieved to see a white man present in the virtually vacant store lot. This was because she had also spotted a black man standing under a lamp post when she drove into the lot alone.

"It struck me when I looked at him that he could be slightly retarded or a little slow," Mrs. Gorney told the judge. She said Joey was wearing metal-frame glasses, a blue jacket, tan pants and sneakers and had a brown grocery bag lying on the ground next to him. She testified that he was gone when she came out of the store some time later and found a commotion going on in the parking lot. That commotion was the result of the Dunn shooting. In response to questions from prosecutor Ranni, Mrs. Gorney testified that Joey's hair color as she was able to observe it the night of the shooting was either "dark brown or light brown." She confirmed that the color of the hair of the peculiar-looking white man she saw sitting outside the supermarket entrance that night was the same as Joey's in several full-color blowups of Joey family photographs that Ranni showed her as she sat on the witness stand.

Mrs. Gorney, who lived several blocks from the supermarket lot where Dunn was killed, testified that she did not tell police she had seen Joey in the parking lot until she was questioned again at her home several days after the murder. She said in the initial police interview the investigators were only interested in learning about the never-identified black man she said had been loitering in the supermarket lot. Mrs. Gorney testified that she was comforted when investigators returned to her house a few days later and she was able to mention seeing Joey at the murder scene. After rethinking the incident, she felt that white man, "might have seen more than I had" in the supermarket lot.

She was followed later that day by Robert S. Oddo, who finally admitted that he positively saw Joey kill Dunn. Oddo, a Buffalo high school dropout just like Joey, testified that he was standing at the entrance of the supermarket and could see Joey some one hundred feet away in the parking lot firing some sort of weapon into an automobile. Oddo said he saw "the flames, the fire from the gun," although he could not recall actually seeing the murder weapon in

Joey's hands. He testified that Joey ran from the lot when he saw him looking at him seconds after the shooting. Joey ran up Floss Street past the home of Oddo's parents in the direction of Weber Street.

Oddo told the judge he had an eight-month battle with his conscience before he finally told investigators he had actually observed Joey shooting the teenager. Oddo claimed he had agonized for about eight months before admitting he had lied at both the police lineup and before the grand jury. Oddo testified that he had gone to the police lineup intent on claiming he didn't see the killer because he felt that would give him a chance to get out of continuing involvement in the investigation. But, he said he changed his mind after concluding that, "I didn't want it on my shoulders for the rest of my life." He told the judge he had a change of heart.

"I didn't want to see somebody let go who did something," Oddo explained. However, Oddo may have had a change of heart after he finally gave up thoughts of receiving a large financial reward for testifying for prosecutors at the murder trials in the case.

After the Dunn shooting, Oddo went right home and told his parents he had just seen a murder being committed. He then returned to the supermarket lot. Oddo said he told Buffalo Police Lt. William Mistal there that he had seen the shooting, but could only provide a general description of the gunman.

Intensively cross-examining both Mrs. Gorney and Oddo, Joey's attorneys noted that Mrs. Gorney claimed the man she identified as Joey wore tan pants and a hooded jacket that may have been of nylon fabric while Oddo said Joey wore dark pants and a blue cloth zippered sweatshirt. Dillon prompted Oddo to say he told the grand jury last May that the killer had blond hair. But, Prosecutor Ranni, on his redirect examination of Oddo, got him to state that as far as he was concerned, there was little color difference between a dirty-blond haired individual and a brown-haired individual like Joey.

The prosecution put its major ballistics evidence before the judge on April 16th. According to prosecutors, ballistics examinations of bullet casings confirmed that the same .22 caliber rifle was used in all three killings. This testimony came from Michael Dujanovich, the firearms examiner at the Erie County Central Police Services crime laboratory.

"They were all fired from the same weapon," Dujanovich said of the shots. Dujanovich told the judge it didn't matter that he was unable to examine the actual murder weapon, because the unique microscopic marks he found on every bullet or casing he examined confirmed that they were all fired from the same gun. Hedging his scientific observations, Dujanovich asserted that "the most probable firearm" used in the three killings was a Ruger 10-22 rifle. Dujanovich told the judge that it was the only weapon capable of leaving the unusual "wedge-shaped firing pin impression" he observed on seven bullet casings found at both the murder scenes and ammunition seized at Joey's properties. The 31st witness during the week-old trial, Dujanovich testified that the missing 10-shot, .22 caliber semi-automatic Ruger Model 10-22 rifle left telltale markings found on all the ammunition seized at Joey's properties. Though the mass-produced Ruger model was normally 3 and ½ feet in length, it could easily be sawed down and hidden in a bag without any loss of firing power, he testified. The firearms examiner told the judge a sawed-off Ruger 10-22 rifle could easily be fired one-handed.

Dujanovich had examined the murder scene evidence September 24, 1980 and the other ammunition on April 22, 1981. He told the judge that a misfired bullet found in a box of ammunition in the basement of Joey's Weber Street home and two spent .22 caliber casings found at Joey's family hunting lodge matched the murder scene evidence.

Joey's attorneys challenged Dujanovich's qualifications as a firearms expert. However, the judge found him to be well-qualified based on the hundreds of bullets Dujanovich said he had examined since joining the county crime lab in 1978. Under cross-examination by attorney Mahoney on his second day on the stand, Dujanovich admitted two of the bullet casings found at Joey's hunting lodge failed to microscopically match two of the three casings found at the Dunn youth's murder scene or any of the three casings found at the Thomas murder scene. Despite that fact, Dujanovich was confident of his conclusions because the unmatchable casings had markings on them identical to other casings found in the probe and those did match what he called "a common third" bit of casing evidence. The firearms expert insisted that while the so-called "cabin casings" found at the Christopher hunting lodge did not match two of the Dunn casings or the Thomas casings, they did match the single casing found at the scene of the Harold Green murder. He claimed such an indirect comparison was a valid method of linking the disparate casings. Dujanovich concluded all the unmatchable casings were fired from the missing murder weapon because they did positively match other casings found at all three murder scenes. However, defense attorney Mahoney characterized the expert's explanation as "peculiar and unusual," undermining the validity of the prosecution's ballistics evidence.

The expert witness took issue with color photographs of bullet casings fired from 18 different Ruger 10-22 rifles in the defense effort to show he had not eliminated the possibility that the bullet evidence could be tied to several rifles. Dujanovich told the judge the angles from which the bullet casings in the defense team's photographs were taken and the types of lighting used to photograph them were far less conclusive than the microscopic firing-pin and other markings he found on the prosecution ballistics evidence.

"I wouldn't base a comparison of bullet evidence on a photograph at all," Dujanovich testified.

Mahoney pressed on in his attempt to discredit the witness. He faulted Dujanovich for his admitted failure to test fire a ten-bullet Ruger rotary magazine seized from the defendant's home under court order in April 1981, suggesting it could have been a cause of some of the microscopic markings on the prosecution evidence.

Mahoney argued for a mistrial, claiming the defense team had not received pretrial notice of what he called the faulty firearms comparisons. He also openly questioned what he called the "logic, integrity and validity" of Dujanovich's findings. But Mahoney failed to get the judge to grant the defense a one-week adjournment so he and Dillon could contact John Sadunas, a former Chicago police ballistics expert they had talked to before the trial.

On April 20, 1982 Robert E. Perrigo, director of the Central Police Services crime lab and Dujanovich's boss, told the judge he concurred with Dujanovich's "inferential" method of linking all the spent casings to Joey. Perrigo, a firearms examiner himself for 29 years, denied defense attorney Mahoney's contention that his lab had felt pressured by public clamor over the racial killings to hastily come up with a ballistics finding based on insufficient testing and lab work. But, Mahoney did force Perrigo to admit that current firearms textbooks did not recommend the use of "inferential" identification efforts. He also admitted that the bullet evidence examined in the Buffalo crime lab was never sent to the FBI crime lab in Washington, D.C. for a confirmation of the local findings.

But, on that same day, two Army psychiatric nurses and two of Joey's stockade guards at Fort Benning made some of the most directly incriminating testimony. They told the judge that, 12 months ago, Joey made remarks to them about killing 13 people, including seven from the Buffalo area. Sgt. Richard C. Morganstern said Joey startled him and Capt. Aldrich Johnson, the stockade warden, by declaring that he "was a mass murderer in Buffalo."

"I did it," Morganstern testified that Joey told him in the stockade about 2:30 p.m. April 26, 1981.

"I did what they said I did in Buffalo. I want to make things right," Morganstern said Joey told him. Specialist Fourth Class Christopher D. Corwin told the judge that while he was guarding Joey in the psychiatric ward at the base's Martin Hospital during the first of Joey's two stays there in the spring of 1981, Joey told him he had "killed seven people in Buffalo" and that he had "killed some people in New York."

Captain Bernard J. Burgess testified that as Joey was being admitted to the psychiatric ward of the base hospital for a second time on April 10, 1981, Joey told him he had killed 13 people. Burgess told the judge Joey's alleged confession came as he was asking the patient some routine questions about medications he might have been on.

"He asked me if I was aware of the killings that took place in Buffalo that had been in the newspapers and on television," Burgess testified.

"I said I hadn't heard of them. He then told me how he killed some people. I asked him how many and he told me 13. I asked him how and he told me had had killed some with a .22 caliber weapon."

Burgess also testified about Joey's mental state. He said that Joey "was frightened, he was paranoid," but that he never learned why. In response to Dillon questions, Burgess testified that, "a person who is paranoid could make outrageous statements in order to keep people away from him." That prompted Dillon to speculate that Joey's statements might have been part of his attempt at either getting out of the Army or being transferred to the Veterans Administration Medical Center in Buffalo.

Capt. Dorothy Henderson testified that three days after Joey's admissions to Capt. Burgess, he told her he was a Buffalo murderer. Henderson testified that she felt the first statement Joey made to her about trying to kill somebody was a possible vehicle for getting back to Buffalo. Reading from a hospital report she wrote on Joey, Capt. Henderson said, "he came into the nurses' station on April 13, 1981 and announced, 'I murdered some people.' I asked him how many and he said he didn't know. He said they were all males. I asked him why and he said there were "signs" and that it was something he had to do." Henderson, who was black, told the judge that at the base hospital Joey showed no signs of hostility toward blacks and he appeared rational during his hospital stays.

The incriminating testimony continued to flow unhindered. Specialist Corwin testified that either in late March 1981 or the first week of April, Joey blurted out from his psychiatric ward hospital bed that he was a killer in both Buffalo and New York City. Corwin told the judge Joey was then was under 24-hour guard as a potential suicide. The testimony of the Army psychiatric nurses and military policemen came as prosecutors were on the verge of completing their case in chief. The judge had allowed their testimony over the objections of Joey's lawyers. Dillon and Mahoney contended that the alleged statements of Joey in the base stockade and its hospital's psychiatric ward were legally privileged and protected from disclosure.

Specialist Corwin told the judge Joey's alleged confession to him came after the suspect woke up in his hospital bed late one afternoon on his first stay at base hospital in the spring of 1981. Corwin explained that Joey had been transferred to the psychiatric ward of the hospital after staging a hunger strike in the stockade. He said Joey simply awoke one day in his bed and asked, "Did you know that I was a mass murderer in Buffalo?" Under cross examination by Dillon, the specialist said Joey was hospitalized a second time because he "attempted to slice his penis off with a razor blade." He also said Joey had his nose broken in a fight at the base stockade with a black guard.

Joey told Morganstern he was willing to talk about the Buffalo killings with an "Officer Molinaro." Joey identified him as a Buffalo policeman. However, Joey abruptly changed his mind and said "Forget it." Though Buffalo lawmen had quickly arrived at the Georgia military base late in April 1981 after being notified about Joey's earlier comments, Morganstern explained that Joey refused to talk to the Buffalo detectives and also refused to give a written confession to Army criminal investigators, dismissing all of them as "clowns."

Defense attorneys pressed witnesses with questions about Joey's condition at the base, perhaps attempting to draw out some other reason behind his extreme, confessional remarks. Under cross examination, Mahoney asked Morganstern if it was true that Fort Benning stockade officials frequently offered prisoners such as Joey "sexual favors" in return for their confessions to crimes. Morganstern dismissed the defense attorney's suggestion as a "rumor." Under cross-examination by Dillon, Burgess acknowledged that a March 1981 nursing report told of Joey complaining of being constantly harassed throughout his three and a half month Army career. That hospital report quoted Joey as saying, "I'm usually not bothered by things, but since I've been in the Army it seems as if everybody is trying to beat me down. I am a man. I don't like it when people insinuate that I'm not a man." That report, prepared by Captain Burgess, also noted that Joey spoke of, "feeling that he was harassed by other members of his unit," and, "that his masculinity was being questioned." As Burgess was being cross-examined, he also described an April 16, 1981 nursing report which documented that Joey said he had committed an act of self-mutilation in the stockade six days earlier because, as he explained, Joey "was tired of confinement." After the Army witnesses completed their testimony, chief prosecutor Ranni called to the stand Buffalo Police Tactical Patrol Unit Officer Eugene Molinaro, who told the judge he had purchased 11 firearms from Joey in May 1980 after Joey's Erie County pistol permit was suspended. The reason for that firearms permit suspension was not disclosed during the trial.

Prosecutors failed to persuade the judge to hear testimony from Army Private First Class Leonard Coles, who had survived the knifing by Joey in their Fort Benning barracks. Prosecutor Knapp argued that Joey was not mentally ill during basic training. He insisted that Coles could prove Joey was in perfect control of his mental faculties at the time of the knifing incident and suffered no delusions that he was really "the queen of England." But the judge agreed with Mahoney that the Coles testimony was irrelevant to the three Buffalo murders. Prosecutors rested their case after calling 38 witnesses who testified over eight days.

THE DEFENSE CASE

The defense case began with a sputtering start on April 21st after Justice Marshall denied defense attorney motions to dismiss the case in its entirety. Dillon argued about what he called a "paucity" of ballistics evidence tying Joey to the Green murder. He faulted prosecutors for failing to put Frenchy Cook on the stand. Cook had allegedly seen the face of Thomas' killer. Dillon and Mahoney reminded the judge that during a police lineup last May in which Joey was one of the subjects, Cook had erroneously picked an assistant district attorney as Thomas' killer. Attorney Michael Stebick had been put in the May 12, 1981 lineup as a decoy to test the accuracy of eyewitness claims.

That wasn't the first time Stebick was a lineup decoy and had been picked as the real killer by an eyewitness. In 1977, after a young man named Richard V. Long had been beaten to death by several later-disgraced and imprisoned off-duty Buffalo police officers, Stebick had also been erroneously picked by an eyewitness as one of Long's killers. [In 2005, Stebick was again in the public spotlight after he and his former boss, State Supreme Court Justice Ronald Tills, transported an illegal alien woman across state lines to work as a prostitute at a Kentucky convention of the Royal Order of Jesters. Stebick was placed on probation for his minor role in the sex scandal. His only criminal involvement was agreeing to use his motor home to drive the young woman to the horny jesters national convention.]

After Justice Marshall refused to dismiss the case, the defense effort began with a thud: the defense's first witness, private investigator Peter M. Vito committed a fairly serious faux pas. In an effort to rebut prosecution ballistics evidence, Vito randomly selected 18 Ruger .22 caliber rifles at the same Cheektowaga gun store where Joey's late father purchased the missing murder weapon and completed tests with them. Vito explained to the judge that he had turned over reports and photographs to Dillon and Mahoney. Rather alarmed, the attorneys told the judge they could not find Vito's reports. Judge Marshall ordered Dillon and Mahoney to bring them to court the next day. But, the next day Vito told the judge he had mistakenly testified the day before about preparing written reports on his ballistic testing.

Vito's belated mea culpa would not be the biggest drama to hit the trial on April 22, 1982. During aggressive cross examination by Prosecutor Ranni, nineteen-year-old Anthony Szymanski, a key defense witness in the Emmanuel Thomas murder, angrily stood up at the witness stand and instigated an altercation with deputies. When Szymanski, another Burgard High School dropout, took the stand, he claimed the killer had a bald spot at the back of his head and wore his balding blond hair shoulder length – in contrast to defense claims that Joey's brown hair was cut short at the time. A Buffalo car wash worker, Szymanski said he heard Thomas' friend Frenchy Cook scream out, "everybody duck!" just before the killer fired the weapon. Emmanuel didn't duck. He was shot once by the balding, blond-haired killer, Szymanski testified.

Speaking in a slow drawl, Szymanski told the judge that police maps of the murder scene that he had been shown by authorities confused him. He said when he saw Joey in a police lineup last May, he hadn't felt Joey was the killer he had observed on the street.

Ranni kept grilling the semi-literate Szymanski. As prosecutor Ranni demanded to know if he was drunk or high on illicit drugs the night of the Thomas shooting, Szymanski took offense, asserting "I don't mess around with nothing like that." As the prosecutor began to present him with a written transcript of an interview he had with police after the shootings – and which court officials were sure he was unable to read on his own – Szymanski got up from the witness stand and started to leave. When a sheriff's deputy tried to restrain him, Szymanski shoved him and barked, "Keep your hands off me!" As other deputies ran toward Szymanski, the judge ordered everyone to "keep calm." Judge Marshall called a recess in the trial after Szymanski told him, "Your honor, I don't want to answer no more questions."

After recess, Szymanski got back on the stand and said he had initially lied to police in both 1980 and 1981. He repeatedly told police that he hadn't actually witnessed the Thomas killing and had actually been in a Zenner Street home at the time. He admitted he also told police he just "forgot" many events linked to the shooting. As to the reason for his fabrications, Szymanski stated, "My mother told me to lie," and, "I didn't want to be bothered with this."

Defense arguments about the color of the killer's hair continued. Joey's maternal aunt, Mrs. Margaret Callari, gave the judge a color photograph she said she took of Joey at a family outing at a relative's Canadian home in October of 1980. In the photo, which the prosecutors tried unsuccessfully to block as evidence, Joey's short hair was dark brown. The defense stressed that in the Callari photo Joey did not resemble the widely-distributed police sketches and artist renderings of the alleged killer. Mrs. Callari told the judge that unlike the long, light brown or blond hair depicted in police sketches released to the public during the investigation, Joey had closely cropped hair for at least a year before the killings began.

U.S. Army Sergeant Paulette Ratcliff, also called to the stand that day by the defense, joined in telling the judge about Joey's hair in

September 1980. An Army recruiter assigned to Buffalo in 1980, Ratcliff told the judge the police renderings did not look like the gentleman she enlisted in the U.S. Army a few days before the first of the .22 caliber killings. Ratcliff first met Joey on September 16, 1980, six days before the first of the killings, when he walked into her office at the Federal Building on West Huron Street in downtown Buffalo. Amidst prosecution efforts to challenge her recall abilities, Ratcliff told the judge she had no trouble envisioning how Joey looked in September 1980. She spent hours with him over three or four days before he was formally enlisted.

"He had such short hair I thought he was in the military already," Ratcliff told the judge about her first meeting with Joey. Ratcliff told the judge that Joey's hair was cut in a severe crew cut style.

Joey on trial. Photo courtesy Buffalo Courier-Express Archive, E.H. Butler Library, SUNY College at Buffalo

She said she told police investigators months before the trial that the police sketches developed during the probe simply did not look like Joey. Though Joey failed a 1978 enlistment effort because he was then recovering from a hernia, Ratcliff told the judge she considered him in 1980 a "hot item" for recruitment because he had passed military aptitude tests the year before and only needed to pass a physical before she could "get him into boots." She told the judge she even drove Joey to his Weber Street home to correct his medical records after he belatedly admitted he had once experimented with marijuana.

The prosecution tried to poke holes in the defense case where it could, calling into question Ratcliff's hair-color-recall abilities. Under cross examination, Ratcliff initially told the judge that the two prosecutors she had met at the District Attorney's office for a pretrial discussion on May 6, 1982 were both brown haired. Prosecutor Stamp clarified to the judge that one of those prosecutors had black hair and the other had graying blond hair. Ratcliff salvaged things by telling the judge she had only been with the prosecutors briefly, but had spent hours with Joey.

As the second day of the defense case was proceeding on April 22, 1982, Dillon complained to the judge of state police investigators and Buffalo homicide detectives "harassing" defense witnesses waiting in the courtroom hallway. During a break in the day's testimony, Dillon went out into the hallway and was seen arguing with Buffalo Homicide Detective Melvin Lobbett about that alleged harassment. Dillon and Lobbett both refused to comment.

Back in the courtroom, Dillon and Mahoney were on the verge of resting their case without calling Joey to the stand. They told the judge they might subpoena at least two other men once regarded as suspects in the probe, hoping to extract testimony on their own racist motivations. But prosecutors won a procedural battle on that issue as the judge informed the defense attorneys that he would only consider racist statements of other suspects in the investigation if they came from the testimony of lawmen rather than from other individuals under suspicion in the case. The judge also told the defense attorneys he would not consider as evidence statements they elicited from Buffalo Police Officer Harold Frank about what he called a "racial" poem penned by another emotionally-disturbed man who was questioned shortly after the September 1980 killings.

Frank had taken the stand and testified that day as a defense witness. He told the judge one of his jobs on the murder task force had been to interview that so-called "poem suspect," a blond-haired 6-foot-tall man, with what Frank described as an "emotional problem." He told the judge that man was questioned after the task force received an anonymous tip about his poem. He said he interviewed that blond-haired man at the Erie County Community College's North Campus in Williamsville north of Buffalo. Frank also interviewed that one-time suspect's father. He did not identify either of those men during his testimony.

Though Joey's attorneys lost on their plan to get earlier suspects in the killings to testify as they ended their case, they urged the judge to "take note of" racist statements taken down by the investigators as they interviewed and then rejected earlier suspects.

The judge told both sides that day – the 10th day of actual testimony – he was not prepared to hear closing arguments until Monday at the earliest. On April 23, 1982, the defense attorneys rested their case, calling to the stand only one of the two Army psychiatrists who treated Joey at Fort Benning. Major Eleanor Smith Law – the 11th defense witness in the trial– told the judge that when she dealt with Joey the previous spring, she felt he had honestly admitted to stabbing a black recruit at that southwestern Georgia military base, but that he may have been "delusional" in claiming to be Buffalo's .22 caliber killer. Major Law characterized Joey as a "seriously disturbed young man."

Regardless of Law's beliefs about whether Joey was the .22 Caliber Killer, there was clarity around the fact that Joey had attempted a murder at the base. Fort Benning authorities had "well established" that he had stabbed Leonard Coles with a stolen mess hall knife on January 18, 1981. She told the judge, "It appeared that he had a sense of guilt about what he had done [to Coles]." Law said she felt Joey exhibited feelings indicating that, "It was a terrible thing he had done." Major Law, the chief of the psychiatric unit at the Fort Benning hospital, told the judge she had been unable to reach a diagnosis on Joey's mental state because he had been uncooperative with her when she interviewed him at the base facility. She told the judge that Dr. Matthew Levine, one of her base psychiatric colleagues, had diagnosed Joey as schizophrenic and that she could not dispute his findings. During both of Joey's hospital stays at Fort Benning staff found him to be preoccupied with religion and displaying signs of "latent and overt homosexuality." He often complained about other GIs taunting him about his manhood, Major Law testified.

Defense attorneys also raised questions about whether at least one of the victims was actually killed as a result of his involvement in the criminal underworld. To counter defense claims that at least one of the three Buffalo victims (Emmanuel Thomas) was actually the victim of a criminal underworld contract killing, the prosecutors called their 39th and last witness, the only rebuttal witness and the 50th person to testify at the trial. Victor Jackson, 20, a Zenner Street neighbor of Thomas, was called to the stand to rebut that defense attorney theory and to tell the judge that his friend Anthony Szymanski had falsely claimed they were together when Szymanski claimed he saw a balding, blond-haired man kill Thomas. Jackson said he didn't know where Szymanski was at the time of the Thomas killing. But, he assured the judge neither he nor his brothers were present and had witnessed that murder. Jackson, admitting on the stand that he had served a brief jail term for stolen auto and assault cases, told the judge he and his brother Terry were watching television in the living room of their Zenner Street home when he heard the "firecrackers" sound of a gun. Jackson denied having any information about Thomas being slain by a professional murderer.

As the case drew to a close, the judge said he would also consider lesser manslaughter charges in the triple murder case. This was a direct indication that Marshall had a clear understanding of the potential problems with the prosecution case. However, Dillon and Mahoney never called to the stand Chicago ballistics expert John Sadunas who they had retained, at taxpayer-expense, to rebut prosecution ballistic evidence linking Joey to the .22 caliber killings. Sadunas ultimately told them he could not successfully rebut the prosecution evidence.

CLOSING ARGUMENTS

In Mahoney's 75-minute closing argument on April 26th, he contended that the ballistic evidence "at best" had suggested Joey "may have had access" to the missing murder weapon, "at some remote period to time," but it failed to corroborate prosecution claims of his guilt. Mahoney attacked Robert Oddo, the only actual prosecution eyewitness to any of the three murders, as a "reward-conscious perjurer." He praised Anthony Szymanski, the only eye-witness put on the stand by the defense team after prosecutors deliberately did not call him, for having testified "reluctantly and possibly at great danger to himself."

Mahoney stressed how Oddo admitted on the stand he had lied to police right after the Dunn shooting and falsely told them he could not actually identify the killer. Mahoney also cited Oddo's claim that the killer of the youngest of the four Buffalo and Niagara Falls .22 caliber killer victims had blond-hair.

The defense attorney called Mrs. Gorney, who had said she saw Joey at the scene of the Dunn murder but did not witness the shooting, "an honestly mistaken eyewitness." Mahoney also reminded the judge that Joey's aunt, Mrs. Margaret Callari, and Army Sergeant Paulette Ratcliff both testified that Joey's hair was closely-cropped in September 1980.

Mahoney found fault with the ballistic evidence, contending that the so-called conclusive evidence proved that only five of the nine casings only indirectly compared to each other under the microscope. He also complained of what he called the well-intentioned but improper "willingness" of witnesses to conform their recollections to fit the prosecution case. Mahoney openly scoffed at what he called the "frailties" of alleged eyewitness claims in recalling in general what they claimed to have witnessed. He told the judge the case against Joey was based, "exclusively on opinion testimony and circumstantial evidence." Mahoney highlighted the opinion of Army Major Eleanor Smith Law, who said Joey's allegedly incriminating admissions might have been the result of delusional thinking.

As Ranni began his closing remarks, he immediately generated angry objections from both defense attorneys by pointing to Joey and declaring:

"There sits the killer of three Buffalo martyrs to racial injustice. Don't let him go!"

During Ranni's 83-minute closing argument he told the judge the "hundreds and hundreds" of corresponding microscopic markings found on spent bullet casings at the murder scenes and Joey's home and hunting lodge were an irrefutable bridge connecting Joey to all three killings. Ranni articulated that the same bullets Joey used to kill each of the three victims were "now being used against him," in a court of law. He highlighted the factual linkages and downplayed any of the apparent inconsistencies brought to light by witness testimony. Ranni hammered home his affirmative case based on the forensics. The ballistics link between the seven spent bullet casings recovered at all three of the murder scenes, two spent casings found at the defendant's hunting lodge, as well as a misfired .22 caliber round found in Joey's Weber Street home, constituted, according to Ranni, "the bridge of irrefutable corroboration linking him to the three crimes."

Ranni maneuvered around the apparent problems with his case. He especially downplayed the eyewitness discrepancies about the hair color of Buffalo's .22 Caliber Killer. The deft prosecutor contended that seeming discrepancies in eyewitness accounts likely came because witnesses, "may have trouble articulating, verbalizing," what it was exactly they saw. He told the judge that this was a problem common to many people. He also reminded the judge that Victor Jackson said on the stand that his friend, Anthony Szymanski, had lied in saying they were standing together during the Thomas shooting. Ranni also argued that discrepancies among eyewitnesses as to whether the killer had dark brown hair like the defendant or blond hair could not be considered meaningful because a person's hair color as it is perceived by others, was "nothing but a reflection of light," at any given moment.

After Ranni closed, Justice Marshall told both sides his impending verdict would, "be based on the facts as I understand them and the law." He would be ruling separately on Joey's fate in each of the three murders.

As the defense attorneys left court after resting their case, Dillon told The Buffalo Evening News that he was "very, very pleased with the way the trial went." He said the decision to call only 11 witnesses for three days of defense testimony was, "a judgment decision based on my assessment of what the proof has been." Dillon felt the prosecution failed to come up with sufficient credible evidence "to convict this man [Joey] of any criminal activity whatsoever."

SWIFT VERDICT

Less than 24 hours later, Justice Marshall found Joey guilty as charged on all three counts of second-degree murder. In a courtroom more-heavily guarded than usual, the judge brought both sides and Joey back into court at 11 a.m. on April 27, 1982 for the verdict. Justice Marshall instructed the parties that the decision was "based upon the believable, credible testimony and the law applicable to this criminal case." Justice Marshall held that the prosecutors had, "sustained their burden of proof and proven beyond a reasonable doubt by legally sufficient trial evidence each and every element of the offense charged and the defendant's commission thereof." Renowned throughout New York State as a meticulous trial judge, Marshall issued a three-page verdict. Sentencing was scheduled for 9:30 a.m. on May 24, 1982, for each of the murder charges.

Joey, who came to court that day dressed just as he had during 10 days of testimony, in a dark blue blazer, green Army dress pants, combat boots and metal-frame glasses, took the verdict calmly and silently. He smiled constantly during the judge's five-minute-long reading of the verdict. He was hastily led from the judge's third-floor courtroom moments later. Joey's widowed mother, Therese Christopher, tightly gripping a blessed Roman Catholic rosary in her hands, also took the guilty verdict calmly.

Within minutes of Justice Marshall's triple-murder verdict, Erie County Sheriff Kenneth J. Braun directed his jail guards, already on 24-hour assignment on Joey to prevent attacks by other inmates or a possible suicide attempt, to keep an even closer watch on the now-convicted murderer.

After Joey was taken back to the downtown jail, Deputy District Attorney Ranni said he felt emotionally relieved, but he maintained that the guilty verdict was the only one, "the judge could honestly reach." In court for the verdict, Erie County District Attorney Richard J. Arcara indicated only that he was satisfied with the result.

Dillon said he and Mahoney were obviously frustrated with the result. Dillon stressed to the media that he and his defense team co-partner, "did not feel that the proof was sufficient." Before they left court, defense attorneys Dillon and Mahoney said they would soon be discussing various legal grounds for an appeal with attorneys for the Buffalo Legal Aid Bureau, who handled indigent appeals. Former district attorney Edward C. Cosgrove calmly said hours after the April 27th verdict, "I feel relief and satisfaction now that the investigation, prosecution and public anxiety have come to an end." Cosgrove continued:

"I am gratified that now the extraordinary efforts of Captain Henry F. Williams and Chief Leo Donovan and their officers of the Major Homicide Task Force can be better appreciated. Their dedication, perseverance and industry in this particularly difficult investigation and prosecution is without equal in the annals of criminal justice in the history of Buffalo and Erie County.

"I am saddened," Cosgrove told The Buffalo Evening News, "at the grief and sorrow suffered by the victims' families and the anguish suffered by Mrs. Christopher and her family. I met and visited with her on April 22, 1981 at her home on Weber Street. She is a fine Christian person. Her family and all of the families harmed need our support and prayers." After the conviction, Buffalo Mayor James Griffin told that same publication, "It's great for the community to know that justice has been served."

Several weeks before Justice Marshall was to sentence Joey, the director of the FBI, William H. Webster, publicly lauded Edward C. Cosgrove for what for the director called Cosgrove's "exemplary" handling of the sensitive murder investigation. In a May 11, 1982 letter to Cosgrove received at his law office, Webster said he wanted "to personally thank you for the fine job you did and to pass along the appreciation of our Buffalo personnel who worked with you on this case." Webster told Cosgrove he found his "assembly and direction" of the murder task force Cosgrove formed to deal with the spree to be "exemplary and contributed significantly to Christopher's identification and arrest." Approached by the local news media when FBI sources alerted them to the Webster letter, Cosgrove, a former FBI special agent himself, told The Buffalo Evening News he was "gratified to receive such a high compliment."

On April 27, 1982, the day State Supreme Court Justice Frederick M. Marshall of Buffalo found Christopher guilty of the three Buffalo .22 caliber killings, Rev. Bennett W. Smith, one of the leaders of Buffalo's black community told The New York Times: "Joseph Christopher sentenced his own self when he chose to be heard by a judge. Had this case been heard by a jury, I'm very doubtful we would have gotten a conviction."

Months after the triple murder conviction, Williams L. Gaiter, a well-known Buffalo black activist and head of the Institute for People Enterprises, raised complaints about delayed efforts to reward the U.S. Army personnel who gave authorities the information that lead to Joey's conviction. Gaiter also admonished leaders for the lengthy delay in doling out the approximately $100,000 in reward money offered by various Buffalo area corporations, charities and governmental units. He contended that any "reneging" by any of those groups, "should be clearly and publicly labeled a copout."

"Not only that," Gaiter told The Buffalo Evening News in late November 1982, "but in 1982, this kind of action smacks of racism. Inasmuch as this type of thing can happen again, a refusal to live up to this commitment could cause citizens to be reluctant to step forward with vital information.

CHAPTER TEN

First Sentencing

B ut the first three convictions were only the beginning, when it came to seeking justice for Joey's victims. In Buffalo alone, Joey also still faced trial for the attempted murders of Albert Menefee on December 31, 1980 and Calvin Crippen on January 1, 1981. He also remained under suspicion for the mutilation murders of Buffalo cabbies Parlor Edwards and Ernest Jones and the fatal stabbing of Roger Adams on December 29, 1980. Niagara Falls, Rochester, the U.S. Army and New York City all had yet to render justice.

Joey faced a single count second-degree murder indictment in the September 24, 1980 daylight murder in Niagara Falls of Joe Louis McCoy, the last of the four so-called .22 caliber victims. But Joey's next trial seemed destined to take place in a Manhattan courtroom, and not a Niagara Falls one. In the midst of Joey's triple murder trial, Niagara County prosecutors began talks with the defense team about the possibility of letting Joey plead guilty in the fourth of the

.22 caliber killings. Both Erie County District Attorney Arcara and Niagara County District Attorney Peter L. Broderick said they would defer further proceedings in their cases against Joey until after he stood trial in Manhattan later in the year. Broderick said he also had to consider the heavy expenses his county government would experience – just as Erie County did – should Joey face trial in Lockport or Niagara Falls for the McCoy killing. The need for heavy security, transportation and living expenses for many of the same witnesses who testified at the Buffalo trial would also come into consideration, Broderick noted.

In the New York City attacks, Joey was charged with fatally stabbing nineteen-year-old Luis Rodriguez in the eye as he was walking on Madison Avenue, and shortly thereafter stabbing Ivan Frazer, 35, several times on a subway train.

Joey's case was docketed for a May 11th hearing in Manhattan with his New York City defense team, which had grown to include a class of New York University law school students who volunteered for the effort at the request of Frank A. Bress, Joey's chief Manhattan attorney and students' New York University Law School professor. However, with Joey facing a possible maximum prison term of 75 years to life from Marshall in Buffalo, no effort was made to ship Joey to Manhattan for the already-scheduled pretrial hearing downstate. The May hearing before Manhattan Justice Benjamin Altman was slated to address defense challenges to the evidence in both fatal stabbings. These attacks were among the eight knife attacks over an eight hour period that day for which Joey had long been suspected, but they were the only ones for which he was indicted due to evidence problems with the three other murders and three other slashings.

Hours after Joey's triple-murder conviction, Manhattan defense attorney Bress told the news media he did not foresee the Manhattan trial or trials taking place for a number of months due to a series of renewed pretrial motions the Joey defense team was filing there.

Spokesmen for Major General Sam Wentzel, commanding officer of Fort Benning, announced hours after the triple murder conviction that proceedings leading to Joey's dishonorable discharge from the U.S. Army would automatically be delayed by what, under New York State criminal law, was the obligatory appeal of the conviction, which could take another year or so to complete. Under Army dictates Joey had stopped drawing Army pay on May 8, 1981 when he was returned to Buffalo on the civilian murder charges. After the conviction, a U.S. Army spokesman told the news media the attempted murder charge against Joey for the January 18, 1981 attack on Coles would be dropped due to the civilian criminal cases he still faced.

While awaiting the verdict at his first trial, Joey displayed a shift in attitude that mildly shocked his jail guards. He started exercising in the Holding Center recreation room and doing pushups in his cell even while remaining under 24-hour-a-day watch. Before, Joey had routinely kept to himself, sitting hours a day in his cell with a blanket over his head. Early in April 1982, guards reported that he began to use the Nautilus machine in the recreation room to lift weights three times a week. According to Erie County Sheriff Kenneth J. Braun, the exercise represented the "totally different" man Joey had been since his return from the state psychiatric hospital for the criminally insane in late February.

Braun, noting Joey had become "more extroverted," disclosed that Joey had even started talking to other inmates and sometimes even to his guards since his return from the psychiatric facility. The sheriff characterized the change in behavior by Joey to be "a 360-degree turnabout" in his attitude.

Regardless of a change of attitude, on May 11, 1982, Justice Benjamin Altman of Manhattan ordered Joey to be tested by New York City psychiatrists to see if he was competent to stand trial for the two Manhattan crimes. Justice Altman refused a request from prosecutor James Fogel, head of the Manhattan district attorney's major offense and career criminal bureau, to rescind his own February 9, 1982 finding that Joey was not yet mentally competent for trial in Manhattan. Altman ordered more examinations despite the fact that on February 17, 1982, Joey had been declared fit for trial after two months at the state's mental hospital for the criminally insane. Altman declined public comment on his new testing order, but court officials told the news media the judge wanted to proceed cautiously with the Manhattan case and establish sufficient psychiatric evidence directly connected to that case before putting Joey on trial for those attacks. After Altman's retesting order, Frank A. Bress said he had yet to decide whether he would seek an insanity defense.

In yet the next abrupt turn in Joey's prosecution, less than 72 hours before Justice Marshall was to sentence Joey in Buffalo, his Buffalo attorneys openly claimed they feared prosecutors had covered up ballistics evidence favorable to Joey's defense in the triple murder case. In an extremely unconventional maneuver, Dillon and Mahoney asked Marshall to rule on May 24th – the scheduled sentencing date – on their bid for a court-supervised search of the voluminous prosecution files in the case.

Mahoney told the news media that he and Dillon launched the unusual pre-sentencing action because of their nagging doubts about the candor of prosecutors with regard to all the evidence compiled in the massive probe. He noted that, despite assurances months earlier in court that prosecutors had no undisclosed evidence when the trial began, prosecutors turned over ballistics evidence they had not previously disclosed to the defense team very late in the proceedings. Erie County District Attorney Richard J. Arcara said his prosecutors would respond to the last minute defense motion on the date of the sentencing.

During the sentencing hearing, the judge refused the defense attorneys' request that he appoint a referee to go through the voluminous prosecution files to see if prosecutors were still withholding evidence favorable to Joey's defense. He also denied a motion by the two defense attorneys to set aside his own verdict in the case saying he was satisfied with the extensive pretrial proceedings handled by his colleague, Justice William J. Flynn.

Vigorously objecting to and denying the defense attorneys claim that prosecutors might have deliberately withheld evidence, Ranni told the judge he considered Dillon and Mahoney to be "chronic paranoid crybabies." Ranni also told the judge he considered Joey to be a "remorseless killer." Ranni called the defense attorneys' talk of hidden evidence that could have exonerated Joey a "worthless, frivolous" defense tactic, designed merely to prolong the proceedings. Ranni told the judge prosecutors had not deliberately withheld any material evidence from the defense attorneys. He contended there was no legal precedent in law or court rulings to support the defense demand for a post-trial search of prosecution files.

Neither defense attorney responded to Ranni's personal insults to their character, but Mahoney refused to concede Joey was the killer of the three victims, telling the judge during the sentencing proceeding that there was no evidence of "premeditated or racially motivated" actions in the three separate shootings, even though prosecutors had "harped" on the so-called racial motive for the killings. Citing Joey's treatment for mental problems in the U.S. Army and his extensive pre-trial psychiatric examinations, Mahoney told the judge that if Joey were actually the killer of the three Buffalo black men his actions were, "the product of an extremely disturbed mind." When the judge asked Joey if he wanted to make a comment, Joey sat smiling and responded:

"I haven't got anything to say, your honor."

Thus, on May 24th, a more-fit and better-dressed Joey was ordered by Justice Marshall to serve a prison term of 60 years-to-life for the first three of the .22 caliber killings. Joey, smiling and wearing a three-piece gray pin-striped suit, rather than the blue blazer and jeans he routinely wore during year-long court proceedings, was ordered to serve the maximum-allowable 25 year-to-life term for the murder of Glenn Dunn, 20 years-to-life for the murder of Harold Green, and the minimum-allowable 15 years-to-life for the murder of Emmanuel Green.

Literally moments after the judge imposed that sentence, the two defense attorneys filed a formal notice to the Appellate Division of State Supreme Court, based in Rochester, for an appeal of the convictions and sentence. And within four hours of the sentencing, Joey arrived in an armed convoy to the state's Attica Correctional Facility some 50 miles or so east of Buffalo. Joey spent that afternoon in Attica's Administrative Protection Company cellblock, which already held Mark David Chapman, the self-confessed killer of rock legend John Lennon in December 1980, the same month Joey carried out the notorious "Midtown Stabber" knife attacks there. Chapman, also 26 in 1982, was only ordered to serve a 20-year-to-life term for murdering the former Beatle, but he would face repeated denials of early parole.

With Manhattan Justice Benjamin Altman already issuing orders that Joey be brought to Manhattan for further psychiatric testing and for a June 1st pre-trial proceeding, Joey was whisked to the state's Auburn Correctional Facility near Syracuse, after spending only a few hours at Attica on May 24, 1982. Joey was driven under heavy guard from the Erie County Holding Center in downtown Buffalo at about 1 p.m. on May 24, 1982, arriving at Attica at about 2:30 p.m. He was driven from there to Auburn around 6:30 p.m. Lou Ganim, a spokesman for the New York State Department of Correctional Services which operates its prison system, told The Buffalo Evening News the move of Joey wasn't based on any "incident" at Attica but solely over concerns about Joey's well-being behind bars. Ganim said that prison system officials felt, "it would be better to remove him from the immediate Erie County vicinity because he's of such notoriety there." Ganim also said the mandatory one to four weeks of prison system physical and aptitude tests used to place an inmate in the state's general prison population would, for Joey, obviously be interrupted by his trips to Altman's Manhattan courtroom. But, Ganim said he expected that Joey would be serving out his long prison term at Auburn.

Richard Fietz, Attica prison's deputy superintendent for programs, said such extra precautions involving the housing of white inmates like Joey convicted of murdering blacks was not unusual given New York State's largely-black prison population. Fietz said he expected Joey to serve out his full life term, given the unlikely chance of him every being granted a pardon by some future governor. He said Joey was kept in Attica's Administrative Protection Company where "very, very sensitive cases" like the Beatle killer were kept, because Joey "might be in danger from other inmates" just like Chapman.

"We handled him a little different than we do the average run-of-the mill inmate," Fietz said of Joey.

Erie County Under-Sheriff Thomas Higgins, a future sheriff of the county, told the news media hours after the sentencing, that his 314-day stay under 24-hour-a-day special guard at the 48-year-old 400-inmate downtown lockup had cost the county government at least $200,000 to $250,000, even with some costs still uncalculated. Higgins told The Buffalo Evening News the average inmate cost the county about $60 a day to guard and house, meaning someone kept in the downtown facility for as long as Joey had would normally cost the county government and its taxpayers about $19,000.

"He's the most expensive inmate who's ever been in this place," Higgins said of Joey, who monopolized the services of three guards in the Buffalo jail.

Separately, Erie County government officials estimated that Joey had already cost local taxpayers more than $1.5 million and counting. He still remained the prime suspect in a continuing multi-agency investigation of the October 1980 mutilation murders of Buffalo cabbies Parlor Edward and Ernest Jones and the December 1980 fatal stabbing of Roger Adams. But, Erie County District Attorney Arcara told the news media that investigators were still not discounting anyone as a possible suspect.

With Joey facing another pre-trial hearing in Manhattan on June 1st, his defense team there learned after Joey's Buffalo sentencing, that only two of the six Manhattan witnesses who had been flown to Buffalo for a May 1981 police lineup had identified Joey. That would be the reason why Joey was only charged with the killing of Luis Rodriquez and the knife attack on Ivan Frazer and not prosecuted for the six other apparently related stabbings in Manhattan that day. The Manhattan defense team also learned that prosecutors had knife evidence stemming from the court-approved searches of Joey's Buffalo home and his family's hunting lodge in the spring of 1981.

Among the many curious twists and turns in Joey's criminal saga, possibly one of the most curious was his plea to the Buffalo judge who had given him three life terms to argue his appeal for him. Facing further mental competency hearings in a Manhattan courtroom, Joey, in a 44-word, two sentence letter he hand-wrote in his cell at New York's Auburn Correctional Facility, the then-27-year-old asked Marshall to "consider representing" him on his appeal. In the undated note that Joey signed "Mr. Joseph Christopher," Joey also told Marshall he wanted to get recommitted to the state's Mid-Hudson Psychiatric Center in the Catskills for further pretrial counseling. In his brief letter to the judge, Joey said he wanted to be returned to the mental hospital because, "when I was their [sic] I was unable to explain my feelings and reasoning." His missive failed to explain why he felt he now had to disclose his innermost feelings and thoughts to state mental health experts.

When asked by the Buffalo news media, Justice Frederick M. Marshall refused to comment on the letter Joey had sent him, telling The Buffalo Evening News, "It's out of my hands in the sense that I no longer have jurisdiction."

CHAPTER ELEVEN

Is He or Isn't He?

By late November 1982, court-appointed psychiatrists from New York City's Bellevue Hospital advised Manhattan Justice Benjamin Altman that they, like the psychiatrists who dealt with Joey for two months at the state's Mid-Hudson Psychiatric Center, found him mentally fit to stand trial without further mental treatments or assessments. Altman gave Joey's Manhattan defense team until December 16, 1982 to tell him whether they wanted to contest the latest psychiatric findings or proceed to trial.

After the usual delays caused by the court docket and lawyers' caseloads, on January 28, 1983, Frank A. Bress disclosed to Justice Altman that a taxpayer-financed psychiatrist now working with Joey's defense team, Dr. John B. Train of Manhattan, had found Joey mentally unfit for trial without hospitalized mental health treatment. Joey, brought back to New York City and housed at Manhattan's Riker's Island Jail for that court session, was in Altman's courtroom, but did not object to his chief attorney's arguments. Altman scheduled a February 22, 1983 court session to address the mental competency hearing that Bress demanded.

At that February 22nd session, Bress told calendar review Justice Stanley Sklar that Joey now needed to be treated for what he called a "thought disorder" that was preventing him from having meaningful discussions with his defense team. Insisting that no trial could be scheduled until Joey received treatment for the new mental problem, Bress insisted Joey could not knowingly aid in his own defense until he received needed treatment. He also challenged the mental fitness determination of court-appointed psychiatrists at Bellevue Hospital four months earlier. Bress informed the judge he was awaiting receipt of a written report from psychiatrist Train, who disputed the prosecution's psychiatric findings.

At the defense attorney's request, Justice Sklar put off further proceedings on the mental competency dispute for several weeks. As frequently happened with Joey's court proceedings, the scheduling of a mental competency court hearing in the case was put off, after Bress and prosecutors argued at a March 4th hearing over whose psychiatrists would take the stand first.

Back in Buffalo in April 1983, Dillon and Mahoney, Joey's Buffalo defense team, billed Erie County taxpayers $24,600 for their court-approved services and $4,000 for out-of-pocket expenses they accrued in defending Joey. Those fees were in addition to the approximately $10,000 his widowed mother had paid for his defense following his arrest in early 1981. Their bill was to the Erie County Bar Association's Aid to Indigent Prisoners program, which funded court-appointed defense counsel in the county and routinely paid such attorneys $750 a case. William J. Diggins, administrator of that legal aid program, said that, as opposed to the standard one-page invoice, Joey's team filed a voucher of more than 50 pages. Diggins

quipped to The Buffalo News, "was like a Court of Appeals brief."
He added, "I've never seen a voucher documented in such detail. It
read like 'The Anatomy of a Murder.'"

Late in April 1983, Bress succeeded in getting a mental competency hearing scheduled for Joey on May 9th. But again, because of
court caseload problems, that New York City court session was put
off until at least August 18, 1983.

By late that summer, Buffalo prosecutors and Joey's lawyers were
fighting over procedural matters in the delayed appeal of his triple
murder conviction of April one year earlier. In the first week of
August 1983, Joseph B. Mistrett, chief of the criminal services division of the Buffalo Legal Aid Bureau, which handled the appeals of
all indigent prisoners in Erie County, complained to officials of the
Appellate Division about a motion District Attorney Richard J.
Arcara had recently filed seeking a dismissal of the appeal effort.
Arcara told the news media he filed that unusual motion to force the
state court system to resolve the case "as quickly as possible."

John J. DeFranks, chief of Arcara's appeals bureau, complained
that Mistrett's team had yet to file any appellate briefs or even contact prosecutors about Joey's case in more than a year. DeFranks
told The Buffalo News that the tardy appeal effort improperly put
prosecutors "in a potentially adverse position" should that state's
higher courts order a retrial of the triple-murder case. The delay
was also unfairly affecting the credibility of witnesses in the case,
"whose memories, dulled by the passage of time, might produce in-
accuracies and unreliable testimony," DeFranks said.

Mistrett publicly rebuked Arcara and DeFranks for what he
called an unprecedented and unfair prosecution motion. He said he
couldn't understand why prosecutors had "singled out" Joey's case for
complaint, knowing full well his understaffed team of four full-time

lawyers and one part-time lawyer legally obligated to handle all area appeals for indigent prisoners had "about 200" other pending appeals, many older than Joey's case.

Despite Mistrett's arguments, on August 10, 1983 the five-judge appellate court set an October 7th filing deadline, so they could then schedule a hearing in their Rochester courtroom. Mistrett, noting his staff was only then about to receive the 5,000-page transcript of Joey's two-week April 1982 trial, said he would undoubtedly "comply with the court's order." But in early September, Mistrett petitioned the appellate court for an extension until early December, given that he and his staff still had a lot of work to do, in assessing the 5,000-page trial transcript and some 250 court exhibits that had to be scrutinized in order to adequately prepare their appeal papers.

"Our problem is that we don't have first-hand knowledge of what goes on at the trial, being assigned in an appellate capacity," Mistrett told The Buffalo News in September 1983. "We have to totally familiarize ourselves with the complete case. I'm looking for the extra time just so we can do the job that should be done in this case," he added. Mistrett said that Dillon and Mahoney, Joey's trial attorneys, had been cooperating with his staff on the appeal effort.

On September 16, 1983, the Rochester appellate court, without comment, extended the time Joey's lawyers had to file their briefs to November 18th and ordered prosecutors, who had sought seven weeks to respond, to respond in four weeks of the defense filing. The court stopped short of setting a date for when it would actually hear Joey's appeal. As the court was granting Joey's appellate team more time to file their appeal, Joseph J. DeFranks, the DA's top appellate prosecutor, predicted the court-approved delay that would put off the actual appellate hearing to January 1984 or February 1984.

September 16, 1983 was also the day The Buffalo News adver-
tised Gene Warner's story on the jailhouse interview he had with
Joey at the Riker's Island facility several weeks earlier.

CHAPTER TWELVE

Voices

J oey did not seriously claim that voices ordered him to attack his victims until a Buffalo, New York judge rejected the insanity claims brought by his attorneys. While hospitalized at Fort Benning, Joey briefly mentioned being ordered to kill, but never displayed any of the unusual behavior that normally accompanies such schizophrenic thoughts. Indeed Joey did not earnestly warm up to defense attorneys' claims about his alleged insanity until well after Justice Frederick M. Marshall imposed a 60 year-to-life term for three of the four.22 caliber killings.

Already serving a life term and feeling, perhaps, as two astute psychiatric specialists later noted, a desire to spend his years in the more therapeutic atmosphere of a psychiatric facility, rather than the harsh conditions of life in a New York State prison, Christopher began pressing his claim that he had been ordered to kill as part of a mysterious, "conspiracy" as he sat in the visiting room of the Rikers Island Jail Hospital on September 12, 1983. Joey explained to Buffalo

News reporter Gene Warner that he killed 13 and attacked 17 men because he was ordered to do so.

In what Warner described as Joey's "bizarre" claims during that 3-hour interview, Joey spoke of a conspiracy involving two groups of an unspecified "they," who he claimed had ordered the attacks as a test of his survival "strength." He called his three-city civilian knife attacks, a form of "guerrilla warfare."

"I was ordered to kill," Joey said in a low-voice. He displayed what Warner called a seemingly "rational manner."

"Who ordered me to kill? Who set up the conspiracy? I don't know," said Joey, who insisted on being called Joseph during the interview. He told the prize-winning journalist that, as a result of his three-state, five-month series of attacks, he had demonstrated that he was strong enough to pass "their" test and was tough enough to survive. The high school dropout, whose peculiar gait likely prompted the first of the taunts that led to his crimes, told Warner:

"I wasn't supposed to be able to cope with having to kill someone after I had been [degraded] for such a long period of time. After I had been able to do what they said I couldn't do, they put me in a system [his reference to state prison] and tried to grind me down, but I just got stronger."

Pressed by Warner in the jail house visiting room, Joey refused to discuss the specifics of any of his crimes, saying, "The reason they kept saying 'more, more, more' was to put more pressure on me, to break me down." Questioned by Warner about the murders, Joey would only repeat, "I was ordered to kill. Again, I was ordered to kill. That's all I'm going to say."

During the Warner interview, which came after months of correspondence between the veteran journalist and the prisoner, Joey spoke of attacking a black man days before killing the 14-year-old

Glenn Dunn on September 22, 1980. Joey told Warner that a day or two before the Dunn homicide – he couldn't recall the specific date – he stabbed another Buffalo black man in the throat.

"The first attack was not Glenn Dunn, but I don't know how badly the [first] person was hurt, because there was never anything in the news about it," Joey told Warner.

"It was downtown and I put a knife in somebody's throat. I don't believe he was hurt badly," Joey added. Joey also claimed responsibility for the gruesome October 1980 murders of Parlor Edwards and Ernest "Shorty" Green. He admitted to cutting out both of their hearts.

But, Joey heatedly denied to Warner that he had tried to kill Calvin Crippen in a Buffalo street incident on January 1, 1981. He had been charged with that crime though never prosecuted for it.

"I was never nowhere near Niagara and Hertel" where Crippen fought off a knife attack.

"That's a degradation against Calvin Crippen," Joey peculiarly told Warner of the claim. Joey pleaded with Warner not to make any mention in the articles he was planning about Crippen, saying curiously, "I don't want to degradate [sic] him. I ask you not to put that in."

Joey told Warner the mysterious "they" had ordered him to kill in New York City in late December 1980 and during basic training at Fort Benning. He curiously referred to his December 31, 1980 near fatal stabbing of Albert Menefee at Main and East Utica streets in Buffalo, but told Warner he didn't want to go into the specifics of any of his other attacks.

"I don't believe that discussing each individual incident would serve any purpose," Joey told Warner.

While refusing to detail each of his other crimes, Joey spoke of being "encouraged" to join the U.S. Army and then being "ordered" to begin attacking dark-skinned men in September 1980 after learning he would not have to report for service for several months.

During the Rikers Island interview, the second of Christopher's meetings with Buffalo journalists, but the only one in which he openly discussed his crimes, Joey took issue with press reports that he became a suspect in the northern state murders as a result of "bragging" to Fort Benning psychiatric nurses. Warner said in his reports on the jailhouse interview that Christopher had a problem with the use of the word "bragging" to describe what led to his eventual arrest. Joey claimed to Warner "I was drugged. All I was doing was talking. I was telling the truth. When I was saying those things [about killing black men up north], I had a conscious thought of trying to stop myself from saying them. They said I was bragging. I wasn't bragging. I don't need people to make myself feel good."

Joey also denied attempting to commit suicide at Fort Benning after his arrest there. He told Warner his slashing of himself in the groin with a razor blade was, "a ploy of getting from one place to another," at Fort Benning.

"I didn't seriously hurt myself," he told Warner. "I was being drugged," he repeated again.

In a letter Joey wrote to Warner shortly after their jailhouse session, he said, "When I went down south [for basic training at Fort Benning] the people said I had to do four more and sent me to New York. Then I went to Buffalo, the people said I had to do more. Then down south again, they said I had to do more and I did."

LOSING HIS PISTOL PERMIT

Days after the jailhouse interview ran, Chief Leo J. Donovan, the renowned head of the Buffalo Police Homicide Bureau, told Gene Warner he had always been convinced Joey's killing rampage was linked to his agony over losing his late father's gun collection. Of course, this loss was a direct result of being stripped of his pistol permit due to his own incompetence. While employed at the college as a maintenance man, Joey began carrying a handgun in his belt and using the school's firing range until a black co-worker turned him into the authorities. But, Joey was forced to turn in his Erie County pistol permit not as a result of this act. Instead, it was his obligation report upon misplacing one of the weapons that resulted in the loss of the collection.

Surrendering his permit meant that Joey had to sell off his beloved gun collection, because it was unlawful to own without a permit, Donovan noted. When Nicholas Christopher, a hunter and gun fancier, died in 1976, his family had been ordered to turn over his gun collection to someone with a permit. At that time, Joey became friendly with a woman who had a pistol permit and officially kept the guns with her until his got his own permit, the chief said.

After Joey was forced to surrender his permit, "the guns that he had a passion for because he had such a passion for his father were lost to him forever," Donovan told Warner.

"I believe that he brooded over this until such time that his mind turned him on to what he became or what he believes his mind told him to do," he added.

Donovan said that he found "no foundation" to support lingering theories that Joey killed blacks to avenge a sex attack on a member of his family, as some had speculated. The veteran homicide detective also told Warner he was certain Joey did not try to kill the black man who reported his workplace pistol-packing because, "[H]e didn't pick on anyone that was close enough to him that the investigation could be directed in his direction."

Mid-spree, Joey switched murder weapons because he knew what he was doing and consciously sought to avoid capture, Donovan speculated. Joey used a sawed off .22 caliber rifle, "until he became aware that we were looking for an individual with a gun. It was printed in the media that I knew it was a sawed-off rifle that was used to kill Glenn Dunn. On the fourth killing, he shot from a paper bag because he knew the casings would be evidence against him," Donovan said. In a statement that underscored Donovan's skill as a homicide investigator, he then told Warner, "I firmly believe he disposed of the gun."

Though Joey refused to tell Gene Warner what he had done with the sawed-off .22 caliber rifle, he later revealed to a court psychiatrist that he had melted down the gun with a blow torch after public reports began surfacing shortly after the four September 1980 shootings in Buffalo and Niagara Falls.

Joey would never be prosecuted for the fatal stabbings of Roger Adams and Windell Barnes in Buffalo and Rochester on December 29 and 30, 1980. But Donovan told Warner those attacks bore similarities to the non-fatal knife attacks on Albert Menefee and Calvin Crippen on December 31, 1980 and January 1, 1981. Donovan said the problem in the Adams and Barnes murders was that possible witnesses could not positively identify Joey in police lineups. When Warner contacted Lt. William D. Mayer, commander of the Physical

Crimes Section of the Rochester Police Department, for his September 20, 1983 post-jailhouse story, he found that veteran lawman agreeing with Donovan about the Barnes murder.

"We have an unsolved crime, although we're pretty well convinced Joey did it," Mayer told Warner.

Warner, for that story, also contacted Erie County District Attorney Arcara, who vigorously disputed Joey's jailhouse claim that he had nothing to do with the attack on Calvin Crippen. "We had enough evidence for an indictment and we believed we have enough for a conviction" in the Crippen attack, Arcara said. Law enforcement sources told Warner that there were witnesses who picked out Joey as the attacker at several police lineups. Chief Donovan told Warner he was sure "[T]he only reason he may have denied Crippen is that he failed to inflict damage on him. In his eyes, he may not want to admit failure."

CHAPTER THIRTEEN

Appellate Fight

As District Attorney Arcara's crack appeals bureau chief John J. DeFranks probably assumed would happen, the Buffalo Legal Aid Bureau sought a third delay in the filing of its appeals brief for Joey's case. The appellate court had given Mistrett until December 10, 1983 to file the appeal briefs. As the date approached, the gifted but overworked appeals lawyer said court officials had not told him and his staff until recently that another 200 pages of court testimony remained to be transcribed and made available for his review. The Rochester tribunal gave the Legal Aid team until December 16, 1983 to file its brief and, as a sort of legal Christmas present, also ruled that DeFranks and his prosecution team would have up to 40 days, rather than the standard 30 days, to file responding briefs.

Lawyers and the press would again squabble – this time in a Manhattan forum. In early November 1983, Joey's Manhattan legal team made a pitch for a court order which would force reporter Gene Warner to testify about his recent jailhouse interview with

Joey and surrender all his notes on that visit to Joey's defense team. Justice George B. Smith quashed the defense team's subpoena based on arguments by Buffalo News attorney John H. Stenger. A highly-respected Buffalo private attorney, Stenger cited New York State's Shield Law which protected journalists and upheld the constitutional rights of a free-press. The Manhattan judge, on November 2, 1983, held that the jailhouse interview wasn't legally relevant to the impending mental competency hearing. Smith ruled, "There is no showing that, at the present time, the reporter Warner, who is not a psychiatrist, can offer testimony that is relevant on the issue of the defendant's competence to stand trial."

Frank Bress, Joey's chief Manhattan attorney, said he hoped the state's higher courts would agree with him that the Warner jailhouse interview and his testimony in court was likely to be the most accurate evidence of the accused's mental state. But, in the end, Warner did not have to turn over his jailhouse notes or testify in Manhattan.

Again in the holiday spirit, the Appellate Division of State Supreme Court on December 26, 1983 granted the Buffalo Legal Aid Bureau's appeals unit a fourth delay in the filing of its appeal brief, this time to January 6, 1984. The appellate tribunal also gave prosecutors until March 6, 1984 to file opposing briefs. John J. DeFranks, Arcara's Appeal Bureau chief, said he didn't oppose the latest defense delays because he had been informed that they would only have been able to file a "skeletal" brief before Christmas Day. Since a "skeletal" brief would have meant that appeal lawyers would have had to file supplemental briefs to expound on their theories anyway, DeFranks told the news media he didn't object to the latest delay: "We thought it would be better for all parties involved that we received their arguments in toto."

In the 129-page brief Buffalo Legal Aid attorneys Joseph B. Mistrett and John A. Ziegler finally filed on January 9, 1984, they argued the Green and Thomas convictions were improper and Joey deserved a new trial solely for the Dunn killing. They also faulted the pre-trial and trial handling of the case by three Buffalo judges for what they called inconclusive and merely "inferential" ballistics work. Mistrett and Ziegler contended Joey should have been accorded three separate trials for the first three .22 caliber killings. They also argued that Buffalo judges should have paid closer attention to his trial attorneys' contentions that he was too mentally ill to make an intellectually appropriate demand for a non-jury trial.

The two appellate attorneys also accused the commander of the Fort Benning stockade of improperly using sexual come-ons to get Joey to falsely make incriminating admissions. They accused Army Capt. Aldrich Johnson, commander of the Fort Benning stockade, of "outrageous" misconduct for admitting under oath that he had offered the jailed Joey the "possibility of having sexual relations" with a female friend of his. They contended that Johnson improperly allowed this friend to talk to Joey after he was thrown in the base stockade for stabbing Coles. Johnson, they stressed, admitted under oath in the Buffalo court to "encouraging" the jailed Joey to ask a female friend, then visiting the officer in his stockade office in January 1981, for sexual favors. The attorneys cited Johnson's testimony about how the officer's female friend declined Joey's specific request to her for sex. They also faulted the stockade commander for admitting he had allowed his female friend to question Joey in his stockade office about the Buffalo killings. Two days later, as he was still sexually enticed by that woman, Joey told her that he was responsible for the Buffalo killings.

Confidentiality violation concerns were also raised by the appellate defense team. They argued that Father Michael Freeman, the
Army chaplain who met with Joey in the Fort Benning stockade,
should not have been allowed to violate his priestly mandate of confessional secrecy and disclose in court that Joey allegedly told him of
having long suffered, "feelings of persecution by blacks." Additionally, statements Joey allegedly made to Army psychiatric nurses at the
Fort Benning hospital after he went on a hunger strike and then
tried to cut off his penis, should not have been allowed in court, having come from an allegedly disturbed patient in a normally confiden-
tial medical setting, they argued.

Joey's convictions for the Harold Green and Emmanuel Thomas
killings should be dismissed, according to the appellate brief, due to
the lack of eyewitness evidence in the engineer's murder and the
allegedly conflicting eyewitness accounts of Thomas' killing. They
contended the evidence problems in the Green and Thomas cases
"created a strong possibility that the convictions were based on a
cumulative evaluation of the evidence rather than upon a careful and
detached consideration of the proof relating to each homicide."

Numerous arguments continued to flow throughout the lengthy
brief. The defense team contended that the seizure of items from
Joey's home and his family's hunting camp went beyond the scope of
the search warrant signed by Justice Kasler. That evidence hunt
resulted in legally inadmissible "inferential" ballistics findings, they
said.

They also faulted Justice Flynn for allowing the allegedly mental-
ly-ill high school dropout to get a single non-jury trial for the three
Buffalo area killings, against his attorneys' advice and demand. They
argued that Flynn erred in refusing to accept offers from Joey's trial
lawyers to allow them to pay out of their own pockets for psychiatric

examinations defense attorneys contended would show Joey was mentally incapable of aiding in his own defense. They also argued that Flynn should never have declared Joey mentally fit for trial with Joey's "outright refusal to even explore" his trial attorneys' suggestions for an insanity-based defense.

They took issue with Justice Marshall's refusal to either declare a mistrial or allow Joey's trial attorneys a brief mid-trial recess so they could hire ballistics experts to challenge allegedly inconclusive prosecution ballistics evidence. The trial team had not been allowed to examine this evidence until the trial got underway. Mistrett and Ziegler asked the Rochester appellate tribunal to both outright dismiss the Green and Thomas murder cases and let Joey stand trial again solely for Dunn's murder.

While appellate prosecutors were in the process of preparing their response, a New York City judge ruled Joey mentally competent to stand trial there for two December 1980 knife attacks. On January 24, 1984, Manhattan State Supreme Court Justice George B. Smith held that Joey "does understand and knows what is going on in the court." Smith concluded from evidence that Joey's "failure to cooperate" with his attorneys' proposed tactics was, "not the result of a mental defect, but is the result of defendant's choice." The judge also noted that, "during the many appearances of the defendant in court, no bizarre or irrational behavior was ever exhibited."

Back in Rochester, Erie County prosecutors filed a 73-page response brief on March 6, 1984 in the appellate case. They complained of what they derided as the "cavalier misrepresentation" of many facts of the case in the Buffalo Legal Aid Bureau's appeal papers. Setting the stage for an April 3, 1984 appellate hearing, the prosecution response brief contended Joey's guilt in the first three of the four .22 caliber killings had been proven "beyond all doubts" by scientifically-sound ballistics evidence. They forcefully asserted that the ballistics evidence was legally and properly buttressed by statements Joey made at Fort Benning to Army psychiatric nurses, the Catholic chaplain and stockade guards.

During an unusually lengthy hour-long appellate hearing on April 3, 1984, Prosecutor DeFranks argued that Justice Flynn had gone to "almost nauseating" lengths in assuring a fair trial. He had made a painstaking inquiry of Joey to ensure that he knew what he was doing in court. DeFranks told the Rochester court that on March 23, 1982, a day before Flynn accepted Joey's waiver of a jury trial, Joey pointedly declared, "I've made my decision!"

Ziegler argued that Flynn lacked any proof Joey was capable of knowingly making such a profound legal decision about his own fate. The pre-trial judge failed to substantiate Joey's "subjective understanding" of what it meant to give up his right to a jury trial. Ziegler argued. He also contended that Justice Flynn committed a "fundamental" legal error during the second of Joey's pretrial mental competency hearings by not allowing trial attorneys Dillon and Mahoney to hire more psychiatrists to test Joey.

Prosecutor DeFranks stressed to the Appellate Justices (Stewart F. Hancock Jr. of Syracuse, James O'Donnell of Herkimer and Reid S. Moule, John J. Callahan and John H. Doerr, all of Buffalo) that Joey was examined by seven psychiatrists and spent two months in a state mental facility for observation before being declared mentally competent to decide himself how he wanted to be tried.

DeFranks argued that the two trial attorneys had no right under state law to make their "illusory" demands for more psychiatric testing. DeFranks told the judges that Dillon and Mahoney had offered to withdraw their mental incompetency claims if Justice Flynn would be willing to turn down Joey's demand for a non-jury trial.

On the ballistics evidence, Ziegler argued that Buffalo firearms experts Michael Dujanovich and Robert Perrigo of the Erie County Central Police Services lab had used an "idiosyncratic method" to match seven bullet casings found at the three murders scenes with a single murder weapon. Ziegler insisted the prosecution ballistics experts had used an unorthodox method of comparing the various bullet casings, failed to take written notes of their efforts, and made unsubstantiated "points of comparison" to link all the casings to a single murder weapon that was never recovered. He also chided prosecutors for failing to alert Joey's trial counsel, prior to the trial, of the nature of the firearms analysis used by the prosecution witnesses so they could have hired experts to challenge that work.

In response, Prosecutor DeFranks argued that Dujanovich and Perrigo's analysis involved, "nothing more than simple logic" to confirm the casings matched, indicating they were fired from the same weapon. While Ziegler argued to the appellate tribunal that only one of two casings found at the hunting lodge had been matched by the prosecution firearms experts to the missing murder weapon and casings found at Joey's home, DeFranks insisted the unlinked hunting lodge casing was "damaged" and because of that was unmatchable with any other evidence.

But in a unanimous ruling on May 25, 1984, the five-judge appellate court upheld Joey's triple-murder conviction and 60 year-to-life prison term.

In a 35-page ruling, Justice Reid S. Moule noted Dr. Wadsworth, after his second court-ordered examination, "altered his previous opinion" and belatedly found Joey unable to assist in his own defense. Dr. Wadsworth was joined in that view by Drs. Joseph and Park. However, Moule noted that prosecutors overheard Joey speaking with his lawyers and demonstrating his ability to assist in his own defense." Drs. Molnar and Rubenstein also found him mentally competent.

Moule called Michael Dujanovich's testimony about the ballistics testing in the case "a critical part" of the prosecution case. He noted the five Army witnesses who testified all said Joey "admitted to them, during various conversations, that he was responsible for killing numerous black men in Buffalo and New York City." The appellate judge rejected the contention that Dillon and Mahoney should have been allowed to hire other psychiatrists to challenge Joey's mental fitness, noting that Joey, "steadfastly maintained that he was competent to stand trial."

Moule cited the prosecution testimony as especially compelling. Joey "was emotionally attached to numerous weapons inherited from his father, including a .22 caliber Ruger 10-22 rifle and assorted hunting knives." He was in Buffalo and New York City on Christmas leave from the Army during the stabbings of men in both cities "by an assailant matching defendant's general description." Also, the "unprovoked attack against a black soldier" at Fort Benning "was similar in nature to the unprovoked attacks against black males in the Buffalo area."

Moule rejected the attack on the search warrant that lead to the crucial bullet casing recoveries. He noted Flynn found that the evidence seized through the Kasler search warrant was "within the scope and obvious intent" of the court warrant. The appellate judge also noted that, contrary to the Legal Aid attorneys' complaint about the search warrant process, "an applicant for a search warrant is not required to provide the magistrate with all the information in his possession."

Moule upheld the single trial for the three murders, noting higher court precedent allowing such joint trials when evidence of one crime is "material and admissible as evidence in chief" in the other crimes. In the appellate decision, adopted by all of his judicial colleagues, Moule ruled that, "while the evidence presented is circumstantial in nature, when considered in its entirety, it is sufficient to exclude to a moral certainty every hypothesis of innocence."

After the appellate ruling came out, both Erie County District Attorney Arcara and DeFranks said they would oppose any further appeal efforts because of the unanimous Rochester court ruling.

"The crimes for which Mr. Christopher stands convicted are of a most heinous nature and worked to upset this community in dramatic proportion when they occurred," Arcara told The Buffalo News, adding "I feel relief for the citizens of Erie County."

Despite the decision of the intermediate-level appellate court, the Buffalo Legal Aid Bureau pressed onward for a final ruling by the state's highest court. On June 28, 1984, John A. Ziegler said he had asked the state's highest court, known in New York State as the Court of Appeals, to review their contention that prosecutors and trial-level judges mishandled the case Prosecutor DeFranks immediately told the Buffalo news media he would argue to the high court that the last-ditch appeal request should be denied because all the issues raised by defense attorneys had already been dealt with at both the trial and intermediate appeal levels of the judicial system.

In a brief sent to Court of Appeals Judge Bernard S. Meyer's New York City office on August 7, 1984, Ziegler attacked the legal adequacy of the judicial findings and asked the high court to review the case.

One of the defense arguments presented in the brief to the highest court had been denounced by the Erie County District Attorney's office as a "stratagem" three years earlier in the case: Ziegler challenged Justice Flynn's refusal to consider Joey's trial attorneys bid for more psychiatric competency examinations because Joey had only spent two months on a state psychiatric hospital for "observation," not formal treatment. He also challenged the adequacy of Flynn's in-court questioning of Joey on the jury-waiver issue. He contended the lack of a clear-cut psychiatric finding on Joey's mental conduct called into question the appropriateness of Judges Flynn and Marshall approving the non-jury trial.

In a responding brief, Prosecutor DeFranks argued that Joey's trial attorneys made a concession in the fall of 1981 that Joey was then mentally competent to face a jury. That act, he argued, "serves to underscore the illegitimacy," of the continuing defense claim that Joey was not mentally competent to give up his right to a jury trial. DeFranks also contended the call for more psychiatric tests by Joey's trial attorneys after two complete court-ordered rounds of such testing could "only be viewed as a stratagem to avoid a non-jury trial." The prosecutor argued in the brief that "the final decision" on jury or non-jury trial "belongs to the defendant" and not his attorneys, because Joey had been declared mentally competent.

The briefs were mailed to Judge Meyer because, under the policy of New York's highest court, a single judge reviewed requests for a further review of a case following a unanimous intermediate-level appellate decision. Because of the mental competency issues clouding the case, Meyer quickly granted the defense leave to appeal.

In late January 1985, the Erie County District Attorney's Office pressed the state's high court to reject the plea to grant Joey a retrial. In a 90-page brief filed with the Albany high court on January 24, 1985, the Buffalo prosecutors insisted court records proved that "a more than adequate defense fund was amassed to ensure that the defendant was adequately represented." Citing sworn affidavits turned over to court officials, prosecutors noted Mark J. Mahoney and Kevin M. Dillon shared $23,897 in taxpayer funds, paid to them through the Erie County Bar Association's Aid to Indigent Prisoners Society, which was funded through a grant of taxpayer funds from the Erie County, New York, government. Another $17,289 was paid to them by Joey's relatives, including over $10,000 his widowed mother provided following his 1981 indictment.

The Buffalo Legal Aid Bureau's claim to the high court that Joey's trial lawyers were improperly denied a third pre-trial hearing on mental competency issues was denounced in the prosecution's high court brief prepared by DeFranks, Jo W. Faber and Rosemarie A. Wyman. They called it a "contrived" and unsupportable defense ploy. From the prosecution's perspective, it did not appear that there was any credible threat to the verdict.

But, following a springtime hearing, a divided high court on July 5, 1985 gave Justice Marshall one of the few setbacks of his judicial career, overturning the three-murder conviction and granting Joey a second trial for those offenses.

Writing for the majority, Judge Meyer held that while a criminal defendant has the ultimate right to decide trial strategy, "it does not include the right to waive a hearing concerning capacity." Meyer said it would be, "a self-contradiction to allow a defendant whose mental capacity is at issue to block such a hearing."

In a vigorous dissent, Judge Richard Simons noted that after two mental competency hearings before the 1982 trial, eleven psychiatrists had examined Joey and at least agreed he was able to understand court proceedings. Simmons insisted that the issue of allowing a 12th psychiatric expert, who Joey's trial attorneys offered to personally compensate, was best left to a trial judge to decide.

In supporting the second trial order and ordering further psychiatric testing, Meyer stressed that New York State law did not permit trial judges such unfettered discretion on competency issues. Further testing of Joey's mental state would be conducted. When the high court ruling came out, Erie County District Attorney Richard J. Arcara was not immediately available for the news media. Speaking for the Legal Aid Bureau of Buffalo, Ziegler told the Associated Press, "We hoped the court would see our way."

Pre-trial proceedings delayed Joey's retrial in Buffalo for almost a year and a half, but in October 1985, a Manhattan jury – the first actual jury to examine the psychiatric issues his attorneys kept raising over his objection – rejected an insanity defense. Following a week-long trial, the Manhattan jury on October 23, 1985 found Joey guilty of second-degree murder for fatally stabbing Bronx messenger Luis Rodriguez on December 22, 1980. That jury of seven women and five men also found Joey guilty of second-degree attempted murder for slashing Ivan Frazer, a 32- year-old Bronx cook, on the west E subway train at 53rd Street and Third Avenue about 1:25 p.m. that same day. Frazer suffered a permanent injury to his left hand.

Manhattan Prosecutor James Fogel told the jury that while Joey was hospitalized at Fort Benning, he had boasted to nurses about killing black men in Buffalo and New York City. Richard Siracusa, one of Joey's attorneys, argued unsuccessfully for an acquittal, telling the jurors Joey was, "not a well person, his vision of reality has nothing to do with ours."

On November 15, 1985, Manhattan State Supreme Court Justice John A.K. Bradley ordered Joey to serve a combined 33 and 1/3rd years-to-life term for those two 1980 attacks. As Bradley imposed the maximum-allowable prison term on Joey, he said, "There is no doubt that the defendant is mentally ill." But, reading a report that accused Joey of stabbing at least six men throughout the day on December 22, 1980, Bradley added, "But it is obvious he is a tremendous menace to society, and it is my job to see that he doesn't menace society again."

CHAPTER FOURTEEN

The Forgotten Victim

J oey boasted of having killed 13 to 17 black men, but there is evidence that he may have been responsible for the death of one more. He would go down in history as a racist serial killer, who used a sawed-off .22 caliber Ruger, knives, a hatchet and a hammer to kill or maim his black victims. However, he was at least indirectly responsible for the death of one white man in his home town of Buffalo, New York – Terence Lee Mills.

By all accounts, Mills was a likable 37-year-old urban planner with a law school degree that he never put to use, except for a short stint as an attorney for the Buffalo Legal Aid Bureau. His real passion was found in his effort to improve the lot of Buffalo's impoverished inner city residents. Mills' efforts to help the less fortunate residents of the city he loved came to a screeching halt about 6:30 p.m. on October 14, 1980, days after Joey murdered his sixth black victim and tried to kill his seventh in the detox ward of a Buffalo hospital.

Mills had finished work for that day at the Central City Restoration Corp., an urban planning group in downtown Buffalo's Genesee Building. He walked to his car parked on Pearl Street near Chippewa Street, briefcase in hand, when two black men confronted him in the dusky light. The one holding a knife demanded to know where Mills' "money was at," the dying victim told police that night. Mills quickly gave the men his wallet containing only $24. Before he died, he told police he had raised his hands and told the bandits, "That's all I have." The man with the knife took the wallet and immediately rammed his knife into Mills' chest, puncturing a lung and his pulmonary artery. Mills was pronounced dead at Buffalo's Sheehan Emergency Hospital about a half hour after the night's events.

People who witnessed the incident from a distance later told police they saw the man with the knife run to the nearby Niagara Square and hop into a cab. Street informants told police the black man with the knife had bragged to buddies hours after the killing that he was going to "celebrate" the murder of Mills with a bottle of booze and a pizza. He was later identified by authorities after his capture in San Jose, California 13 months later by the FBI, as Larry "Too Tall" Barnes, a 20- year-old former resident of Buffalo's Northland Avenue

Informants told police that the 6 foot 4 inch Barnes said that, as he had been cleaning the bloody knife in an East Side pizza shop hours after the killing, he had boasted of having "yoked" the white dude wearing a sport coat.

"And I'll yoke another one if I have to," informants claimed Barnes said, as he was being congratulated by friends for having done the right thing. Their feelings seemed justified by what the then-still-unidentified killer was doing to black men around the city.

Instead of simply robbery, Barnes' motivation appeared to be retribution for the continuing, unprovoked attacks on black men.

An intense police search of the crime scene led to the recovery in Main Street sewers of Mills' driver's license, his credit cards and the knife – the alleged murder weapon – which bore the inscription "007." Barnes was indicted in absentia, but Buffalo Police Homicide Bureau Chief Leo J. Donovan, already deeply connected to the search for Joey, had indictment warrants for Barnes sent to Los Angeles after he and FBI agents developed leads that indicated Barnes had fled to Southern California.

Months after Mills was murdered, veteran Buffalo Homicide Detective Edwin A. Gorski, one of Donovan's top men, told Buffalo News reporter Dan Herbeck that the real tragedy in the death of the warm and personable Mills was that he had been dedicated to rebuilding the inner city, only to end up a backlash victim to the racial violence the still-unidentified murderer was continuing to provoke until his arrest. Gorski called Mills, "the forgotten victim of the .22 caliber killer."

Mills' grieving mother, Amy Averill, of the Buffalo suburb of Tonawanda, told Herbeck in the summer of 1981 that the irony of her son's death was that he had been an honors law student at George Washington University, but passed up a lucrative legal career to work for considerably less money trying to rebuild Buffalo. Ms. Averill told the reporter that months before her son was murdered, she had asked him if he ever regretted not going into the law. He said he never gave it a second thought.

"He was a brilliant man who could have made lots of money," she told Herbeck.

"His great love was people. Money never impressed him," she said of her late son. At the time of his murder, Mills was involved in an ultimately successful reconstruction of the Willert Park area, one of the more depressed areas on Buffalo's East Side. Mrs. Averill told Herbeck that she and her husband, Damon, who had been vacationing together in Manila at the time of her son's murder, said the family received scores of compassionate calls from architects and city planners across the nation. But she said the most gratifying letters sent to her family were from the mostly black residents of the Willert Park area, who told her how much they cared about her son and his efforts to better their community.

"Too Tall" was captured by armed FBI agents in San Jose, California on November 2, 1981 in the offices of a janitorial company, where he was then working under a false name. He was extradited back to Buffalo, but the case would take years to resolve. Finally, on November 5, 1986, Barnes accepted a prosecution plea offer to a reduced charge of first-degree manslaughter. He admitted to Justice Vincent E. Doyle that he actually had stabbed Mills as he and a friend attacked the urban planner. The judge told Barnes his reduced plea was victory enough. Doyle also told him the killing of Mills was the type of "non-panic, deliberate act" that didn't merit leniency. After the manslaughter sentencing, Prosecutor Ernest G. Anstey said the Erie County District Attorney's office agreed to the plea to spare the victim's family a third trial and to guarantee Barnes could not challenge his conviction again. Barnes never identified his unarmed accomplice, who has never been tracked down and prosecuted. After almost 17 years behind bars for the Buffalo street killing during Joey's reign of terror, Barnes was paroled on July 8, 1998.

CHAPTER FIFTEEN

The Third Pretrial

Dillon and Mahoney had both come to enjoy more lucrative legal careers by the time Joey's third trial rolled around in 1986. Neither relished the thought of having to spend more months dealing with the uncommunicative and at times hostile Joey, who refused to follow most of their legal advice.

Because New York's high court in July 1985 had overturned Justice Marshall's 1982 conviction and faulted Justice Flynn for not letting Dillon and Mahoney hire another psychiatrist just before Joey's first trial, another Buffalo judge had to be assigned to take over the case. On January 10, 1986, Erie County Judge Joseph P. McCarthy, once the top prosecutor in the Erie County District Attorney's office, was selected to preside at Joey's retrial. McCarthy's ability to handle complex criminal cases, and the fact that he was one of the few available judges in Buffalo's higher courts who hadn't yet been involved in Joey's earlier local court proceedings, were factors in his appointment, court officials said. McCarthy, who was destined to assume the unpaid but crucial role of supervisory judge for all criminal courts in the area's court system in 1993, ordered state prison officials to return Joey to Buffalo from state prison by February 24th.

McCarthy quickly conducted a closed-door session with Dillon, Mahoney and Deputy District Attorney Albert M. Ranni. All participants in that one-hour, closed-door session refused to comment afterwards, but it was clear that Dillon and Mahoney were busy with other clients by then and not keen to resume dealing with Joey. Mahoney made clear that he wanted to be excused from the case because of what he correctly called his "overwhelming obligations" to other clients. He and Dillon met with Joey at the Erie County Holding Center again on February 24, 1986 and with Judge McCarthy four days later.

In early February 1986, McCarthy told the news media he was leaning toward letting Dillon and Mahoney withdraw from the case saying, "It's quite clear the defendant must and should have able and competent counsel" fully committed to his case. The judge also wanted to get the case moving swiftly.

On February 28, 1986, Mahoney and Dillon both submitted written requests to Judge McCarthy to be removed as trial counsel, citing the lengthy work that they had already done for him and citing the apparent "personality conflict" between both of them and Joey that might "cloud" pending court proceedings and mental competency examinations. As a result, the judge on March 7, 1986, assigned another pair of distinguished Buffalo defense attorneys, David G. Jay and Sean D. Hill, to serve as Joey's taxpayer-financed defense team at the upcoming retrial. McCarthy delayed the next round of mental competency examinations, mandated by the Court of Appeals ruling of the previous summer, to give Jay and Hill time to, "attempt to communicate with Mr. Christopher," who had once again had stopped talking to counsel. The judge urged Jay and Hill to try to "make a bond" with Joey.

Mahoney went on to set international criminal law precedent reversing the conviction of an Austrian doctor who had been convicted of smuggling millions of dollars worth of military helicopters into Iran. Mahoney also went on to active representation in numerous highly political cases, which included the trials of Daniel Morrison, publicity director of the Irish political party, Sinn Fein. He also defended a wide range of political activists representing peace and nuclear disarmament movements, artists, environmental activists and even Critical Mass bicycle-ride participants arrested for disturbing the Buffalo peace in 2003. His eminence as a top criminal defense lawyer became firmly etched in stone upon the exoneration of Michael Rigas, the only member of the Rigas family acquitted of criminal activity, in connection with the family's former Adelphia Cable Television dynasty. And on behalf of the National Association of Criminal Defense Lawyers, Mahoney authored the successful amicus curiae brief in a landmark New York Court of Appeals case in 1985 which foreclosed the use of the so-called "Good Faith" exception to the exclusionary rule in New York and ultimately in other jurisdictions nationwide.

Attorney Kevin Dillon went on to an illustrious career as top prosecutor and judge. When Erie County District Attorney Richard J. Arcara, a Republican, resigned that job in late May 1988 to accept a lifetime appointment as a U.S. District Court judge in Buffalo, the Democratic governor of New York State, Mario J. Cuomo, appointed Kevin Dillon as interim Erie County district attorney. Dillon went on to retain that job until the end of December 1996, when he began the first of his two 14-year terms as a New York State Supreme Court justice. Governor Cuomo had come to regard Dillon's father, Michael F. Dillon, both as a close friend and as a judge whose legal opinions he deeply respected. Michael Dillon was himself Erie County District attorney for a decade through 1972 and served on Gov. Cuomo's advisory council of judges in his capacity as the longest-serving presiding judge of the Fourth Department Appellate Court in Rochester. He died on July 9, 1991, while making a speech in Albany with his eldest child, then-District Attorney Kevin, in attendance. Governor Cuomo altered his entire work schedule to come to the Buffalo suburb of Lackawanna, New York – Mike Dillon's hometown – to speak at his Mass of Christian Burial.

With the then-30-year-old Joey in court for a March 7th hearing, Judge McCarthy told him he understood that he "may wish to exercise free choice" and refuse to talk to Jay and Hill, but he urged Joey to "participate" with his new attorneys. While Joey had a constitutional right to remain silent during the latest round of the 5 and ½-year old prosecution effort, McCarthy noted from the bench that Joey's silence had "psychiatric overtones." The then-bearded Joey simply slouched in his chair at the defense table and maintained a silent smile throughout the 20-minute hearing, refusing to respond or even acknowledge the judge was talking to him.

On September 2, 1986, Jay and Hill told Judge McCarthy that, should psychiatrists advise them that the insanity legal theory would not apply, they might drop their planned insanity defense. McCarthy set a November 5, 1986 start for the jury retrial and directed Joey's lawyers to "expeditiously" decide whether they would pursue the insanity claims. In August 1986, Jay and Hill had filed the insanity claim with McCarthy as they sought court approval to hire a psychiatrist to aid in the defense. But raising doubts for the first time publicly about the advisability of an insanity defense – already rejected by the Manhattan jury which convicted Joey a year before – Hill told McCarthy that "if our doctor does not find" the insanity claim "is viable, it's going to be the end to it," as a defense strategy.

A month earlier, McCarthy had already granted the defense team's request to hire a psychiatrist to look at Joey. Also, that month, McCarthy, much to the consternation of prosecutors, limited prosecutors to a single psychiatric rebuttal witness should the insanity defense be used. But McCarthy also gave prosecutors the right to videotape all of Joey's future mental exams for use as evidence at the impending jury trial.

Erie County prosecutors made a bid to have Joey, his attorneys, and their local psychiatrist, flown to New York City at taxpayer-expense for a more current examination by Dr. Richard Wiedenbacker, the prosecution's mental health expert at Joey's Manhattan murder and attempted murder trial in 1985. Deputy District Attorney Ranni told the judge that Buffalo prosecutors wanted to use Wiedenbacker as their key witness, but his work schedule and long-confirmed New York City area commitments made a trip to Buffalo impossible for months. However, that attempt was opposed by defense attorneys and rejected outright by Judge McCarthy October 16, 1986. With the retrial set to begin soon, the judge told Ranni that prosecutors could have Joey available "any time" to be examined by a local psychiatrist. Attorney Jay told the judge that Dr. Brian Joseph, the Buffalo psychiatrist he and Hill were using in pushing their insanity defense, met with the jailed Joey "on almost a daily basis."

The start of jury selection at the retrial was moved back from November 4th to November 10th because Dr. Russell W. Barton of Rochester, the psychiatrist prosecutors brought into the case, could only examine Joey on November 4th.

Barton, former director of the Rochester Psychiatric Center and a frequent prosecution expert in criminal insanity cases in Western New York had just played a key role in the trial of 18-year-old John D. Justice. At age 18, Justice had been convicted of murdering his mother, Mary, and neighbor Wayne Haun. But, Justice was ruled innocent by reason of insanity in the killings of his father, John W., and his 13- year-old brother, Mark, the same day.

Joey had been silent during all of his earlier pre-trial sessions before Judge McCarthy. But on November 5, 1986, the bearded and paunchy Joey, then 31, told the judge in a low voice that he did not object to the decision of both his trial lawyers not to come and observe his examination by Barton. Dr. Barton's pivotal psychiatric examinations took place at the Erie County Holding Center November 6th and 9th.

.

CHAPTER SIXTEEN

The Skeptical Alienist

Since the Empire State's highest court mandated a second trial, Joey would face one more psychiatric examination – the one that would count. Joey's last, and determinative, court-ordered forensic examinations were conducted by Dr. Russell W. Barton, the most veteran of the court-appointed psychiatrists who examined Joey after he was initially identified as the .22 Caliber Killer. A former director of the Rochester Psychiatric Center and a frequent prosecution expert witness in criminal insanity cases in Western New York in the late 20th century, Barton, an Englishman, had originally come to the United States in 1969 to teach.

When he first met Joey in the dank conference room at the Erie County Holding Center about 1 p.m. on November 6, 1986 for the first of their two pre-trial sessions, Barton identified himself as a psychiatrist. He explained that he did not come to the session with any pre-conceived notion of Joey's mental health, either at present or six years earlier during the rampage. The examinations were videotaped, as Barton deftly teased out rational thoughts from the irrational; and the impulsive ones from the planned.

"Psychiatrist must be a bad name for you," he said to Joey, who was dressed in his jail green shirt and pants and was smoking the first of a number of cigarettes he had during that two and one-half hour session. The University of London-trained physician noted that he had found, since he began taking on such court assignments, that, "everybody thinks that the district attorney has me in his pocket." Barton said to Joey, "I try to be fair." Joey was, at that point, smiling at the openness of this doctor. Barton quipped that prosecutor Albert Ranni, who was in the room along with defense psychiatrist Brian Joseph, had called on him to, "try to find out how your brain was doing" six years earlier.

Barton's skillful examination would traverse a range of subjects, emotions and motivations. His depth of experience allowed Barton to let Joey reveal certain critical features of his mental state. Barton observed everything. He noticed a constant twitching of Joey's fingers and inquired about these other physical symptoms. Joey told him that his feet moved all the time. Joey said he had complained about the involuntary tremors in his fingers and feet to the doctors examining him at the state's Mid-Hudson Psychiatric Center. They had prescribed him Nervine and Cogentin.

Barton asked him about his experience with previous psychologists, perhaps in an effort to build trust. Joey said, "I wasn't talking to them at all at first." When Barton brought up the name of Army psychiatric expert Dr. Eleanor Smith Law, Joey said again, "I didn't talk to her." Barton asked him why he wouldn't talk to the medical experts assigned to deal with him and Joey said, "I don't know. I didn't say nothing to nobody. I used to sit in the corner." He explained that when he started taking medication last summer, his attitudes changed and he began talking to doctors.

Barton bounced from small talk to serious topics. When asked how he was eating now, given that he went on a hunger strike at the Fort Benning stockade, Joey said, "It's institutional food, not like cooking yourself." Changing to another topic, Barton asked him what he thought about the just-concluded national elections. Joey said he didn't pay much attention to the elections or sports, claiming that "I don't watch TV too much." He told the doctor that when he and other inmates are near televisions, "I let them watch what they want." However, Joey admitted he got into a fight at the Marcy hospital the previous summer with a "crazy" Puerto Rican guy, who he said started swinging at him for no reason after the guy moved a table. He said they exchanged punches before hospital attendants separated them.

Barton inquired about family and personal relations. Joey said there was a time for two years when he didn't talk to his widowed mother, either, even refusing to talk to her when she came to see him in custody.

"I was mad at her," he said of his mother. But he added, "I had no reason to be mad at her."

Joey pointedly denied having proposed marriage to Mary Louise Montesano. Joey insisted she was not his girlfriend and that he "I never told nobody" he wanted to marry her, despite whatever the records Barton was using said. Joey told the psychiatrist that, after being out of work for some time, the girlfriend who he was then living with got him a job on the maintenance crew at Buffalo's Canisius College where he would "mop the floors." He said that at the age of 16, he began working in car lots washing cars and doing repairs and "tuning them up." His interest in cars grew to the point that he had his own 1967 Camaro and he "souped it up" with help from friends. Joey said he became skilled at working on car engines and doing body work on vehicles, which prompted Barton to say he was, "a better man than I am," mechanically.

The conversation veered into a discussion of another mechanical item – firearms. Joey admitted that while he was at the college, he would carry a pistol around campus for security. He told the doctor his live-in girlfriend was a firearms instructor on the campus firing range. Joey said he met her in the neighborhood, when she hired him to put up a door and renovate her bathroom. When he refused to take as much money for the work as she offered, he said she took him out to dinner. Their friendship grew. Barton never inquired about how their relationship came to an end.

However, Joey said that, as he got older, he became somewhat of a loner. "[A]t times" he felt people were against him. Barton asked Joey point blank if he had anything against black people. Joey said he did not. He noted that at the college, he worked with a black man named Smith and they used to get high together. Joey continued on describing his history with illicit substances. "I did drugs for a seven-year span," from age 18, after he had begun using marijuana with friends.

He told Barton he had done "quite a bit" of LSD. He said he recalled taking acid 10 to 15 times and undergoing flashbacks during which, Joey explained, "you analyze things." Joey said on his worst acid trips, "I was running and everybody had ugly faces down the street." Joey said his last acid trip took place before the killings began. Joey said he used cocaine once in a bar but had never used crack cocaine. He told the doctor he used to smoke marijuana "every day," doing "three bags a week" at costs ranging from $20 a bag to $56 a bag. He began using marijuana when he quit high school and began hanging around friends who used it. In an uncharacteristic episode of preachiness, Joey told Barton that marijuana. "...leads to other stuff. That's what's wrong with it."

He said he took angel dust "quite a bit" for a while and it made him feel, as he described, "spacey."

"I'm an alcoholic," Joey continued. He said he drank beer, rum and cokes and other "mixed drinks."

Barton then told Joey that he did not want "to trick you into anything." Joey responded to the doctor's assurances by telling him he would sometimes in the past have memory lapses which he felt were linked to his drug use. He said such drug-related problems would last, "for a couple of months sometimes."

VOICES

When Barton told him he wanted to talk about the events of January 18, 1981, Joey responded matter-of-factly that that was, "the day I stabbed a guy in the barracks." That prompted the genteel doctor to initiate another line of questioning about Joey's attitudes towards other races.

"I like black women," Joey said. As to black men, he stated, "They don't make no difference to me."

Joey told the Barton he had never been troubled by seeing ghosts or having hallucinations, but he had heard "voices" telling him what he should do on the streets to combat his enemies. He said the voices started talking to him in July 1980. Joey would return to this topic again and again over the rest of the examinations.

"I had voices coming from the TV saying I was being drafted in the Army," he said. "I went to the Psychiatric Center" on Forest Avenue in Buffalo, "trying to be admitted, but they wouldn't admit me." He said that this rejection prompted him to try to enlist in the Army. Once enlisted, he thought, "I was on a mission" and was "supposed to kill people."

In his rambling talk, Joey then told Barton he had "melted down" his late father's used .22 caliber rifle and went around shooting people and after that "I killed a cab driver." Barton asked him why he attacked the cabbie. Joey replied, "I thought he was the devil so I cut his heart out." He described driving a stake into the organ. Barton asked him if he was familiar with human anatomy and Joey, smoking another cigarette, didn't directly respond. He just said that he had "pounded the stake in his heart" after getting the first victim to drive him to an office park near the airport. After stopping at a deserted building, Joey explained how he attacked the cabbie "with a hatchet on his face." He said the elderly cabbie swiftly grabbed a metal bar to defend himself but, "I kept hitting him with the hatchet," Joey stated. Barton asked him if the visible scar Joey had on his face was due to the cabbie striking him in self-defense, but Joey said he got the scar earlier in his life while working on a truck.

Barton asked him why he chose a black cab driver as a victim. "I thought I was on an Army mission. I thought he was the devil. It was wrong with me," Joey responded, in his own disjointed and grammatically incorrect parlance. When Barton told Joey that stakes were often driven through the hearts of vampires to kill them, Joey seemed to agree: "I thought that's how to kill the devil." Asked what he did with his victim's heart, Joey calmly said, "I threw it in a field right next door" to the scene of the attack. Though he was not any more precise with the psychiatrist about the site of the second cabbie attack, Joey told him he had used a hammer and, "put two holes in his head." After the hammer blows, "Shorty" Jones fell to the ground. Joey said he "cut through the ribs" and "reached in and grabbed the heart." He impaled the severed organ with one of the three wooden stakes he had made specifically for the attacks.

Pressed by Barton on the reason for the second cabbie killing, Joey repeated, "I thought I was on a mission." He said he walked home about three or four miles after abandoning the cab all the while feeling, "terrified that I was going to be attacked," by black people for what he had just done. But, he immediately denied harboring ill feelings toward blacks.

About 40 minutes into the first examination, Barton asked Joey to explain the relationships between a number of words he gave him. These exercises included, for example, the relationship between a cat and a mouse. Joey was able, for the most part, to explain them properly. As to the cat/mouse relationship, Joey said, "They don't get along." When the doctor asked him to add the numbers 49 and 121 Joey, lighting another cigarette, told him, "I'm not good at math, unless I study."

At almost an hour into the examination, Joey's hands became very sweaty. He told Barton that sweatiness was probably due to the Newport cigarettes he was smoking. Building the relationship, Barton told Joey, "I used to smoke three packs a day." He then pointed to the Lifesaver candies he now used to take his mind off cigarettes.

They next discussed various past courtroom dramas. Coming back to the examination after a bathroom break, Joey said he did not want a jury trial in 1982 because, "I thought they [the jury] were going to do something to my mother. Now that I think about it, it was stupid." As Barton pressed him on his irrational concerns about the jurors, Joey got irritated and said he would not talk about that issue any more. Barton challenged Joey, saying that that his general attitude, "makes it look like you're concealing stuff," and that activity like that would, "determine how this interview comes out."

"I'm not going to answer your question," Joey responded. Civilly, Barton scolded, "I hope to be reasonable and polite to you."

With this statement, Joey managed to open up. "I don't believe this stuff happened to me. It's hard to believe I would do something like this," he said of his violent attacks. Joey told the doctor that he had, "stabbed a guy in the barracks" because, "I thought he said I was a homo." Joey said he heard a male voice that he was convinced was the devil. That disembodied devil voice was saying, "He's going to sodomize me."

When Barton asked him if he had read books on psychiatry, Joey quickly responded: "I'm not a good reader."

After another bathroom break, Joey returned and lit another cigarette.

FIRST MURDER

Barton then inquired about the first murder in the Tops supermarket parking lot, which began with Joey sitting quietly on a ledge outside the store.

Joey told Barton he had melted the barrel of the .22 caliber rifle his father had left him with an acetylene torch and hid the gun in a paper bag. He said he had accomplished that task just a few hours before the Dunn shooting. He hadn't even test-fired the gun before he used it for his first murder. Joey then boasted of having been a pistol instructor. He also bragged about having been a deer hunter, experienced in butchering his kills. That naturally got Barton back to inquiring about the cabbie murders. Joey said, matter-of-factly, "One I put in the trunk [Edwards]." He said he left the other victim, "Shorty Jones," on the ground.

The questioning returned to the Dunn shooting. Joey said he walked up to Dunn as he was sitting in the driver's seat of a parked car and shot him in the head. Joey said he then went down a side street towards home, which was a short distance from the super-market lot – "the next block over," he recalled.

When Barton asked Joey why he immediately left the Tops lot after shooting Dunn, Joey said, "I thought I'd be attacked ... I thought I was at war."

"Why at war?" Barton asked him. Joey said he did not think about the reasons why. He simply claimed the devil had told him he was at war and had to kill Dunn. He said he did not think at the time that it was wrong to kill Dunn.

"Now I believe I was wrong then, but didn't then," Joey said.

As Barton pressed him on his feelings about what he had done, Joey said that if he had thought it was wrong at the time of the crimes, "I wouldn't have stabbed the private in the barracks where everybody knew me." Barton, revealing his growing skepticism about Joey's insanity claims, said that it seemed Joey was trying to convince him of his mental derangement six years earlier. When Barton asked Joey if he had the ability six years earlier to know it was wrong to have done what he did, Joey said, "I don't think so."

"I had no intention of doing what I did, for myself," Joey said. Like I was told to do it," he repeated. Joey told the doctor that he recalled that at about the same time of his attacks he had been walk-ing down a street and saw a garden hose looped like a noose. He interpreted this as a sign that, "I was supposed to go strangle some-body. And I did. Someone in the hospital." He said his intended victim "kept on breathing" as he was strangling him with "a wire noose" he claimed he had taken off a bicycle. Somewhat circularly, Joey added that his theft of the bicycle wire had then struck him as a sign he was supposed to strangle someone.

As he was trying to accomplish that task at the Buffalo hospital, a nurse had walked into the room. "I'd been there a long time and he wouldn't die," Joey said. That unexpected guest caused him to rapidly exit the room and successfully flee the hospital.

Joey then told Barton he slept with his late father's .22 caliber rifle in 1980 because he thought that he was going to be attacked. While he recalled using the sawed-off .22 a couple of times, Joey also claimed that back around the time of his attacks, he had also cut down a 20-gauge shotgun, which he never used to kill anyone, but which he also kept in his bedroom.

When Barton asked Joey about the killing of Emmanuel Thomas, the defendant repeated, "I thought I was on a mission." He recalled another guy standing right next to Thomas when he shot him. He said he had tried to shoot the other guy, too, but that "he ran away." Joey said he then got into his sister's Dodge, and drove away right after killing Thomas. Joey said he recalled having left the shells at the scene.

When Barton asked Joey about the fourth killing of Joe Louis McCoy in Niagara Falls, Joey once again repeated, "I thought I was on a mission." Like a broken record, he insisted that at that time he was certain that, "the Devil was against me." Joey said he recalled shooting McCoy in the back of the head after toting the sawed-off rifle in a bag. After that shooting, he said he went around the corner to get into his car, which he had parked about a half block from the site of the shooting, and drove back to Buffalo. Of the Niagara Falls killing, Joey said he did not know his way around Niagara Falls, but he killed McCoy because "I was on a mission, like I was supposed to be killing," as if Barton hadn't gotten the message yet.

CHRISTMAS BREAK

Lighting up another cigarette, Joey said he remembered leaving Fort Benning for his 1980 Christmas break in New York City. Joey told the doctor that he simply did not remember how many men he stabbed in New York City. But he complained about the surviving victim testifying at his 1985 trial, "saying I ran from him [after the stabbing]." Instead, Joey boasted, "He ran from me."

Recalling his trip home in December 1980, Joey described stabbing a few people, killing one individual at about 7:30 in the morning one day. He said he was then using a knife and was thinking, "I was supposed to be doing it."

When Barton asked him about the Rochester trip on his December 1980 northern visit, Joey recalled, simply, "I drove there and stabbed somebody." He said it had been his first time ever in Rochester and he was "just walking along" until he saw a black man he decided to stab with the hunting knife he was carrying. Joey was clear to the doctor: "When I went to Rochester, I was intending to kill somebody." Joey emphasized that he was again hearing "the voices," but he could not articulate exactly what they were telling him. But he pointed out, "I thought I was doing what was right."

Barton mentioned the December 31, 1980 attack on Menefee back in Buffalo. Joey said he recalled Menefee was standing on the corner when he asked that victim for the time and then stabbed him in the chest. But when Barton asked about the January 1 stabbing of

Crippen, Joey immediately denied that incident, saying "I didn't do it. I was nowhere near him." When Barton said Crippen told police Joey said, "You fucking nigger," as he tried to stab him, Joey insisted that he "was never near Hertel [Avenue]" the day Crippen was stabbed. He would always deny any involvement in that attack.

ATTEMPT ON PRIVATE COLES

Barton then turned to questions about Joey's return to basic training at Fort Benning on January 3, 1981. The doctor mentioned that a recruit named Juan Feliciano reported to military investigators that Joey told him, "I'm tired of everyone messing with me. I'm going to fuck around with the next one," at some point before the January 19, 1981 stabbing of Private Coles.

"I don't remember saying that," Joey responded. Of the Coles stabbing, Joey repeated, "I thought I was on a mission" because Coles was black. He was against blacks everywhere at that time.

At that point, Dr. Barton remarked that Joey seemed to remember some things that happened over a half decade earlier very clearly, but about other things "you just black out." Joey replied, "I answer your questions as best I can." Barton reminded him he was making his professional observations of Joey's statements based on his four decades as a psychiatrist. It would be very difficult to pull the wool over Barton's eyes.

Barton began a thread of discussion about blacks in the Army. Somewhat contradicting his earlier statements, Joey said he stabbed Coles in the barracks because he thought Coles had called him a "fairy." Barton calmly mentioned another white recruit telling Army investigators that, at a bar during basic training, Joey had told him, "If the nigger fight with me, I'll kill him." To that, Joey had no response.

The good doctor, finding some inconsistencies in Joey's responses, brought up the fact that in the Fort Benning stockade, "you cut your penis with a razor blade." Joey acknowledged that he did that, offering the explanation that he, "wanted to go to the hospital because I thought they were poisoning me [in the stockade]." Joey insisted he made only a small cut on his penis and, at the base hospital, they had sewed it up.

Joey said that he did not recall why he had spoken of his northern killing spree to a male nurse at the base hospital in April 1981. He said he believed the hospital staff gave him some drug that made him talk, "because I don't talk to people," he told Barton. The doctor noted that, at Fort Benning, Joey had bragged of having killed 13 persons by either shooting or stabbing them. Joey couldn't get clear on why he had made that claim. "I probably said it," Joey responded, "I don't understand why." Barton also noted that on April 13, 1981, Joey was listed as telling a black female nurse named Anderson about his killing spree. " She was nice," Joey said in recalling Nurse Anderson. He agreed when Barton told him he had told Nurse Anderson of his spree: "I knew I had to do it. None of them was white."

COMPETENCY SELF-ASSESSMENT

Barton noted that in May 1981, back in Buffalo, Joey had been ruled mentally competent to stand trial. Asked to comment on the first four Buffalo psychiatrists who examined him when he was returned to Buffalo, Joey said "I don't have any opinion on them." When Barton asked Joey what it was like to be under guard and examined by psychiatrists at New York City's Bellevue Hospital before his 1985 jury trial there, Joey just said it was "a zoo" with "all kinds in there." Barton asked him if he told his chief psychiatric examiner at Bellevue in 1985 about hearing voices ordering him to kill. However, Joey said he had stopped talking to that shrink. He claimed the voices stopped talking to him in February 1986 when he started taking a medication to deal with his hand and leg tremors.

Pressed by Barton, Joey admitted that as a kid he had liked blacks and even had sex once with a black Buffalo prostitute named "Judy." Joey said he had met Judy on the street where she was plying her trade in 1978, and during the escapade, they had smoked marijuana. In response to a question from Barton about whether he was sexually interested in men, Joey smiled and denied being a homosexual. He called them "faggots," labeling such men as both "funny" and "sad." Joey told Barton he considered homosexuality to be "a waste," without expanding on his statement. But he told Barton the voices were clearly telling him he was a faggot.

Joey said of his Fort Benning stabbing victim, "I didn't like Private Coles" because he was "boisterous" and "cocky."

Joey explained that, as a kid, he got into fights in his neighborhood "as much as anyone else." He vehemently denied reports that he had been a bed wetter and walked in his sleep as a kid. Joey told Barton that he got into arguments with his father, when he quit high school at age 18 after failing his junior year twice. He said his father had been a mechanic for the Buffalo city government and had taught him welding. His father got him to attend an auto repair school in Buffalo for a while. Joey said the death of his father when he was 21 hit him hard. "People said I was different" after the death of his father, "but I didn't notice it."

When Barton asked him again how he felt about blacks in the U.S. Army, Joey said, "Except for that one that I didn't like [Coles], the others didn't bother me." Joey said he liked being in the Army even though "I didn't get out of boot camp."

At that point in the examination, Barton mentioned he was noticing Joey's hands and feet involuntarily "working more" as he spoke. Joey told Barton he had gone to the Buffalo Psychiatric Center in August 1980 and saw a doctor and a social worker during a half hour visit. Joey lit another cigarette and repeated his claim that when he went to the psychiatric center in August 1980, "I asked to be admitted the first time I went there." That prompted Barton to ask him, if he had been admitted for treatment, "Do you think all this would have happened?"

Joey just shrugged.

At that point, Barton reminded Joey that nothing he told him during the court-ordered mental examinations could be used against him in court, except as to his insanity defense. Barton then offered to buy him cigarettes, but Joey told him "I have a whole carton upstairs" in his cell. Someone had been providing him with some spending money.

Joey told the psychiatrist that, like it was during all his court-ordered hospital stays in recent years, he was "restricted" from associating with other inmates at the Erie County Holding Center, the downtown Buffalo pre-trial lockup.

"Being in jail is rough," Joey said.

When Barton then asked Joey if he thought he had been insane during his violent crime spree six years earlier, Joey replied in the affirmative. He pointed out that Dr. Brian Joseph, his defense-hired psychiatrist, believed he was schizophrenic. Joey told Barton he was currently taking nerve medication and pills to deal with his involuntary tremors. He said that he had, for a time after his arrest, been administered a liquid form of Prolixin, an anti-psychotic medication used to treat schizophrenia and psychotic symptoms such as hallucinations, delusions and hostility. He said the drug gave him "a pain sensation."

At that point, Dr. Barton went out into the hallway and conferred with Albert M. Ranni, Erie County's deputy district attorney and Joey's chief prosecutor in Buffalo.

DEEPER QUESTIONS

When Barton returned, he spoke of "anomalies" in Joey's comments. He asked him further questions about his history of fights. Joey admitted a fellow stockade inmate broke his nose in 1981, but then quickly changed the subject. He began complaining again about the stockade food having had poison in it. When Barton asked him why he was convinced of that, Joey said "I don't know. I thought I felt different," after eating the stockade food. He claimed that for a time after each of his stockade meals, he literally "couldn't talk."

Then Barton asked him why he had opted for a non-jury trial in Buffalo against the advice of his own attorneys. Joey repeated his belief back then that jurors would hurt his mother. When Barton then asked him how he thought court jurors could hurt his widowed mother, Joey petulantly replied, "I am not going to answer."

Barton then told Joey that he could not understand his claim that he killed under orders from disembodied voices, pointing out that,

"You wouldn't obey your attorney" about trial tactics. Burton highlighted the inconsistency in Joey's ability to take orders. To his attorneys, Joey was "independent and stubborn," yet he blindly obeyed the commands of faceless voices. In response, Joey just said, "I thought that it was real. I thought I was in a war. I was convinced."

Upping the ante, Barton queried, "How come you were so meek, such a wimp? So namby-pamby? It doesn't add up to me."

Joey said blankly, "I don't know."

Barton then noted Joey had been periodically pausing before responding to some of his questions during that day's examination. He told Joey he found him capable of standing up to psychiatrists and yet caved in to body-less voices. Barton pressed Joey on why he had not stressed to other doctors with whom he had been dealing about how voices controlled his criminal actions.

"Sometimes I do things impulsively," Joey said in response.

Barton told Joey the medications he had been put on since his 1981 arrest may have been giving him a "kind of synthetic sanity." But he added, "I really don't know yet."

"You're an enigma," Barton told Joey.

SECOND SESSION

As a second session got underway, Barton asked Joey how he was doing on cigarettes. Barton stressed that he wanted to be as agreeable as possible in his determinations on his mental status. To that, Joey, somewhat in the third person, responded, "Joe is all right." Barton went straight to questions about the absence and appearance of Joey's mental delusions. He noted that, on this topic, at first, Joey said that he didn't have any. Joey responded that, "Most people, I wouldn't talk to at all." But, Joey elaborated to Barton. He said he started hearing voices in July 1980. They were male voices which, "first started telling me I was being drafted."

"Well, what did they actually say?" Barton asked.

Joey said they were "telling me to go down to the Army office. That's about all I remember." Then he added that they also told him, "that I was at war and a whole bunch of other stuff."

Barton asked him if the voices, "ever make a commentary about what you were doing?"

"Not that I recall," Joey responded.

When Barton asked Joey who the voices told him he was at war against, Joey immediately said, "black men." That prompted Barton to ask him if he liked black men now. Joey responded that black men, "don't bother me one way or the other." The doctor noted that all his victims had been black. Joey said, "I knew they were black. Because I was at war with them."

Joey claimed he was hearing "more than two voices," which seemed to talk to others, too.

"What did they say?" Barton asked.

"I don't recall," Joey said.

Asked if he had any delusions in July 1980, Joey asked, "Like what?"

"Well," Barton said, like "Something strange" happening.

"Like the Devil was behind it?" Joey asked, adding, "I don't recall if I remember" if the Devil was one of the July 1980 voices talking to him.

When Barton asked him if, in July 1980, he felt anyone was out to get him, Joey quickly responded "Yes, black men."

"Why?" Barton asked. Joey said, "No reason why. Now I don't believe it's reasonable that they were out to get me. At one time I thought that it was a conspiracy against me."

"How come this did not come out before?" in earlier forensic examinations by other psychiatrists, Barton asked. "You've seen a lot" of psychiatrists, he noted. Joey just said, "I don't know. I didn't talk" much to psychiatrists in the past.

At that point, Barton told him his responses were raising questions in his mind about whether Joey was "faking it" on his alleged mental problems.

"I believed like the TV could hear what I was thinking and I believed people could imprint things into my head," Joey told him.

"Thought insertion?" Barton inquired.

Joey then interrupted this particular line of questioning. He announced that he had stopped exercising in jail about six months ago. His weight had ballooned from 170 pounds to 212 pounds.

But Barton did not get thrown off course. When Barton asked him if he ever thought he was in control of his surroundings in a God-like way, Joey said, "Yes, on and off."

When asked if he felt persecuted back then, Joey said yes, but by no one in particular. Barton then said he read that Joey had lived with a girl, which prompted him to make a strange response about feeling persecuted by "everybody," but mainly by "the Kennedys."

"Voices," Barton said.

Joey said that's what he was referring to. He admitted, "I don't recall exactly what they said," adding that they spoke about "everyday things." Joey insisted that he could think rationally about things now. When Barton asked him if he ever had strange thoughts, Joey said, "The question doesn't have any relativity to anything I think."

"I was like a different person from what I am now," Joey said. "Seems like jail has made me tougher," he added.

When Barton asked him if he talked to his fellow prisoners, Joey said "sometimes," adding that most other inmates know why he is in prison. He then said, "I don't feel I'm a racist," but he contended that a lot of his fellow inmates feel that way about him.

Barton told Joey that he thought that he was capable of logical thought. Joey emphasized that he did not feel he could think logically in the past, before he began getting medications.

Barton asked him if his mind ever went "blank." Joey replied in the affirmative, lighting another cigarette.

When Barton asked to talk about his feelings and emotional experiences, Joey said, "Now they are kind of guarded," because, "you don't trust other people [in jail]."

"I don't find myself getting angry at people," Joey said, adding that in jail you "don't get much" to laugh about, except "just stupid things, that's all." When Barton asked Joey if the medications he was taking affected his feelings, Joey said, "Not that I've noticed." He told the doctor he felt he had "improved a lot" since 1980.

"I was like a different person" at that time, he added.

After Barton then asked him if he had had a knife or a sawed-off rifle on him now, "[D]o you think you'd polish me off?"

Joey said, "No. I'd throw it away."

Barton then asked what had prompted him in the past to feel "betrayed." Joey responded that he had broken off with friends because they were not loyal to him anymore.

"This whole experience has been prettying frightening," he said, referring to "what happened before."

"I thought I was going to be attacked," Joey said.

He said that at that period of his life, "I didn't have a job. I was mowing lawns for people and was down on myself."

CABBIE REPRISE

Getting back to the killing of the two black cabbies, Barton asked Joey why he attacked Parlor Edwards with a hatchet.

"I had already thrown away the gun," Joey told him. When Edwards had driven him to Sugg Road near the Buffalo airport, he hit him in the face with a hatchet that his late father had kept in their garage. But that the victim fought back.

"He was hitting me with an iron bar and I was hitting him with the ax." Their fight seemed to have lasted about five minutes.

"I was crazy," he remarked, about the death-match with the elderly cabbie. He said he had not felt any of the cabbie's blows to him with the iron bar. Joey said after he killed Edwards, he put him in the trunk of his taxi and left it in a field below a nearby Thruway overpass, cutting down some tree branches to try to cover the taxi from view of passing vehicles. When Barton asked Joey why he had tried to hide the taxi after the killing, Joey said, "I don't know. It was an afterthought." Joey claimed he had not been following any news accounts of the murder, saying he was not reading newspapers and turned off the television when news reports started.

"We didn't get the papers" at home either, Joey said.

He told Barton he used a hammer to attack "Shorty" Jones because the hatchet he used to kill Edwards had broken during that struggle. He said the hammer also broke as he attacked and killed the second cabbie.

"It was like a driving thing that I had to do, like an obsession," Joey said in explaining his use of the wooden stakes on the hearts of the two cabbie victims. Joey said, "I was like energized, like super-charged, like I was real strong."

Barton said that it seemed that in 1980, Joey had felt cold and unemotional for the most part. Joey agreed that assessment, claiming, "I was afraid for me." He felt generally terrified. He agreed with Barton when the doctor said Joey had been looking for the "sinister" or "harmful" meanings behind anything people said to him at that period of his life.

Joey said that when he was drinking and using drugs, he would lose his temper, get mad and often throw things. However, he insisted, "I had stopped drinking" months before the 1980 attacks began, "because I knew I was having a problem."

He said he got tattoos on the then-seedy Chippewa Street red light district in Buffalo when he was 17 and he now regretted it. He said he got tattoos because "people I was hanging around with" got them, "so I just...," trailing off. He stopped without completing that thought and randomly began telling Barton he, "didn't like the Catholic Church at all," even though Barton had reports that Joey used to go to attend mass with his widowed mother frequently.

Further discussing his life before the killing spree, Joey told the doctor he had been close friends for ten years with a man he identified as Dave Robinson. He said, "I just stayed away from him about the time I started to get sick," and began avoiding people in general.

Barton observed aloud that Joey seemed to have an ability to stonewall people. But Joey said he just didn't answer anyone's questions after becoming mentally ill.

At that point in the examination, Joey grabbed one of the Lifesavers Barton kept popping in his own mouth.

Barton then told Joey he had seemed to have a poor self-image. Joey agreed, saying he was just drifting through life with only a few friends. He said that he had even thought of suicide due to "all this trouble I've got" before the attacks began.

Barton asked him if he experienced "magical thinking." Joey told him he didn't, saying he was not superstitious. When the doctor asked him if he felt clairvoyant and able to tell the future, Joey said no, but that he thought other people were planting thoughts in his mind around the time of the killings. He also felt his feelings were being broadcasted to others. Also, he claimed that as he walked past street signs in New York City in December 1980, they were telling him to kill five people.

Joey recalled the murders there. He said he remembered that one black man he attacked at a subway station ran away from him

Barton said if he had "had a command" to kill that victim in the subway station, then why didn't he run after him "to finish him off?" Joey responded that "it wasn't specifically" that man he had attacked in the subway station that he had to kill, "It was anybody. If it wasn't him, I had to get somebody else."

Barton asked Joey if he ever felt the presence of a "supernatural force" around him.

"Yes," Joey said. "I don't know how to explain it. Like feeling electricity near me." He said it felt like "a pleasant buzzing sensation" and that happened frequently. Last February, during one of his hospital stays, Joey said that was the last time he felt the presence of a "supernatural force" around him.

Barton asked Joey if he had ever felt "unreal," like he was watching a film rather than living. He had felt that way during his last stay at the state hospital at Marcy, saying "I thought the film could change magically and give me messages." Joey explained that he kept quiet about his "film" experience to the doctors treating him there.

Joey claimed the voices seemed to stop for good when he went on his hunger strike in the Fort Benning stockade in January 1981. Barton then asked him if he ever felt he had a mission in life, to which Joey replied that his mission was war with the blacks.

When Barton began inquiring about Joey's feelings towards all the lawyers who had been representing him, Joey said, "I didn't feel they were on my behalf," adding that he did not talk to or trust most of them. But he said, "I don't think that now," believing that medications he began taking in March or April 1986 changed his view. Joey told Barton the shots of Prolixin he was given to treat his alleged schizophrenia "slowed me down." They were administered against his will, but under court orders.

When Barton asked Joey why he drove to Cheektowaga to fatally shoot Harold Green, Joey said "I don't know." After Joey said he could not remember why he drove to Niagara Falls for the daytime killing of Joe Louis McCoy, Barton accusing him of "being cute" with him in his remarks. That prompted Joey to say he had "no recognition of what you are saying now." Joey also told Barton he could not recall ever telling any of the psychiatrists who had dealt with him that he felt he had to have been insane to have carried out his attacks.

When Barton then asked him if he wanted to make any final statements, Joey first said no, but then claimed, "I don't sleep good, but I eat everything they give me" in jail. As the session was winding to a close, Joey said he no longer heard voices and felt "pretty normal."

Barton reported the session coming to an end at 3:33 p.m., Sunday, November 9, 1986.

CHAPTER SEVENTEEN

Third Trial Begins

As the trial got underway on November 14, 1986, defense attorney Sean D. Hill told that jury of seven men and five women that Joey fatally shot the three black men in September 1980 because disembodied voices told him to kill. Hill made the case that these symptoms were the result of untreated paranoid schizophrenia. He told the jury those voices "haunted" Joey and instructed him, in September 1980, that he was "going to war." Hill illustrated how Joey lived, "in a world filled with shadows, a world haunted by voices." He argued that Joey committed the killings because he was "severely, gravely, profoundly, mentally ill." Hill told the jury he and co-counsel David G. Jay would be presenting testimony about Joey's demented mental state that would, "make your hair stand up on the back of your head." He told the jury that Joey's mental deterioration began with the death of his father in 1976.

In Deputy District Attorney Albert M. Ranni's opening statement, he made no mention of insanity. Ranni insisted that he and co-prosecutor Thomas J. Eoannou – with whom Ranni had teamed up to obtain John D. Justice's murder conviction the month before – would prove the "perfect" ballistics match between crime scene shell casings and the still-missing .22 caliber rifle.

On November 17th, Army Capt. Dorothy Anderson again testified that on April 13, 1981, when Joey was in the psychiatric ward at the Fort Benning hospital, he casually walked up to her and announced that he had killed. Once again, Anderson testified that Joey told her he could not remember exactly how many men he had killed. That same day, Christopher Corwin, the Army private assigned to guard Joey in the psychiatric ward, testified that Joey had told him he was "a mass murderer" in Buffalo and killed "seven people" in Buffalo and "some people in New York," just as he had testified years earlier. Out of the army and working as a civilian youthful-offender counselor in New Paltz, New York, Corwin told the jury that when Joey made his murder claims to him, he "appeared to be disgusted with himself." Under cross-examination from defense attorney Jay, Corwin told the jury that even though he had already been guarding Joey for eight hours a day for about a month, the only time Joey talked to him was when he made his murder claims. He told the jury, as he had told the original trial judge, that he would see Joey periodically, either sitting up in his hospital or laying on it, shake his head in his hands and say to himself "Christopher, Christopher, Christopher."

Prosecution witness Madonna Gorney told the jury that Joey had what she described as a "rather dull or blank" look on his face when she walked past him near the entrance to a supermarket at Genesee and Floss streets in Buffalo moments before Glenn Dunn, 14, was shot dead at about 9:30 p.m. on September 22, 1980.

Joey ages in jail. Photo courtesy Buffalo Courier-Express Archive, E.H. Butler
Library, SUNY College at Buffalo

Firearms expert Michael Dujanovich told the jury that same day that all three murder victims were shot in the head with a Sturm-Ruger .22 caliber rifle. Bullet casings found at the murder scenes matched spent shells and a misfired bullet seized from Joey's Buffalo home and his family's hunting lodge in the Town of Ellington in Chautauqua County, New York.

On November 20, Robert S. Oddo returned to tell the jury he saw Joey shoot the Dunn youth. The only prosecution witness to identify the killer positively, Oddo admitted he never actually saw the murder weapon in Joey's hand, but he did see three or four gunshot flashes as Joey reached into the car in which the Dunn youth was sitting. Oddo confirmed that he watched Joey run out of the supermarket parking lot onto Floss Street and toward Weber Street where Joey lived.

After Oddo testified, the prosecutors rested their three-day-old case. On November 20, McCarthy denied defense motions for an immediate dismissal of the triple murder case, saying sufficient evidence "both direct and circumstantial" had been presented to the jury to allow it to reach a verdict.

That day Dr. Brian S. Joseph, a Buffalo psychiatrist and the first defense witness, testified that Joey told him that he had cut the hearts out of the two cabbies, Parlor Edwards and Ernest Jones, and had attacked his other victims because he was "on a mission against the devil."

Dr. Joseph also revealed that Joey had made homosexual propositions to hospital workers and to a fellow patient at Fort Benning's base hospital in 1981. He said Joey gave the explanation that those homosexual advances were actually attempts to get a guard out of his hospital room so he could attempt suicide. Joseph found Joey to be a paranoid schizophrenic.

Joseph told the jury Joey had said he felt "terribly sorry" for having stabbed a black recruit, but he had also said there that "People are trying to control me. . . . I'm not myself right now. I'm guarding myself." The defense psychiatrist told the jury that Joey had actually lived with a woman in Buffalo for about two years in the late 1970s, but at Fort Benning, he "felt his masculinity was being questioned." He complained of fellow recruits in his unit harassing him. Joseph told the jury some psychiatrists believe that "homosexuality and paranoia go hand in hand.

Resolving a burning issue in the investigation of Joey's crimes, Dr. Joseph told the jury Joey told him, during the October examination, that he had used a blow torch to melt down the rifle he used in the four .22 caliber killings. Joseph told the jury that in 1980, Joey was "terrified" of being attacked by unknown assailants and feared he was being followed. The jury also learned through Joseph's testimony about Joey's pre-spree attempt to get himself admitted to a mental hospital. The defense psychiatrist said that, just in the last month, Joey became willing to talk about his crimes because he felt he finally "needed to tell somebody."

On his second day on the stand, Joseph insisted Joey's responses to doctors about why he wanted a non-jury trial in 1982 and his starvation and mutilation efforts in an Army stockade in earlier 1981 may have seemed to be rational, but merely masked his insanity. He insisted Joey gave other psychiatrists what he characterized as superficially logical responses to questions because he "wanted to be seen as not mentally ill." Due to Joey's long-standing paranoid schizophrenia, he did not always understand what he was randomly telling psychiatrists, Joseph told the jury. Joseph also stated that Christopher demanded a non-jury trial in 1982 because he had a demented fear that a jury would sexually molest his widowed mother.

To counter the defense psychiatrist's assertions, prosecutors Ranni and Eoannou produced Army records that indicated Joey told Fort Benning doctors in March of 1981 he refused to eat at the base stockade and mutilated himself because, "I couldn't take the confinement, the crowds." He told Army doctors he "wasn't thinking" when he nearly castrated himself in the base stockade. The prosecutors also produced documents revealing Joey told a state psychiatrist in 1982 that he did not want a jury trial not because of fears of his mother being molested, but because he felt a judge would know the law and a jury could be swayed by news reports. The prosecutors also introduced a February 1982 psychiatric report in which Joey was quoted as telling one of his psychiatric examiners, "If I'm smart enough to make up some [expletive deleted]," to fool some psychiatrists, "I'm OK."

But Dr. Joseph testified that it was "quite conceivable" Joey's alleged insanity was dormant when he was sent to the state's Mid-Hudson Psychiatric Center late in 1981 before his first Buffalo trial. He insisted that Joey's claim to Mid-Hudson psychiatrists that he had attacked a number of men in Manhattan in late December 1980 with a 10-inch kitchen knife he had purchased at Macy's because he "had to kill people," was also a sign of his mental illness.

After Joseph got off the witness stand, Judge McCarthy told the jury that they could not use any of Joey's admissions to Dr. Joseph during the October 27th and October 31st examinations or to Dr. Barton on November 6th and November 8th in deciding whether he was to be found responsible for the first three .22 caliber killings.

Prosecutors Ranni and Eoannou used sworn statements from Rev. Michael Freeman, the Catholic priest who talked to Joey in the stockade and two former soldiers who had been there with him to counter defense attorneys' claims that he did not hate blacks and killed only because of an alleged twisted belief he was at war with the devil. Joey told fellow prisoner Robert Travis that he and a friend had "wasted" some blacks in that northern city. According to soldier Terry Potter, Joey had had a "slap fight" with a jailed black soldier and afterward told Potter that if that black soldier actually tried to fight him, "I'd take care of him." The jury learned from the Father Freemen statement that Joey had told that priest he had a "great deal of hostility" toward blacks because in high school they had bullied him.

Neither the trial prosecutors, nor District Attorney Arcara ever commented on Joey's alleged boast to fellow jailed soldiers at Fort Benning about allegedly having an accomplice in the 1980 attacks.

BARTON TAKES THE STAND

Dr. Russell W. Barton took the witness stand on December 1, 1986 to deliver his testimony.

Barton told the jury that during his two recent mental exams, Joey told him he had "no feelings against black people," but had attacked because he felt he was at war against blacks and the devil. Barton rejected previous psychiatric claims that mental illness had caused Joey to refuse food at the Fort Benning stockade. Barton said he also rejected defense claims that the "superficial" wound Joey inflicted on his penis to get out of the Army jail and into a base hospital was a sign of insanity. Regarding Joey's starvation attempt, Barton stated that Joey's belief that Army food was poison was actually "a very common belief," among servicemen used to their mother's home cooking. Joey's "superficial" mutilation attempt was a "fairly common" act by someone pretending to be mentally ill, Barton told the jury. Barton diagnosed Joey as suffering from a personality disorder which caused him to be unable to relate normally to other persons. But he stated that Joey had a firm grasp on reality.

On his second day on the stand, Barton told the jury that Joey "cooked up" what he called the "bizarre" cabbie murders because he wanted front-page headlines. Joey wanted the notoriety about his exploits to remain alive in the minds of the public. Barton called the cabbie killings a sign of Joey's long-standing personality problems and his overall feelings of "unimportance and insignificance," but not insanity. Barton said his examinations convinced him that Joey considered himself "a nobody." Psychologically, Joey's feelings about himself were an "almost perfect fit" for a borderline personality disorder that left Joey sane, but overly sensitive and difficult to befriend, Barton testified.

Joey carried out the cabbie killings in a "very bizarre" manner, Barton testified, because it gave him the feeling of being "a very powerful person," a feeling which he lacked in his everyday life.

Barton rejected defense claims of paranoid schizophrenia based on his own review of Joey's medical records. Barton told the jury the records he examined revealed that Joey want to the Buffalo Psychiatric Center two weeks before the first killings complaining of depression. He said there was nothing in the hospital records to indicate Joey in the 1980 visit made any mention of the delusions and hallucinations that routinely accompany schizophrenia. That day Joey merely complained to psychiatrists about being unable to "deal with the pressures of society," unable to hold a job and wanting to live "independently" so no one could interfere with his life, Barton said. The reports prepared by doctors on Joey's September 8, 1980 unscheduled visit to the mental hospital presented "very strong evidence" Joey was lying about hearing voices, Barton told the jury. In examining Joey, Barton told the jury he found Joey seeming to be "searching" for exactly the right response to his questions.

The Rochester psychiatrist also told the jury that while Joey spoke during his November examinations of having been told by voices that he had to kill, during six years of court-ordered periodic mental examinations by psychiatrists, Joey had pointedly refused – including as recently as last month's exams – to take psychological tests capable of indicating whether he was lying. But as Joey told Barton, he had refused to submit to any psychiatric tests recommended since early 1981 by any of the psychiatrists or psychiatric nurses who dealt with him in the courts and the U.S. Army. In fact, Joey refused to take even medical tests capable of revealing the cause of his tremors. Barton speculated that the involuntary and bothersome hand and leg tremors Joey complained about could have been the result of a never-diagnosed manifestation of Parkinson's disease. Joey was only treated with mild nerve pills for the tremors. The mental deterioration could also have been caused by Joey's admitted alcoholism and years of using every available hard drug he could get his hands on.

Barton testified that Joey had told him he killed eight black men in Western New York and an untold number in Manhattan in 1980. Barton said that Joey was currently dismayed by his conduct of six years earlier. Barton said during the examination, Joey admitted killing the two black cabbies, fatally stabbing Roger Adams and Windell Barnes at bus stops in Buffalo and Rochester and trying to strangle Erie County Medical Center patient Collin Cole, even though he had never been, and never would be, charged with any of those attacks. During the November 6th examination, Joey also said he began attacking black men because he had begun hearing voices telling him he "was on a mission." He revealed that he slept with a sawed-off .20-gauge shotgun near his bed because he feared being attacked by blacks. Barton said Joey told him that as he fled from his attacks on black men, he said he was always "terrified that I was going to be attacked by other black people." Yet, he added that Joey denied being a racist and had admitted to him, "I like black women." Joey also told Barton he used to "get high" with a black maintenance worker when he worked at Canisius College.

On December 4, 1986 the prosecutors played for the jury the 90-minute long videotaped mental examination conducted on Joey by Dr. Barton. On the tape the jurors heard Joey telling the doctor he felt "supercharged" and "real strong" when he was attacking the two black cabbies. Joey was also heard telling the psychiatrist he pounded foot-long wooden stakes through the hearts of both cabbies after cutting them out of their bodies because "it was like a driving thing that I had to do." The jury also learned that Joey had made three pointed stakes – one he never used – the day before his October 8, 1980 attack on Edwards. Joey told the psychiatrist he had previously gutted deer when hunting with his late father, but until he cut the hearts out of the two cabbies, "I never gutted a human." Barton contended that Joey was sane during his 1980 murder and stabbing spree. The jurors heard Joey speaking in a clear, strong voice as he told Barton he now found it hard to believe he could have carried out such attacks.

"It's hard to believe I would do something like this," Joey could be heard telling the psychiatrist. "I thought I was on a mission. I thought I was at war. Now I believe I was wrong in doing it, but I didn't then."

Barton told the jury he found many "inconsistencies" in Joey's claims to other psychiatrists during earlier court-ordered examinations. Barton said he discounted Joey's claim to him that the anti-psychotic drugs he was now taking made him realize he had committed the attacks in a fit of insanity. He said that while he felt Joey was generally being honest during their four hours of talks in November, he concluded Joey was lying when he spoke of being compelled to kill by disembodied voices. Barton told the jury he rejected Joey's insanity claims because Joey's "repetitive and limited description" of the so-called voices was incredibly vague in comparison to his candid talks about many other aspects of his personal life.

Barton also told the jury that despite five prior years of intensive scrutiny by psychiatrists, Joey never spoke about having heard voices until his latest team of attorneys convinced him to go with an insanity defense. The expert said it was clear to him that "these killings [the first three] had a motive" in Joey's "distress of feeling he was a nobody."

Barton believed Joey's ulterior motive in now claiming openly that he was insane six years earlier lay in the fact that he had learned from lawyers and fellow inmates that he would stand a greater chance of getting released from custody after spending time in mental confinement than he did in getting paroled from prison.

As defense attorney Jay began cross-examining Dr. Barton on December 5, 1986, he cited Army reports on Joey's mid-morning barracks knife attack on Leonard Coles. Witnesses described Joey as "staring, as if he were not aware of what was going on" during the attack. Jay read Army witness reports of Joey "screaming, struggling." appearing "upset" and "shaking as though he was in a convulsion" at he attacked Coles. Jay read the jury an Army investigative report that quoted another black recruit as telling investigators that Joey might have mistaken Coles for him because the night before the attack, Joey "had wet his bed and I kidded him about it."

After Jay cited all the Army reports on the Coles attack, Barton testified that Joey might have been shaking during the attack on Coles because of his emotional "rage" rather than insanity. Citing what he called Joey's mention to him of his apparent desire to become a priest even though he was a high school dropout, Barton told the jury Joey's problems in the Army were indications that "he was trying to find an identity in both the Army and seminary." Barton insisted Joey's criminal conduct in 1980 and 1981 supported his own view that Joey was sane and afflicted only with a personality disorder that made it hard for him to cope with many situations.

CLOSING ARGUMENTS

On December 5, 1986, Judge McCarthy ruled that when jury deliberations begin as scheduled on December 9th, the panel would decide whether Joey was sane when he killed the three men. The panel would also be given the option of finding him guilty of first-degree manslaughter if jurors decided he was acting "under the influence of extreme emotional disturbance," rather than insanity. Such a verdict would mean he would be facing three 25-year prison terms instead of facing three possible life sentences. Attorneys Jay and Hill said that, while they would not shy away from their insanity defense, they felt it appropriate the jury be given the chance to opt for the lesser felony crime if it viewed the evidence as showing uncontrollable, but still reprehensible conduct.

In closing arguments to the all-white jury of seven men and five women on December 8th, Jay explained that the main issue in the nearly-three-week-long trial was "why did it happen?," and not "who did it?" because there was no question that Joey killed Glenn Dunn, Harold Green and Emmanuel Thomas. But Jay argued that "madness – absolute madness" led Joey to kill. Joey was "sick" with paranoid schizophrenia "and getting sicker by the minute." Jay, a gifted criminal trial strategist and defender of civil rights– which had gained him a national reputation – told the jury Joey killed because he was legally insane and "had no control" over himself due to delusions. The counselor told the jury that the signs of Joey's worsening mental condition were evident in his unsuccessful attempt on September 8, 1980 to get admitted for treatment at the Buffalo Psychiatric Center. The defense attorney insisted Joey made no effort to cover up his attacks, noting that he spoke of having delusions to Army hospital personnel in the spring of 1981 and told them he was a mass murderer. By late 1980, Joey was "a very troubled young man, who felt the world was coming at him," Jay stated. He argued that Dr. Barton, in rejecting his insanity claims, was deliberately "very selective" in his review of signs of Joey's mental illness.

Jay told the jury that at least 10 psychiatrists who had examined Joey in the Army and after he was brought back to Buffalo either diagnosed him as a paranoid schizophrenic or discovered signs of mental illness. Jay also noted that Dr. Joseph, the only defense witness, said Joey had only recently become able to talk about his illness because of the strong anti-psychotic drugs he recently started taking. If Joey was faking mental illness, he would have been able to give a much fuller explanation of the disembodied voices he insists have been haunting him, Jay told the jury.

Deputy District Attorney Albert M. Ranni urged the jury to convict Joey, arguing that his attacks on black men were attributable to years of sexually-related harassment he felt he had endured from them.

The jury went into several days' worth of deliberations. On the jury's second day of deliberations, they had court stenographer Mildred Scott re-read the March 31, 1981 diagnosis of Dr. Eleanor Smith Law, the Army psychiatrist who found Joey to be suffering from a non-psychotic personality disorder when he was hospitalized after refusing to eat stockade food. Before retiring for the night, the jury also had Ms. Scott read back portions of psychiatric testimony about Joey's feelings toward blacks.

A FINAL DECISION

After 11 hours of actual deliberations over two days, the jury finally found Joey guilty of first-degree manslaughter in each of the three .22 caliber killings. They cleared him of second-degree murder, but rejected his insanity defense claims outright. The jury ruled that Joey, who did not react emotionally to their verdict, killed all three victims during fits of uncontrollable rage while sane, but "under the influence of extreme emotional disturbance" that clouded his judgment, but did not cloud his view of reality.

After the verdict, Erie County District Attorney Richard J. Arcara refused to set a timetable for Joey's next prosecution either for two Buffalo stabbings or the fourth .22 caliber killing in Niagara Falls. Arcara told The Buffalo News, "The important thing for us at this time is to make sure that everything is done to make sure this man never gets out of prison."

Niagara County District Attorney Peter L. Broderick, who had to decide on whether to prosecute in Niagara Falls, faulted the jury's analysis, contending that Joey should have been found guilty of murder. Broderick told the media he felt the manslaughter convictions would have been reasonable only if Joey's attorneys had presented evidence of some "relationship" between Joey and his three victims. While Arcara that day lauded what he called the second Buffalo jury's "fair and just" verdict, Broderick said he viewed all four .22 caliber shootings as "random, ambush-type killings," which demanded a verdict of either "murder or insanity."

Weeks before Joey's January 20, 1987 sentencing, Arcara asked Judge McCarthy to impose the maximum-allowable prison term of 25-to-75 years on the triple-manslaughter conviction. He said that Joey's conduct warranted a sentence that would keep him behind bars, even for parole-consideration, until he was almost 90. Arcara blasted Joey as, "a racial assassin who terrorized the entire community of Western New York," through a reign of "horrendous conduct over an extensive period of time that constituted a serious threat to the long-standing goodwill and peaceful relations that existed in the black and white community."

On January 20, 1987, Judge McCarthy ordered Joey to serve the maximum-allowable 25-to-75 years for his triple-manslaughter conviction, in addition to the 33 1/3 years-to-life he was already serving for the December 1980 Manhattan murder and attempted murder. McCarthy denounced Joey for killing the first three .22 caliber victims, "solely because of the color of their skin," telling him he deserved to spend the rest of his life behind bars for having "terrorized the community for months." Dressed in green work clothes, the bearded 31-year-old Joey, who had his hair cut extremely short after the verdict, simply responded "No, sir," when the judge asked him if he had any comment. McCarthy ruled that the sentences would not begin until after Joey completed his term for the two December 22,

1980 attacks in New York City. Joey's attorneys vowed that they would appeal.

Judge McCarthy told Buffalo News columnist Ray Hill after the sentencing that he had anguished over some sentences he had imposed, "but not this one."

"This community had to be satisfied that the criminal justice system would respond in kind," the judge told Hill. "Christopher's acts were so grievous that my duty was clear," he added. Judge McCarthy, having himself lived through the community's days of turmoil, doubt and fear prior to Joey's arrest, told Hill the just completed trial established *what* Joey did, "but I don't know that we found out why he did what he did."

THE COMMUNITY RESPONDS

After the sentencing, Buffalo's Episcopal Bishop Harold Barrett Robinson told columnist Hill he remembered the fear Joey had created in the community – among blacks, the fear of a racist killer on the loose, and among whites, the fear of fear itself. He also remarked about the racist killings' long term effects on the community.

"The black community and much of its leadership had come to believe that the justice system belonged to the white man and that it was unable and even unwilling to bring the killer to justice," Bishop Robinson told Hill.

Bishop Robinson recalled that black and white clergy of all faiths had walked down Jefferson Avenue in the heart of the city's black community, often in pairs, urging blacks to give "the System" a chance. After Karl Hand made national headlines by announcing his call for a white supremacist rally outside of Buffalo's City Hall on Sunday, October 19, 1980, Bishop Robinson and the city's other religious leaders had assembled the crowd of about 5,000 whites and blacks in front of Buffalo City Hall despite a cold, biting wind. With Buffalo's Roman Catholic Bishop Edward Head on center stage, the crowd locked arms and sang "We Shall Overcome," the universal anthem of the oppressed.

Bishop Robinson, who Hill praised for having put together a coalition of local clergy and lay people who could debate the issues that the attacks had provoked without destroying the Buffalo community as a whole, told the columnist after the January 20th sentencing that there was much to be salvaged from Joey's racist rampage.

"That there were people – black and white – that would come together at a time when emotions might have prevented unity, was the best of signs," the bishop said.

"It had never been done before and now, having done it, we know it can be done again. In the end, we saw justice work and we are now able to dispel the honest doubts of those who said that there was a system of justice for whites and another for blacks. If Christopher taught us a lesson it was that we must constantly work for racial unity."

Rev. Robert Beck, one of the co-chairs of Buffalo Interracial Task Force created by Bishop Robinson and which was composed of white and black clergy, noted to Hill after the January 1987 sentencing, that the task force continued to function.

"Perhaps it's not as dramatic as those meetings we had when the .22 Caliber Killer was still on the loose," Beck said, "but it continues to function, dealing with latent racism that crops up in the private and government sectors, especially in hiring." Rev. Beck told Hill that Joey's mindless hatred of blacks should serve as a reminder that the community must keep working to stamp out prejudice and Joey's likely life term "should give us some encouragement."

Soon after the sentencing, John A. Ziegler, head of Buffalo Legal Aid's appeals section and Kay Huff, an appeals attorney for the Legal Aid Society of New York, began working separately on appeals of both the Buffalo and Manhattan convictions. But in his long-standing fashion, Joey, who was not prosecuted for any other attacks and who grew very overweight in prison, refused to cooperate with either the Buffalo or Manhattan appeals lawyers who tried to craft new trial arguments on his behalf. Though Joey received mental health treatment in state prison, he never granted authority to prison officials to allow any of his prison medical records to be released to the appellate bureau.

In 1991, the First Department Appellate Division of New York State Supreme Court unanimously upheld the Manhattan murder and attempted murder convictions. The Fourth Department appellate court in Rochester unanimously upheld Joey's triple manslaughter conviction and the stiff prison term imposed by Judge McCarthy.

In its February 1, 1991 decision, the Rochester appellate tribunal made clear that it was bothered by prosecutor Albert M. Ranni's aggressive handling of evidence at the retrial. The Rochester tribunal described McCarthy as the "saving grace" of the 1986 retrial, due to what the appellate judges cited as his handling of countless instances of "inappropriate and improper conduct" by Ranni, which even the district attorney's appellate team had been prompted to acknowledge during a hearing over a month before the appellate ruling was issued. The Rochester court faulted Ranni for constantly referring to legal and fact issues not in evidence, making himself an "unsworn witness" with his repeated comments to the jury and his flouting of rulings McCarthy made throughout the trial. The five-judge panel said Ranni's trial misconduct "detracted from the seriousness of the proceedings," adding that "although we cannot condone the trial assistant's behavior, we find that the judge's firm control over the trial obviated any prejudice to defendant that might have resulted from the prosecutor's misconduct." The prosecution and the defense would rest for good and there would finally be some measure of justice for Joey's victims.

CHAPTER EIGHTEEN

Joey and Leon

Among the ironies of Joey's bizarre saga were the similarities between him and Buffalo's other infamous killer, Leon Czolgosz. Nearly one hundred years earlier, the self-professed anarchist Czolgosz fatally shot U.S. President William McKinley on September 6, 1901 before a horrified crowd in the Temple of Music at the Pan-American Exposition, a world fair held in Buffalo that was illuminated by the unprecedented sight of thousands of light bulbs encrusting all of its buildings. Both killers accomplished crimes with serious social and political implications for their time, but the similarities did not stop there.

Both killers refused to cooperate with their trial attorneys – in Joey's case with Kevin M. Dillon, the attorney his mother had hired for him, and Mark J. Mahoney, the other talented attorney Dillon brought into the case early on. Leon similarly refused to talk to his court-assigned attorneys, Robert C. Titus and Lorin L. Lewis, prominent Buffalo attorneys of that era. Lewis told the jury at Leon's trial of his refusal to cooperate with his own attorneys. An avowed anarchist, Leon told his jail guards he would refuse to talk with anyone he viewed as related to the evil government he hated, including lawyers and judges.

Both were tried in Erie County Hall on Franklin Street in downtown Buffalo. Joey was brought from the Erie County Holding Center to the courthouse through an underground tunnel which was a much-improved version of the underground tunnel prepared for bringing Czolgosz to the court house. The tunnel was created so that Czolgosz could be transported under the feet of the angry crowds that had gathered on Delaware Avenue calling – accurately as it turned out – for his quick execution.

Both used inexpensive, common firearms to carry out their foul deeds. In Joey's case, it was the dearly loved Ruger .22 caliber rifle his late and idolized father had purchased used for $69. In Leon's case, it was the .32-caliber Iver-Johnson "Safety Automatic" revolver he had purchased for $4.50 four days before he carried out his assassination plan. There were even some similarities in the deaths of their victims. McKinley died seven days after he was shot twice by Leon during a daytime attack. Harold Green, the only one of Joey's .22 caliber victims who survived for a time after also being the victim of a daytime attack, died five days after Joey shot him twice.

Both killers were boastful and arrogant on their first appearances in court after their indictments. Joey demanded to act as his own lawyer; Leon initially demanded to plead guilty. When Joey made his demand to New York State Supreme Court Justice Samuel H. Green on May 11, 1981, that judge ordered a forensic mental examination for him to ensure that he was mentally competent enough to assist in his own defense. When Leon, on the day of his trial, September 23, 1901, demanded to plead guilty immediately, Judge Truman C. White instead entered a "not guilty" plea into the record.

Both Joey's attorneys and Leon's attorneys argued at trial that their client was insane. Lewis actually admitted his client was guilty of killing the president. He framed the question for the jury as follows: "The only questions that can be discussed or considered in this case is whether that act was that of a sane person. If it was, then the defendant is guilty of murder. If it was the act of an insane man, then he is not guilty of murder but should be acquitted of that charge and would then be confined in a lunatic asylum."

At Joey's higher court-ordered triple murder retrial in 1986 – at which he was convicted of first-degree manslaughter counts after the jury determined he was out of control during the three Buffalo area .22 caliber killings – David G. Jay, one of his attorneys, stressed his alleged insanity. Jay told that Erie County Court jury before Judge Joseph McCarthy that Joey was hearing voices from his television set telling "a very troubled young man" to kill. Both killers underwent court-ordered mental competency examinations before their trials. Leon was examined by three noted mental health experts of his day and the Buffalo Police Department's surgeon who maintained all records of Leon's mental and physical health while he was in custody. Joey was examined by numerous Buffalo, New York psychiatrists at New York State's mental hospital for the criminally insane, New York City's Bellevue Hospital and by psychiatric nurses at the U.S. Army's Fort Benning military base in Georgia.

The connections between Leon and Joey even had a real estate link. Edward C. Cosgrove, the district attorney whose command of the investigations led to Joey's prosecutions, ended up owning the Buffalo office building once occupied by one of Leon's three court-assigned mental health examiners, Dr. James Wright Putnam. Cosgrove purchased the Buffalo building at 525 Delaware Avenue used by Putnam for his private law firm after leaving public office. Putnam, who did post graduate work in both neurology and psychiatry in clinics in Germany, was one of the prosecution psychiatric experts at Czolgosz's jury trial.

The initial verdicts came swiftly for both killers. At Joey's first trial in 1982, Justice Frederick M. Marshall took one day to issue his verdict and rule Joey guilty of three counts of second-degree murder. The jury at Leon's trial deliberated only one hour before convicting him on September 24, 1901 – 18 days after the president was shot – and unanimously recommending the death penalty. Both Joey and Leon's significant convictions took place on the second floor of Erie County Hall in what would have been adjacent courtrooms. Neither displayed any emotional reactions to their jury verdicts, according to news accounts.

In the official report on Czolgosz's mental state to Thomas Penney, Erie County District Attorney in 1901, Putnam, acknowledged by the news media of that day as "an expert of wide experience in mental diseases," joined with Police Surgeon Joseph Fowler and Dr. Floyd S. Crego, also a well known Buffalo specialist in mental and nervous diseases, in saying of Leon:

"He is the product of Anarchy, sane and responsible."

Dr. Carlos Frederick MacDonald, chairman of the New York State Board of Lunacy Commissioners, who was brought in late in the prosecution of Leon and who also examined him, concurred with the three Buffalo experts. Czolgosz was electrocuted at New York State's Auburn Prison on October 29, 1901. Before being killed by three jolts of 1800 volts of electricity, Czolgosz's last words were: "I killed the president because he was the enemy of the good people – the good working people. I am not sorry for my crime." As the prison guards strapped Leon into the electric chair, according to press reports, said through clenched teeth, "I am only sorry I could not get to see my father."

Dr. MacDonald publicly noted that the post-mortem autopsy on Czolgosz by Dr. Edward Anthony Spitzka of New York City, "revealed no evidence whatever of disease or deformity of any of the bodily organs, including the brain which was normal in size, shape, weight and appearance and was well developed in all respects, a conclusion to which by all of the physicians present, several of whom had witnessed the execution." Leon was buried on the prison grounds. Prison officials poured sulfuric acid into his coffin so his body would be completely disfigured, a process the prison warden estimated took 12 hours. Leon's letters and clothing were burned, according to contemporary newspaper accounts.

Joey's last words were not recorded by anyone. Unlike Leon, the corpse of Joey wasn't disfigured by sulfuric acid, but it took months to get him six feet under upon his eventual demise.

Of all the chilling connections between Buffalo, New York's nearly century-apart killers – lastly and maybe leastly– both Joey and Leon's last names began with the letter C.

CHAPTER NINETEEN

Early Release

Joey never went through any more courtroom dramas. Though two judges had ordered Joey to spend a minimum of 58 and one-third years behind bars, he cut short that mandate by 16,868 days.

After 4,423 days and over 12 years in jails and prisons, in the U.S. Army, in Buffalo, at the city's chief downtown lockup, at New York City's Rikers Island jail and in several New York State prisons, the 37-year-old Buffalo high school dropout died in New York's Great Meadow Correctional Facility at Comstock, near Glens Falls, almost exactly at 3 p.m. on March 1, 1993.

Joey, who had ballooned in prison to about 250 pounds had been transferred to Great Meadow five months before his death. He spent most of his time in that prison's infirmary. In announcing Joey's passing Arthur Leonardo, superintendent of that prison, announced to the media, "It was definitely natural causes. It was nothing that anybody did to him. He was here for several months. Most of the time he's been here he's been a very sick individual."

Virginia Parrott, a registrar in the Washington County town of Fort Ann near the Great Meadow facility, told The Buffalo News the autopsy performed after Joey's prison death confirmed that fact. Even Joey's death set him apart from others. Like many, he died of cancer. But, it was a cancer more regularly known to afflict women: Joey died of a rare form of male breast cancer.

Many individuals involved in the case spoke out about Joey's death. By 1993, Kevin M. Dillon was Erie County's elected District Attorney.

A young Joey, seated farthest to the right. Photo courtesy Buffalo Courier-Express Archive, E.H. Butler Library, SUNY College at Buffalo

"It's probably a blessing from his point of view," Dillon told The Buffalo News concerning Joey's death.

"My heart goes out to his mother, who was just wonderful, a very nice person," he added. Dillon said he heard that Joey was fatally ill in February 1993, telling The Buffalo News his former often-combative and unresponsive client, "was as complicated a person as I ever had to deal with"

"There's not much doubt he was a very, very disturbed person," he said of Joey.

"He could sit in a jail cell with his eyes closed and two hours after the guard came on Christopher could tell him what time it was. He could tell [time] by constantly tapping his foot."

Mark Mahoney, the other member of Joey's first defense team, felt inspired to question what he called the waste of taxpayer money in the pre-trial procedural actions of the first judges and prosecutors in the case.

"How many hundreds of thousands of dollars did Judge Marshall, Judge Flynn and the district attorney cost taxpayers by running roughshod over him to get this to trial?," Mahoney asked rhetorically.

"Nobody ever ruled out the possibility that Christopher had delusionally popped himself into these cases," he added. Edward C. Cosgrove, mastermind of the task force that paved the way for Joey's convictions, disagreed with the defense attorney's contentions.

"We got the right guy. I was saddened by his death. God Bless his soul but he was an unfortunate wretch," Cosgrove told The Buffalo News in March 1993.

Joey was buried in the hunting country south of Buffalo that he had grown to love with his late father. His relatives had a private Mass of Christian Burial for him at St. Joseph's Roman Catholic Church in Holland, New York on March 4, 1994. Rev. Matthew S. Wendzikowski, pastor of that rural church, told a Buffalo News reporter who had come to try to witness the service to just, "Let it rest. There has been enough publicity. Let the family have some peace."

Because of heavy snowfall that year Joey's body was not buried in that church's cemetery until the weather cleared in the spring. Joey always claimed he attacked 17 black men, but police never conclusively confirmed more than eight deaths. His true motives and the exact number of his victims went to the grave with him.

But, Joey's unexpectedly early death prompted Buffalo News reporters to recall essays he had sent the newspaper a decade earlier. In one, they recalled him comparing his killing spree to a sporting game, having written: "So, it was a baseball game. Seventeen hits and 13 dead, if they are dead." In another 1983 essay Joey sent to the newspaper, he wrote, "My father told me a long time ago what 'they' were going to do to me. Except I had no idea what his stories meant."

Some continued to speculate that Joey's emotional collapse began the day his beloved father and hunting buddy, Nicholas Joseph Christopher, died on May 21, 1976, two months before Joey's 21st birthday. For months after his father's death, Joey went to his grave almost daily, breaking down in tears as he contemplated his loss and hating himself for never getting really close to his father in his last years. However, other experts opined that Joey had acted on the basis of a different motivation altogether.

Dr. Michael M. Baden, one of America's most noted forensic experts of the late 20th and early 21st centuries, was so convinced of Joey's homosexual lust for black men that he included references to him in his 1989 Random House autobiographical book, *Unnatural Death: Confessions of a Medical Examiner.* Baden would be consulted as an expert witness or serve as chief pathologist on many famous cases, including the deaths of John Belushi, Sid Vicious and David Carradine. He also famously participated in the investigations of the assassinations of John F. Kennedy and Martin Luther King., Jr., and gave testimony at the trial of O.J. Simpson.

Baden, a former chief medical examiner for New York City and the founder in 1986 of the New York State Police Forensic Science unit at the request of New York Gov. Mario Cuomo, was so certain of Joey's homosexuality that he told a reporter for The Buffalo News in June of 1989 he found it revealing that many of Joey's victims were similar in build and general body features. Baden also disclosed that after Joey was jailed at Fort Benning, he had committed acts of sodomy on black inmates in the stockade and "made a pass at" the black Army captain who ran the stockade.

Baden, who was called in by the .22 caliber task force to perform autopsies on both of Joey's cab driver victims, asserted in his 1989 book that Joey's homicidal attacks on black men were linked to both his homosexual desires and his attempt to establish in his own mind that he was "macho" and heterosexual like his late father. As much as Joey may have been concocting ways to "get even" with the black men who had allegedly taunted him for his more feminine behavioral traits, it was still possible that he harbored sexual feelings for them. Joey may have struggled with himself for months before deciding in September 1980 that the only way he could lead a satisfying life was to drill his mental anguish into his social and sexual antagonists – black men. Baden said that, "Whatever Joey's mental state was at the time of his multi-state criminal rage, his sexual attraction toward black men both excited him and disturbed him to the point that he began his homicidal spree to "try to destroy the thing that was tempting him."

Epilogue

A decade after Joey's killing spree which, in the words of Buffalo News reporter Charles Anzalone, "brought the city to the brink of racial strife," Buffalo was still divided along racial lines. Henry Louis Taylor Jr., the black director of the Center for Applied Public Affairs Studies at the University of Buffalo, told Anzalone for his September 16, 1990 look-back story that the .22 caliber horrors "was not just an isolated incident."

"Those acts were symbolic of deeper tensions that still exist in Buffalo," Taylor said, continuing, "If you don't see the connections you don't understand the source that feeds these criminal acts."

Anzalone wrote that, a decade after the killings, many Buffalo area black leaders still questioned whether Joey was caught as quickly as he would have been if he had been a black man indiscriminately shooting white people. Warren K. Galloway, president of the Buffalo chapter of Operation PUSH, said: "A lot of people feel there was not as big of a push on their part to resolve it. There always will be a general distrust of the criminal justice system in Buffalo and the United States."

Barbara Banks, publisher of the Challenger, Buffalo's black newspaper, said in September 1990: "This is not just one thing that happened, a madman who shot some black folks and now it's over. It reminds black people there is a double standard. It reminds them of where they are. They can still be killed and not receive total justice. Some of these cases have never been solved," referring to the two cabbies, Joey's murder of two additional black men in Buffalo and Rochester, the Niagara Falls .22 caliber killing that never went to trial, and the deaths of four black men in New York City.

"Joseph Christopher is a manifestation of what society has always done to black men, on one level or another," Banks told Anzalone. "Get rid of them. Destroy them," she added.

"Black people unfortunately have a tendency to forget" wrongs done to them, Ms. Banks told Anzalone, adding "They have suffered from historical amnesia. It's a survival technique. Joseph Christopher is still with us on so many different levels. I don't know if he'll ever go away," she added.

Mark J. Mahoney revealed to Anzalone in September 1990 that even other local defense lawyers told him back in 1981 it would have been easy to pick a jury for Christopher in the first trial because his legal colleagues felt a Buffalo jury wouldn't be so quick to convict someone of killing black men in that era.

New York State Supreme Court Justice Samuel L. Green, the first judge to arraign Christopher after his April 1981 indictment and who, by 1990, had become one of the state court system's top appellate judges, and who also happened to be black, told Anzalone that in the fall of 1980 he had been, "Very concerned about going out at night."

"Every black man on the street or in a profession was worried," Green said.

"You just didn't know who this person was going to hit next." Green said in the autumn of 1980, he had been walking to lunch in downtown Buffalo with a black lawyer when he felt a man next to him who he said "was so close, I could smell him." Green said he grabbed for the pistol he had started carrying in his right pocket as the .22 caliber killing spree was underway and nearly pushed his lawyer friend into nearby bushes. That action led the white man who had been crowding the two black men to run away down Delaware Avenue.

"There was no reason to think it was Joseph Christopher, but that's how scared I was," Green said. "It was a very scary time," the judge added.

"If there is a lesson to this," former Buffalo Episcopal Bishop Harold Barrett Robinson told Anzalone, "it's the only way to solve these problems is for blacks and whites to work together."

In March 1993, several days after Joey died in New York State's Great Meadow Correctional Facility in Comstock at the age of 37, Frank Mesiah, a longtime black civil rights leader in Western New York, said he didn't know if the families of Joey's victims could "ever be made whole."

"Myself," Mesiah said, "I see the close of a certain period in Buffalo that carried a great deal of anxiety and pain for the African-American community. If there's a good side and a bad side to things then the good side is that the Black Leadership Forum, a cross-section of religious, business, community and political leaders developed from this," and stayed alive years after Joey's murder spree.

In the end, the .22 Caliber Killer, may leave more questions about the society he inhabited than of his personal motivations. In Frank E. Dobson Jr.'s historical fiction volume, *Rendered Invisible: Stories of Blacks and Whites, Love and Death* (Plain View Press), Dobson portrayed a fictionalized account of Joey's killing spree. Dobson depicted the murders as having been carried out by a pathological white racist-turned serial killer, who intended for his crazed reign of terror to spark a race war. One of the characters in Dobson's book put it bluntly: "Here we talkin' bout thirteen dead black men and nobody knows it happened. How the hell that happen, man? Thirteen black men, men of color murdered, and this killer is not infamous? They ain't made no TV movie 'bout this here! The dudes that he killed, it's like their lives meant nothing."

ACKNOWLEDGEMENTS

The author would like to express his gratitude to the following individuals and organizations that provided assistance in the creation of this work:

Daniel DiLandra, Buffalo State College archivist and special collections librarian; E.H. Butler Library, Buffalo State College, Buffalo, N.Y.; Buffalo Courier-Express, Buffalo, N.Y.; Buffalo Evening News, later The Buffalo News, Buffalo, N.Y.; Buffalo and Erie County Public Library; Edward C. Cosgrove; The New York Times; The Associated Press; Time Magazine; the late Buffalo homicide detective Eddie Gorse; and NewspaperARCHIVE.com.

ABOUT THE AUTHOR

Matt Gryta is a veteran crime reporter based in Buffalo, New York. A staff reporter for the Buffalo News for four decades, Gryta has spent his entire career covering gritty stories of crime, punishment and violence in the Western New York region. Early on, Gryta served as a U.S. Army war correspondent on the Vietnam battlefields. While calling in reports on the battalion's battle field successes, he was brought to Chu Lai to serve as the officer in charge of the writers and photographers in the Public Information Office of the Americal Division.

More recently, he has appeared on E! Entertainment Television and Investigation Discovery to shed light on remarkable cases he has covered. Gryta is also the author of The Real Teflon Don: How an Elite Team of New York State Troopers Helped Take Down America's Most Powerful Mafia Family, available through Cazenovia Press.

Gryta was one of the principal reporters covering Joey Christopher's saga in Buffalo.